Vagabonds

and

Strolling Dancers

The Lives and Times of Molly Lake and Travis Kemp

by

NAOMI BENARI

With contributions by Molly Lake and Travis Kemp

ISBN 0900484 62 4

Published under the auspices of Imperial Society of Teachers of Dancing.

Printed by Avon Litho Ltd, Masons Road, Stratford-upon-Avon. (0789) 415500
and 112 Bermondsey Street, London SE1 3TX 071-378 1579

For

Sheena

at Travis's request

Acknowledgements

My first thanks must go to Joyce Sherlock, without whose encouragement and advice on writing in general, years before I began work on this book, I would never have dared to attempt it.

I have been overwhelmed by the willingness of everyone I have come in contact with, to give of themselves in every way possible to help me complete the work.

I cannot express strongly enough my gratitude to Kathrine Sorley-Walker, who continually gave of her time, reading through the manuscripts on several occasions, patiently and tactfully making comments, and filling in many gaps in the appendix.

My grateful thanks are due to Dame Ninette de Valois who obligingly spared the time to talk to me with great charm about her memories of Molly and Travis as dancers and teachers; to Dame Alicia Markova whose revealing memories of them as dancers were most enlightening; to Jane Pritchard, archivist of Rambert Dance Company who kindly researched the roles which Travis danced while with the Ballet Club and Ballet Rambert, and gave me the exact dates for each; to the staff of the Theatre Museum, who put all relevant material at my disposal; to Mrs Judith Osborne, who read the finished manuscript with very great care, and made very valid suggestions about style; to Chris, who read the manuscript and uncomplainingly made numerous copies and collated them; to Peter Michael, who very kindly wrote at length about his memories of Molly and Travis while he was a dancer with the Markova-Dolin Company and with Ballet Intime.

I feel particularly privileged to have had the opportunity of talking at length with the late Robin Howard. He talked most interestingly not only about his admiration for Molly and Travis, but also about his ideas on dance training, and on dance in general.

Above all Travis, who unstintingly gave me his time, talking about his experiences and his reactions to them, putting all his archival material at my disposal, and helping to decide the names of chapters and of the book itself. He took an active interest in every aspect of its preparation, often writing whole chapters because he felt the only way his story could be told was in his own words. Without Molly and Travis there would have been nothing to write about, but without Travis, there would have been no book.

Contents

Contents

Introduction

Molly Lake and Travis Kemp are not names widely known outside the ballet world. Yet during their careers as dancers, directors and teachers which spanned over seventy years, they danced with the great — with Pavlova, Spessivtseva, Markova and Dolin, and many others.

Their memories and diaries give a picture not only of a changing England, but also of Europe and other parts of the world in which they toured. Molly describes her tours with Pavlova in the United States and the Far East, work in revue in Munich at the beginning of the Nazi period, and life in an ENSA ballet company, following the allied armies into Holland, Belgium and Germany at the end of the Second World War.

This book has resulted from many conversations with Travis and with Molly during the last few years of her life. She never understood why anyone would be interested: programmes and press cuttings existed for anyone who wanted to know the historical facts, and beyond that it was "just my life, and there you were. It wasn't anything that stood out for me." She kept detailed diaries during several periods, and these were consulted and have been quoted extensively as were the programmes and press reviews.

Molly and Travis were always pioneers. Molly toured the world with Pavlova, dancing on concrete floors and by the light of car headlights. For de Valois they worked "all hours that God sent, for 4½d"; with the Markova-Dolin company they visited almost every corner of the British Isles, bringing dance where it had never been seen before, and working under conditions which many dancers today would find impossible; at the beginning of the war, they were among the first to give lunch-time concerts while firefighting at night. As part of an ENSA tour, Molly danced in nissen huts and aeroplane hangers, and Travis, as a soldier, found himself doing his daily barre in a roofless cowshed or a partly demolished brick kiln. When they taught in Turkey and asked if they could hold a double-work class in the holidays, they were given permission as long as the girls worked in an upstairs studio and the boys in a downstairs one.

They gave lectures in schools and matinees for schoolchildren forty-five years before this became accepted practice in this country.

They discuss the situation of dance, and stress repeatedly their view (held fifty years before the Gulbenkian Report on Dance Education and Training reached a not so very different conclusion), that in England the over emphasis on syllabus in exams "is killing dance". Travis is one of the very few still teaching today who actually worked with the great choreographers and dancers of this century: Fokine, Nijinska, and many others and, for him, dance no longer exists the way he and Molly knew it. Yet, to watch him work is to realise that he is capable of restoring it.

They certainly fulfilled their ambition of bringing the enjoyment of dance to a wide audience, and yet they did not gain national acclaim or honours as did many of their contemporaries. They did not receive grants or subsidies, nor did they have any independent means; they worked and lived solely from what their audiences paid them — surely a proof of their success.

In later years, whenever Travis gave a talk about ballet or opened a competition, he always referred to an act passed about three hundred years ago which has never been rescinded and which described musicians, actors, singers and dancers as vagabonds and strolling players who could be arrested on street corners without a warrant. He expressed his belief that *"all worthwhile artists have within them something of the vagabond, the vagabond for whom the smell of the theatre means home"*.

Molly and Travis were never of the establishment: they were vagabonds until the end, and their lives were always hard but, as Travis says *"it had its advantages, it took us round the world and kept us young, at least in spirit"*.

London, January 1990

As It Was in The Beginning

Travis remembers Molly's account of her early life and how she began to dance:

"The Red House was definitely haunted. Molly's brother Peter had seen and described accurately the little old miser who had lived in the house some hundred years before. In the rose garden the bushes swayed violently when there was no wind and the sound of blows and heavy breathing could be heard. Footsteps came up to Mrs Lake's bedroom door every night, the door handle turned, but the door never opened. Molly's governess swore she had been pulled out of bed by the hair. Mr Lake said it was all nonsense, but even he admitted to hearing the slamming of doors which, on inspection, had been found to be open. The dogs hated the house; one of them appeared to have been thrown down the stairs and was found in a shivering heap at the bottom.

"Molly was born on the third of June 1899 at Lowfield Heath in Sussex, but shortly after her birth the local council erected a gas lamp on the village green and Mr Lake, considering the place was becoming far too suburban, moved his family to the Red House, a red brick Queen Anne farmhouse at Wissett in the wilds of East Anglia. It stood on top of a hill about a mile from the village which consisted of ten cottages, one Norman Church and three pubs. The villagers obviously had their priorities right.

"Molly's mother was an orphan who had been brought up by two very religious half-sisters. She was rather a fey creature with huge limpid brown eyes, while Molly's father was in every way a most practical man; Molly described him as a most un-Cornish Cornishman.

"When he was in England, Mr Lake spent most of each week in London, coming to Wissett only for the weekends when, to his wife's irritation, he usually brought with him numerous business friends whom she was expected to entertain. Peter went away to school at a very early age and during the week the house, even with a cook, two maids, a French governess for Molly and a page boy, seemed empty. Life for Mrs Lake and Molly was very lonely, and East Anglia could be very cold. All her life Molly hated the cold, but as a child it sometimes had a fatal fascination for her: she would sleep with her window wide open so that ice would form on her water jug, and often in the early morning she would steal out and run barefoot through the snow.

"Her one joy was her pony, and she rode daily. Unfortunately Mrs Lake also insisted on giving her a daily piano lesson, and these lessons coloured her life: she dreaded them. Mrs Lake's method of teaching was to rap Molly's knuckles every time a wrong note was

played; more raps led to more wrong notes and more wrong notes led to more raps. It was rather a vicious spiral. Molly considered that her lack of self confidence in later life stemmed from these lessons.

"Molly first had a French nurse, then an English one whom they called 'Old Bobtail', followed by a string of French governesses. Molly grew up speaking French with ease, and she recalled her father teaching the more attractive of her teachers to skate on the horse pond.

"Of course there were moments of excitement for Molly: Peter home for the holidays, chasing her round the garden potting her with an air gun and Mr Lake saying 'Don't interfere with the children, let them sort it out for themselves' (Molly swore later that her rapid movement on the stage came from dodging Peter's air gun pellets); stealing moorhen's eggs; Peter falling into the pond and, having hung up his clothes to dry on a bush, being chased naked through the village by the gamekeeper; Peter having been objectionable to the village school master, being beaten by his father and then taken out riding; Peter and the page boy fighting round the garden until they both fell into the pond, Mr Lake, considering the fight a draw, giving them both a shilling saying they were good entertainment value; Molly and Peter managing to push over 'Old Bobtail' and lift her skirts to determine whether or not she wore red flannel bloomers. She did. Then there was the time when

> "Mother in a fit of enthusiasm had my ears pierced, to which I took great exception: turning those 'sleepers' round hurt like hell. A few days after the piercing my father noticed the little gold rings. The barbarism shook him considerably: 'For God's sake, you'll put a ring through the child's nose next, or you will encourage her to become a ballet dancer'. Not that he disapproved of the theatre, he liked it, but ballet was something about which he knew nothing and was determined never to know anything. 'Blighters in Catskins' summed up his view, but it possibly put an idea into Mother's head."

"There was Mr Lake's feud with Fred, his head groom. Fred would slowly move things from the front of the stable to the back, and if by the time they had reached the back nothing had been said they would quietly disappear. Many times Molly would go into the stables to find Fred and her father sitting each side of the feed bin while on the bin reposed the latest objects that Mr Lake had found on their migration to the rear of the stable. Neither said a word; they just looked at each other, and the articles would be put back in their rightful places, possibly to start re-migration at a later date.

"One of Molly's pet hates was taking Sunday dinner to the old people of the village. She was always accompanied by the bulldog who on more than one occasion knocked her down and cleared the dishes. He, the bulldog, also liked beer, and was regularly brought home drunk by the village policeman: he would sit behind the bar in one of the three village pubs and drink the dregs from the glasses as they were thrown into the slop pail.

"Then there was the time that Mr Lake suddenly realised that Molly and Peter had never been baptized, so he hurriedly arranged with the Vicar for them to be, as he called it, 'done'. Molly and Peter had been out with the dogs so they tied them to the church railings, unfortunately not tightly enough, as during the most important part of the service the dogs rushed madly down the aisle barking furiously and deposited themselves on Molly's and Peter's laps. The service broke up in an uproar, and Molly was never quite certain whether or not she had been baptized.

"Molly's bedroom had been the 'cheeseroom' and as far as hauntings were concerned, was quiet; nevertheless Molly dreaded the moment when the light was put out and her mother's footsteps retreated down the stairs. Many times she would creep to the bannisters and listen to the conversation from below. Mostly, to Molly's distress, there would be arguments between her mother and father, and Molly grew up to mistrust the relationship of marriage.

"Molly's father was a mining engineer — Molly said he knew every inch of every mine in Cornwall; he spent much time in the farflung outposts of the Empire. He was made a Knight of Franz Joseph for services to Austria, he was given the order of the Medici by Abdul Hamid, the last Sultan of Turkey, during the disturbed latter part of this sultan's reign, and remembered crossing the Galata Bridge when a body hung from each lamp post. He was decorated in Persia, he had crossed Siberia five times, he had mapped most of Johore and had been in China during the Boxer rising. He had seen Chinese pirates gobbling up their last grains of rice before being beheaded. For him the Red House and its farm, where he 'could not see the smoke from another man's house', was a haven to come home to. For Mrs Lake, who had no interest in the country or the farm animals, it was a prison, and almost one of solitary confinement. In later life Molly understood the cause of the rift between her father and mother, but as a child it made her very unhappy.

"However one night seemed very different: her father and mother seemed in complete accord. They were enthusing about something they had just seen and appeared, almost for the first time, to have some feeling for each other, and that in itself caused Molly to listen with greater attention. They had just returned from London where they had seen Anna Pavlova as part of a variety bill at the Palace Theatre. Their enthusiasm was enormous, and it was as though each was trying to outdo the other in the use of superlatives.

"Molly listened enraptured, and slowly in her mind's eye began to see this wonderful creature. Her eyelids drooped but still the vision remained. Slowly and quietly Molly crept back to bed, but before she sank happily to sleep Molly promised herself that one day she too would be a dancer.

"In the cold light of dawn Molly's determination had in no way diminished, but problems began to arise. Firstly there was her father's attitude to ballet — she remembered his remarks over the pierced ears. Secondly, how did one start to become a dancer when even one's nearest friend with whom one could discuss it lived six miles away.

"There were five dogs in the house: the airedale, the bulldog, two dachshunds and a griffon called 'Bojum'. There was a great upheaval in the house when the cook cut off Bojum's whiskers because, after drinking, he would spray water over her clean kitchen floor. Only the fact that she was a very good cook saved her.

"Once a week Molly spent the afternoon with her friend Emma. Fred the groom drove her over in the pony and trap, accompanied on these occasions by the airedale, who was a good friend of the pony and always ran a couple of yards in front of him. Unfortunately she would suddenly stop to scratch fleas and the pony, in order not to over run his friend, would rear up and deposit the occupants of the trap, if they were not ready for the manoeuvre, into the road.

"Emma's parents had also seen Pavlova, and Emma had friends in London who attended a dancing class given by a Mrs Wordsworth. Things were progressing. Then as Molly related:

> "Unfortunately for father, I had to be educated and later sent to a finishing — what an ominously apt description — school in France or Germany; my brother was at boarding school, I had passed the nursery governess stage and was of an extremely enquiring frame of mind, so up to London we went every winter. I went to an extremely good and interesting school in Queens Gate, then kept by a Miss Douglas."

"At the end of each day Miss Douglas would sit in her carriage across the road and watch her students leave the school and woe betide a girl who dropped below her standard in dress or deportment. Miss Douglas had quite advanced ideas on education, and engaged as French mistress a well-known actress from the Comédie Française. Because Molly had had a series of French governesses, she spoke French quite fluently, and was put into a class two years in advance of her age. She always said that her appalling writing dated from this time, from trying to keep up with the copious notes which had to be taken.

"Molly and Peter had been brought up on Kipling and the school had Molly's final approval when she found that at assembly each morning instead of singing a hymn they recited Kipling's 'If'. The literature teacher however never recovered Molly's respect after saying in reply to a question that Yes, she believed there was someone called Kipling who wrote some kind of verse.

"The great moment came: Molly asked if she could take dancing lessons. The idea planted in Mrs Lake's mind by her husband's remarks over the pierced ears had taken root, she readily agreed, and Molly was enrolled in Mrs Wordsworth's 'Dancing Class'. The journey had begun."

The Consequences Of A Strike

The chain of events which led to Travis becoming a dancer were also indelibly printed on his memory:

"The ambulance passed me as I was turning into Derby Road; I had not seen an ambulance in Rolleston Drive before, at least not one with one of the new electric bells. Having negotiated the corner with some difficulty, it dashed off down the Drive, its new electric bell ringing wildly. I wanted to follow it, but I was already late for school, and anyway it would be something exciting to tell Mother when I got back. She might even have found out where it was going. I was sorry for whoever was having a problem, and I never dreamt that such things could ever affect me.

★ ★ ★ ★ ★

"I was born at 1 a.m. on 23rd of May 1914 in the front bedroom of a small semi-detached house (19 Highfield Road, West Bridgeford, Nottingham). There was a laburnum tree in the front garden and even at an early age I thought a laburnum was rather suburban and wished we had a lilac. I can't think why; maybe it was the play of the words 'Laburnum' and 'Suburban', or maybe I had been reading Mother's copy of J. B. Priestley's 'Laburnum Grove'.

"An iron railing divided our front garden from that of the neighbours, and I used to swing on it by my legs until I fell off onto my head. To this day, should I do anything unusual, relatives say that that fall on the head accounts for it.

"One of my earliest memories is of an uncle home on leave. Someone had given me a water pistol, and I pointed it at him and said 'Uncle, do you like my new gun?' His teeth chattered, his body shook all over, and he passed out completely. It took my mother two hours to bring him round. Even we who took part in the Second World War tend to forget the horror that was shell-shock.

"My father came from a long line of Lincolnshire farmers, but he left the land and became interested in electricity. He was a quiet, rather gentle man, totally unfitted for the cut-throat life of commerce; often to the fury of my mother, Clementina, who was of Italian descent, he would punctiliously pay his own debts, but never demanded payment from those who owed money to him; thus Clementina, who was a much stronger personality than he, would regularly have to act as debt collector. I inherited something of both their characters.

"One of Clementina's brothers was a tailor, but between the wars became interested in boxing. He promoted weekly matches at the local swimming baths and later opened a

gymnasium to train local talent. I trained there for a time, and what I learnt stood me in good stead, first in the Scouts and later in the Army.

"The boxing matches went so well that my uncle gave up tailoring and bought his own hall for his promotions. As the fights took place only once a week, he opened the hall for the rest of the week for dancing, calling it the Victoria Ballroom. This was so successful that he retained it only as a ballroom and took his fights back to the local baths.

"Clementina's elder sister Pauline became a school teacher. She married Arthur Bush, who later deserted her. They had one daughter, Noreen who, I do not know how or why, became a dancer, training with Edward Espinosa and dancing in the musical shows that Espinosa and his wife Eve Kelland presented at that time. Pauline was a maths teacher, but considered that if one could teach one subject one could just as well teach another, and she established, in a house in Fishpond Drive under the rock of Nottingham castle, a dance school which later became known as the 'Pauline and Noreen Bush School of Dancing'.

"I never attended lessons in my aunt's school, but was always 'raked in' to help in end of term performances if someone wanted a male elf or a tin soldier. I enjoyed being in the shows and always received one or two boxes of chocolates. At the end of the show masses of boxes of chocolates and bunches of flowers were brought onto the stage. Names were read out and each dancer came forward to receive his or her present from relatives or hopeful admirers. It became a great competition as to who received the most boxes of chocolates — so much so that certain girls used to collect chocolate boxes throughout the year, fill them with sand and send them up to themselves; but when they started to receive twenty or thirty boxes supposedly filled with chocolates, the audience used to make derisive comments and the number of boxes per person was limited to four.

"After the performance there was always a dance; chairs were removed from the auditorium which became a ballroom. All the small girls wore pink or white fluffy dresses and the small boys wore Eton suits and white gloves. Everyone had a card with a small pencil attached, on which you wrote the names of the girls you were having the various dances with. You would make the rounds saying, for instance, 'May I have dance number 9?', choosing the more clinging types for the waltzes and the more boisterous ones for the polkas and gallops. The girl might say 'I am already booked for number 9, but could let you have number 4 or number 10 instead', and so on. There was always great competition amongst the girls to see who got her card filled first. And from the boys' point of view you always hoped that you could kiss your partner behind the stage after the dance. You always tried to be near the entrance to the back of the stage when the music stopped so that you could disappear quietly into shadows.

"When I was nine we moved to Rolleston Drive, on the north side of Nottingham. The move had obviously been planned for some time as the house was built to Mother's design. I left the council school and went to a preparatory school, and Father bought a new car, a

four-seater Clyno. Obviously family affairs were improving. We acquired a black cat called George and a spaniel called Waddles.

"On March 19th 1924, my brother Bill was born. George had three kittens on the same day and his name was hastily changed to Georgette. The household paid far more attention to Georgette and her kittens than it did to my Mother and my brother. On that day, too, a school friend charged me sixpence for telling me the facts of life. I didn't believe him, and fought him and got my sixpence back.

"I joined the local scouts. I had to provide my own uniform and as I always had very little money, I bought a second-hand one. The hat was too small, the trousers too long and the shirt rather threadbare. Later Mother told me that if ever any member of the family saw me coming in my scout uniform, they would hastily dodge up a side street rather than own me.

"I fell in love for the first time with the sister of one of my fellow scouts. Jane had a beauty that even a hideous school uniform could not disguise. I used to steal roses from the garden, a thing strictly forbidden, and would throw them through her bedroom window at night. I learnt later that Jane married a curate, went out with him to South Africa and died at a very early age of some form of bush fever. What a tragic waste. I still have an autograph album in which she wrote:

When the summer sun is setting
And your mind from care is free,
When of others you are thinking
Will you sometimes think of me?

Oddly enough I still do.

"For me the 1926 General Strike was most exciting. Normally I always walked the two miles to and from school. I used to find these periods the most exciting of the day, but now cars stopped to offer you a lift and normally you did not say no. Also you were always meeting your friends' elder brothers driving a bus or tram.

"For Father it was different. He now dealt in electrical installations and one of his main contracts was to supply and install the electrical equipment for the Nottingham and Derbyshire coal mines. With the strike his business dropped to almost nil, but instead of laying off his men, Father kept them all on. It actually broke him and he went into liquidation. He worried himself sick and the worry caused his untimely end. I suppose in a way that my lack of sympathy with unions and strikers dates from that period.

★ ★ ★ ★ ★

"But as I said, the ambulance passed me as I turned into the Derby Road. Coming from school I contemplated the meaning of the ambulance heading towards my own home.

"When I did arrive home the house seemed quiet, dark and empty. Mother was waiting for me at the top of the stairs and she was crying bitterly. She beckoned me and led me into her bedroom, and I then knew the meaning of the ambulance: while out, Father had had a stroke and the ambulance had brought him home dead. I was just thirteen and a half years old".

Molly Spreads Her Wings

Along with other little girls in pretty frilly dresses and a boy called Algernon Harcourt Essex, Molly attended the lessons given by Mrs Wordsworth in an

> "enormous and very slippery hall in Harrington Road, where twice a week all the daughters and occasionally sons of the respectable, were instructed in the arts of skipping, wielding Indian clubs, the pas de basque, the polka, the waltz, and various other mysteries. What bliss! I was on the way to becoming a ballet dancer!" (Notebook)

No one ever wanted to dance with Algy (who many years later danced under the name of Harcourt Algeranoff), and Molly was often obliged to struggle with him through the waltz and the polka, avidly watched by her mother (who always sat next to a Mrs Stannus). They and all the other mothers jealously observed the classes, worried lest their precious darling should appear less able than the others. But Molly soon found that the classes were not demanding enough.

> "I was very energetic, and despite the fact that I only attended in the mornings and spent the summer as before in East Anglia, I found that after a year or so I had digested all the available mysteries and was looking out for more. In the class I had become friendly with Edris Stannus, afterwards Ninette de Valois, who was already moving towards professionalism and the great career which was to become hers afterwards." (Notebook)

Their families became friends and Edris and her brother Trevor (her other brother later became Gordon Anthony the photographer), used to come and stay at Wissett. Molly used to ride on the back of Trevor's bicycle, but one day it collapsed, Trevor knocked his front teeth out, and Molly cut her knees very badly and was spanked for having dared to ride on the bike. The children would surreptitiously help themselves to coconut ice at the vicarage tea parties, and when they were taken to Harrods by Molly's mother, Molly and Edris used to steal sweets. Sometimes Molly stayed with Edris and her family. Edris's mother had two very large dogs, and was known in the area as "The Squiress of Earl's Court".

Molly was still not satisfied with her dancing lessons:

> "Was I to be left repeating the polka and the pas de basque? This was unbearable. My mother and I conceived a plan: she would pay for two extra

lessons a week out of the housekeeping money, nobody would be the wiser, and no bones would be broken. So I found myself having the joy of lessons with Miss Euphan McLaren in her attic studio in Onslow Gardens. How I loved those lessons. Still came the wrench every summer, when I was taken back to East Anglia, back to the Red House on the hill with its roses, honeysuckle and nightingale, its walled kitchen garden hedged with forgetmenots and mint, and hay fields with their ponds full of roach and newts, its muddy roads and beautiful lamplit rooms with a fairly active ghost to each of them."

"I begged for a barre to be put up in the school room; I bought a pair of pointe shoes with 3/6 saved from seven weeks pocket money; I hung on to that barre for hours on end, staggering on to my points, heaven knows how much harm I did, but I was 'on my toes'. Father spent his week in London, only coming down on Friday evening so was unaware of the subversive activities going on under his own roof.

"To cut a long story short, educational difficulties became unsurmountable as Mother refused thank heaven to send me to boarding school, so poor Father was forced to sell his beloved and beautiful home where 'he could not see the smoke from another man's house'. I can see him now, leaning over a 5-barred gate in the winter twilight, gazing at a limitless expanse of ploughed field with rapt attention. I wish I had felt more for him at the time.

"From now on we rented various houses in London, an uneasy existence during the unsettled period between the wars, and I went to Seraphina Astafieva." (Notebook)

Astafieva had a studio in Chandos Hall, Maiden Lane, off the Strand. In an article which Molly wrote forty years later for 'Dance and Dancers', she described the surroundings in which the classes were conducted:

"On arrival at the murky entrance I was directed by a depressed individual with a very red tie down a dark passage to the dressing-room. This was nothing more nor less than a cellar into which one plunged at a breakneck angle down a flight of wooden steps. It was dark and dirty with a very low ceiling; the stone floor had a few strips of decrepit coconut matting scattered about, some wooden chairs and a long wooden table. The aspect generally seemed, to my youthful imagination, secretive and rather sinister.

"Having emerged from this dungeon, the new pupil pushed open a very tall door painted a dingy brown, and entered the Hall itself. It was large and, like the dressing room, dirty. It had drab walls and torn oil cloth on the floor. At the far end was a platform raised very high on which stood the piano. Generally one can hardly imagine a less congenial atmosphere for a great teacher to work in."

Luckily, soon after Molly began taking classes with her, Astafieva moved to a large and airy studio in the King's Road, Chelsea, known as 'The Pheasantry'. In a talk she gave many years later Molly spoke about this wonderful dancer and teacher and the training she received, and compared it, as she was to do so many times, with that of the teaching of the present day:

> "As a teacher, she demanded a depth of movement, a length of line and that basic rhythm which gives continuity and spread of pattern on the floor and in the air, an ability to create an illusion of flight, which today has virtually become a lost art! The wings of our dancers have been clipped, their magic imprisoned in the tense and rigid muscles of their torsos and in the arch of their straining backs....
>
> "Is the pull of gravity so much stronger now than it was in those days? Had we but an Astafieva to teach us, would we not regain something of our lost elan, both physical and mental? A class from Astafieva would, I think, be a revelation to most of the present generation of ballet students.... They would be expected to cover the ground easily and rhythmically, with accurate placing.
>
> "They must jump, pausing for that fraction of a second at the top of the movement — they must have vitality, speed, great bravery of attack, and pride of carriage."

Molly described these as being 'the basic equipment' of any ballet dancer, without which they would be merely acrobats:

> "Performed merely at 'tricks', with an uncompromising pedestrian approach, as they are so often now, Astafieva would dismiss the executant with 'She is a strong girl', then with a shrug of her shoulders, 'She has no school'. Her classes were exciting, her pupils even more so: Anton Dolin, Alicia Markova, June Tripp — well known as 'Little June', Keith Lester, etc. Arnold Haskell, a frequent spectator, sitting huddled up in a corner looking rather sad; but it was Astafieva herself who always claimed the leading role by sheer force of personality and the eccentric beauty of her appearance: very tall, really quite out of proportion with her immensely long and slender legs and tiny feet in very high heeled shoes, covered by grey woollen leggings, pulled up carelessly, and the rest of her clothes I frankly do not remember. I never got beyond those astounding legs and the tiny little head, always tightly swathed in a soft coloured turban, the whole vision to me was just legs and minute head, and the long and elegant stick which she always carried; a general figure of unbelievable neglected elegance.
>
> "Her lessons were strong and vital with all the command of the Imperial Russian ballet behind them, she a creature from the designs of Bakst and the

music of Rimsky Korsakov; she brought colour and evocation of sense of the theatre with her. Tell me, where can our young dancers find these qualities now, when can they recapture the colour, the illusion, the excitement, the breed and elegance of the great Russians collected together in the greatest ballet company of all times — the Diaghilev company.

"I suppose that what you have not seen or heard you do not miss, but what a pity that they do not miss it, try to visualise it, try to realise what a great blank is left in the competent and commercial often very dull ballet of today. The magic has gone.

"I had not been with Astafieva very long when the Diaghilev company made one of its dazzling visits to London, and with Diaghilev came Enrico Cecchetti, perhaps the greatest living teacher. I asked Astafieva If I might have a short course with Cecchetti to which she agreed. But when I returned to her she did not approve of the alterations which Cecchetti had made in my way of dance: "My poor Molly, what you do now!". So I went back to Cecchetti to his studio in Shaftsbury Avenue."

Molly studied with him until he left to rejoin the Diaghilev company, and when he settled in London, took class with him whenever she came home, until he left in 1928. He was very fond of Molly, and wrote here affectionate letters until the end of his life, and on one occasion recommended her to the theatre manager Sir Oswald Stoll. In May 1920 he wrote from Paris asking her to go and see his landlord to ensure that his room would be ready for him on his return, and also requesting her to inform the owner of his studio in Chandos Street that he would be working from 10 a.m. until 4 p.m.

Cecchetti would arrive every morning with cat food in one hand and a couple of bottles of milk in the other for his adored cat Mamie after whom he named one of his adages. At Cecchetti's classes Molly was

"lucky enough to be brought into contact with all the greatest dancers of that, or any other, day — Diaghilev's dancers. We, Maestro Cecchetti's personal students, shared their classes, their dressing room, watched them with envy, admiration and despair, while they were treated and criticised with the same dispassionate frankness as were we, 'the brats, the getters-in-the-way'.

"We all stood in a semi-circle moving round one place every day. On Monday you might be lucky enough to be standing behind Vera Nemchinova, a few days later unlucky enough to be standing in front of Alexandra Danilova, clothed in a well deserved sense of our own inadequacy; Lydia Lopokova to watch, Lydia Kyasht, Felia Dubrovska, Lubov Tchernicheva, Ludmilla Schollar, Alice Nikitina, and above all, Olga

Spessivtseva (later simplified to Spessiva by Diaghilev) — I remember Cecchetti watching her fine-drawn beautiful delicate hidden strength, coming from perfect placing and understanding, then saying almost to himself 'Voilà la danse'. She was so beautiful too: medium height, thin almost to emaciation, the bones so apparent and so fine that they helped rather than hindered the beauty of her body, legs and arms too long for anything but ballet, little long fingered hands and small high-arched feet, smooth black hair, a very serious small face with large dark sad eyes, which seemed always to look beyond the limit of our vision. There was always something tragic about her, a foretaste of the shadows which were later to cloud her mind. Lopokova (who used to disappear into the dressing room if there was an exercise she found difficult), gay, vital and exuberant, fair hair, tip-tilted nose, very short strong muscles, almost plump, dancing with gaiety and enjoyment — not the accepted idea of the prima ballerina, but what a lovely happy thing to watch. Dubrovska very tall and thin with endlessly long legs and long arched feet, legs that unfolded so expressively that they might have stood for the telling old Russian expression of "educated legs". Tchernicheva, another tall beautiful figure with long golden lion's eyes, a dramatic forceful personality — each so different in type and in dance, and all welded together to make the fantastic Diaghilev ensemble.

"There they all were in class with us; we watched and tried to learn from them; we heard their corrections, we absorbed their attitude to the theatre, and we hoped to absorb something of their style and tradition. Nostalgic figures whose quality has vanished just as surely as Imperial Russia has vanished. So much beauty lost; until we can learn to build on what we have been given without destroying completely first, what real improvement can there ever be? And those dancers had 'breed', not in the social sense, breed I think has nothing to do with social superiority, but in their values, humility regarding their out and out genuine sense of service — how lucky we were to have known them.

"Known them too with Cecchetti as master of ceremonies. His very short rotund figure, usually cheerful rosy apple of a face, not unlike one's idea of a family coachman, his very earthy and realistic view of ballet, no pretensions, no illusions, plenty of hard work and abuse. To me one day: 'Vous êtes jolie belle fille, mais un morceau de bois" accompanied by a dance of sheer rage and the vicious swish of his cane as he threw it at me; and through it all a great benevolence and liveliness, and above all an incomparable logical approach as a teacher. How lucky to have come in to the last brilliant magic display of the pre-revolution Russians and their teachers, still held together by what was for them an undying tradition, a way of life, a way of ballet, whatever you like to call it."

Whenever she taught in later years, Molly always based her classes on Cecchetti's teachings which were so very rich and varied.

Molly was about thirteen when she had her first job, a solo in a ballet, "Before Dawn", to a poem by Swinburne — "... for a day and a night, love played to us, sang to us...". It was at the Coliseum and lasted about four weeks. Her second engagement was in the play "Holofernes" at the Kingsway Theatre, in which she had a short dance.

While Molly was growing up and pursuing her dream, the world was plunged into war, thousands were dying, and members of the family were being injured. Travis tells the story:

"During the Battle of the Somme, Mr Lake, who was now a Colonel, received two communications. The first was from Divisional HQ, and announced that certain equipment was badly needed at the front. Everyone said it was impossible to get it there, but Colonel Lake did get it there and received the CMG for his success. The second communication was from Mrs Lake begging him to find Peter. He did find Peter. Peter at eighteen was second in command of a field battery and Colonel Lake found him wandering disconsolately round his guns, one of which had been knocked out by a direct hit; the others were out of ammunition. I always think of Peter when I read Rudyard Kipling's 'Epitaph to a Battery Out of Ammunition':

'When you see them in the workshops say
We died because the shift kept holiday'"

A week later Peter was gassed. The day after he was due for home leave, and rather than miss this he decided to go home instead of going for treatment. As a result he spent the latter years of his life attached to an oxygen machine, as his lungs had burnt out.

In 1921 Molly's father decided that if Molly was serious about her dancing, then she should go and study in Paris and furthermore must make her own way, so Molly was sent off to begin her adult life.

In Paris Molly lived on the Rive Gauche and made her way every day across the city to study with the former Maryinsky ballerina Julie Sedova. She always trained with professional dancers, and this was to remain for her a very important point. Like Travis she did not believe that dance should be taught by anyone who had not danced professionally. Sedova taught on the top floor of the Olympia Music Hall in the Boulevard de la Madeleine.

One day in 1921, a magical day the details of which Molly never forgot, the legendary Anna Pavlova came through the stage door, admired a troupe of performing dogs who were rehearsing nearby, and went up the rickety stairs to the studio, accompanied by two men, Pianovsky the ballet master and Victor Dandré, her manager and constant companion. She wore a plain grey dress, and looking elegant and serene she crossed the studio floor and sat and watched the class intently. At the end, she called Molly over to her and asked "Why you dance off the music?". In retrospect Molly felt her answer had been "very stupid and very young", for she replied: "I don't dance off the music". Luckily this response amused Pavlova and was obviously what she wanted, for she and Dandré laughed heartily, and gave Molly a contract. Molly felt Pavlova had decided that:

> "my length, my enthusiasm and my gormlessness might be *made* to fit into her company — she only had two sorts of dancers 'little gels and big gels' and I was definitely a big one, and *made* was to be the operative word.... It was hard, very hard. I had an incredible amount to learn without the age or experience to enable me to do it without great stress. Clustine was ballet master at the time, a kindly but erratic personality and a disorganised choreographer. I did not remember his lessons, I think I was too harassed to take them in. There was always the flying figure of Pavlova driving through class or rehearsal like an icy wind or a flame; nothing was ever good enough. I understand now how dreary we must have been to her, respectable mostly rather dull English girls, always blunting the sword of her desire to make us understand the meaning of ballet. Resentful and frightened of her whip-like tongue, not understanding what she had to give, and taking it regardless of the misery that went with it."

Molly remembered Pianovsky with great affection and respect. She particularly admired his character work, his rhythm and the way he danced the Kracoviak and other Russian dances which all the dancers were "brought up on".

The girls were given one pair of pointe shoes a week.

> "and that had to be enough. We never complained about it, but of course if our pointe shoes made a noise on stage we were fined. Today the clatter of the pointe shoes is sometimes such that it takes the magic out of dance."

Molly began dancing with the company immediately, at the Trocadero, and in the open air in the Bois de Boulogne. In one ballet with choreography by Ivan Clustine, which the dancers called "Chevre Pied", "quite the most appalling thing I have ever seen", the dancers wore goat skins. One evening it poured with rain and the skins were soaked, as was the audience. The skins began to smell and were most uncomfortable to wear, and the poor dancers were most relieved when they were pulled off the stage and the audience sent home.

Molly returned to London and was appearing in a few concerts for Lydia Kyasht, when she suddenly received an invitation to dance with Tamara

Karsavina. She felt very honoured and found Karsavina 'perfectly sweet'. She used to invite Molly to her house in Albert Road, and taught her many short dances. Molly was introduced to Karsavina's husband, H. J. Bruce, who was equally pleasant: 'They were such an enchanting pair, no conceit, nothing'. On March 10th they began a two week season at the Coliseum in London in a 'fantasy' written specially for Karsavina by Sir James Barrie entitled 'The Truth about the Russian Dancers'. This was given as the second part of a variety show, in which George Robey, Little Tich, Grock, and a hypnotist by whom the girls used to try to be hypnotised, appeared in the first half. Molly was given a long dancing part and in pre-production publicity, which stated that there would be a corps de ballet of eight, she was mentioned by name together with Margaret Craske and Dorothy Coxon.

Molly re-joined Pavlova's company on a short tour of England, which included Cardiff where Molly appeared in the corps in a dance called 'Primavera' to music by M. Helmund, and Blackpool, where she took over the part of Mlle Lafrenchi in a 'Pas de trois' in 'Snowflakes' too late to get her name printed in the programme.

Two years later, in 1922, between the tours with Pavlova, Molly again danced with Karsavina, touring England for several weeks, during which Bournemouth, Edinburgh, Glasgow and other large towns were visited. In this programme, Molly had her first opportunity of choreographing professionally, when she created a few short dances which she performed with two other girls while Karsavina changed her costumes. After this, Molly was invited to join Pavlova's company for a tour of the Far East. She walked up the North End Road to Ivy House, signed her contract, and was given her first lesson on dancing the Mazurka, which was very different from what she saw in later years: it had a smooth gliding movement, "not that hop skip and a jump bit". While struggling with the dance, Molly suddenly realised that Pavlova was watching from the balcony, roaring with laughter at Molly's "galumphing around". Molly was not at all hurt and told me years later: "She was a wicked thing, but a darling. She and Cecchetti had something in them that was the same: that wickedness".

What Shall We Do With Travis?

The evening his father died Travis was packed off to his aunt's school until the funeral was over. As well as all the day pupils, there were about ten residential students, girls whose ages ranged from about 18 to 24. They were wonderful to Travis ensuring that during the day he never had time to think, and at night taking him into their beds until he fell asleep. Travis emphasises that their attention was strictly maternal but says that never again was he in bed with so many beautiful girls all at the same time.

However, keeping Travis amused seemed to necessitate a great deal of noise far into the night, so much so that all the neighbours complained, a deputation visited Travis's aunt stating that they did not mind the noise until ten o'clock but after that time they would like to get some sleep. That night promptly at ten, every window in the house was thrown open and a head was thrust out of each window. They sang "God Save the King" in unison, the windows were slammed shut and you could have heard a pin drop for the remainder of the night.

When Travis's father was brought home dead his mother had exactly two shillings and sixpence in the house and no means of getting more. Early the next morning she went out and sold one of her most prized possessions, a Crown Derby tea service. She received five pounds for it which tided her over for two or three weeks.

Some time earlier Travis's father had taken a partner into his business. The partner claimed everything, even asking if he could borrow the car (to which Clementina unwillingly consented), and having driven it to the factory claimed it was part of the business. The only fortunate thing was that the house in Rolleston Drive was in Clementina's name. So she had at least a "roof over her head", but nothing to keep it there.

It was the day after the funeral that Travis went into his aunt's office and overheard the tail end of a telephone conversation. His aunt was obviously talking to his mother, and she stopped as soon as she saw him, but not before he had heard the words "There is plenty of time to worry about Bill, but what shall we do with Travis?"

Travis's father had been a Mason of long standing, and the Masons rallied round Clementina when her husband died. As soon as he was old enough, Bill would go as a boarder to the Masonic school at Bushey, and Travis was to be trained for banking. Fortunately, his aunt offered an alternative by offering to train him as a dancer. When the alternatives were put to Travis, he was not too sure that he wanted to dance, but he was very sure he did not want to go into a bank, so Travis became a dancer rather as he said "from a negative than a positive point of view".

Clementina sold the Rolleston Drive house and rented one next door to her sister's school, for which she was to make costumes for many years, and in the spring of 1928, Travis was enrolled as the first male dancer at the Bush School of Dancing.

He remained there for two years. The training consisted of three classes a day: from 10 o'clock until 12.30, from 2.00 till 4.00 and a third class from 5.00 till 7.00. He remembers:

"It was rather the survival of the fittest. One was thrown in the deep end and told to get on with it. In actual fact that was how I learnt to swim at school. All the boys were thrown in at the deep end and you actually swam or were scraped off the bottom by one of the bigger boys."

Pauline and Noreen Bush's pupils were given opportunities for public performance whenever possible, and Travis would dance with them in what was known as "Ciné-Variety". This was a performance which consisted of a film and a variety show in roughly equal quantities. It was very hard work: the dancers would arrive at the theatre at 11.30 in the morning, dance at two-hourly intervals, leaving the theatre at midnight having performed five times. This type of show was so popular and so widespread that the *Dancing Times* used to list them under "Cinema Dancing Shows".

In the winter of 1928–29 Pauline Bush died and on her deathbed asked Travis's mother to look after her daughter Noreen. In consequence Clementina put the money from the sale of her house into the school, moved it into a larger house in Forest Road Nottingham, and took in a greater number of both residential and day pupils. The school prospered until Noreen married Victor Leopold. He was a very good looking juvenile lead who had appeared in Skegness with Clement Concert Parties. He drove a red sports car and was the heartthrob of every girl in Skegness. Travis remembers:

"Noreen had demanded that Victor be brought into the school as a partner, so Mother agreed, providing I could be too. Noreen would not accept this, and insisted that the partnership between herself and Mother be dissolved. Amongst other things, Mother had put all her furniture into the school, and she wanted to buy certain items back, but Noreen insisted that they go to auction, and Mother never did get them back.

"Victor wanted a musical act of his own, and Mother financed it because I was to be in it. It had its own running tabs — its own stage curtains — which travelled with us. Victor performed a tap dance and sang, and I did a Spanish dance with a girl from the school, and an adagio act, choreographed by Noreen. Like other acts around at that time, it had very fast acrobatic lifts, as for instance where the girl rushed at the boy, put one foot in his clasped hands, he threw her up, she twisted in the air and he caught her in a fish dive."

In May 1929 they appeared at the Nottingham Palais de Danse in cabaret. The local paper considered Travis and his partner to be "very clever young dancers", and printed a photograph of them with the girl sitting on Travis's shoulder in what was described as "a difficult pose".

The local press followed his progress proudly, and in 1931 a reporter felt that he shared "the family gift for corybantic display", and reported that he and his partner would next be performing in London, at the Commodore Theatre, Hammersmith. It was while he was there that a friend made a chance remark which was to change his whole life:

"Would you like to come and watch a rehearsal of a performance of ballet that is being put on in a theatre in Islington by somebody called Miss de Valois?" In those days I was not quite certain as to whether he said Mister Valois or Miss de Valois. I soon found out. I went to the rehearsal, and while I was there a very charming lady came up to me and said "Look, do you dance?" It reminded me of the story "A man said to me 'Do you dance?' I said 'dance?', he said 'Yes', I said 'Who?' he said 'You', I said 'Me?', he said 'Yes', I said 'No', He said 'Oh'". But on this occasion I said "Yes, I do" and she said would you like to take part in the next performance and I said I would, so I did a half dozen rehearsals and on 25th January 1931, I danced in a ballet called 'Cephalus and Procris' and I drew my fee of half a guinea and returned to my cabaret act at the Commodore Theatre with Victor Leopold and Company, in 'Artistic Song and Dance Scena', never anticipating to hear anything more. Three or four days later I received a postcard — would I go to a certain address for a costume fitting and underneath were the letters J.O.B., and it was signed by somebody called Ursula Moreton. I looked at it and thought "how nice, somebody is offering me a job" and it was not until I got to the fitting that I realised that it was pronounced in the Biblical way 'Job'. 'Job' really was a fantastic ballet. It was something (the production in general and Dolin's performance of Satan in particular) that I will remember for the rest of my life, and I am sorry to say that although other people have danced Satan nobody has ever performed it the way Dolin did. 'Job' was a ballet that most ballet companies would not have attempted until they were well established, but de Valois considered that she had to make an impact and establish herself later, and she did."

The *Morning Post* agreed with Travis:

> "In such a production as 'Job' for example, the choreography of Ninette de Valois, the dancing of Anton Dolin and other British Dancers, and the Music

of Dr. Vaughan Williams, do the highest honour alike to British creation and British accomplishment''[1].

It was at this time that Travis made his first television appearance, in a concert which featured Helen Bates (''Songs and Dances'') and Fred Wildon (''Entertainer''), for which he was paid £2.2.0, an enormous amount at that time. He recalls:

''In those days television was in its infancy. The television studio was a small basement room in one of the houses just at the back of the BBC, it was like a witch's cavern. At that time they used the Baird system; you danced in a totally darkened room, with a square flickering light, like a shimmering spot, on you. The spot moved with you, and as only the area of the spot was seen on screen, you ran but appeared to be staying in the same place; also, owing to the delay between transmission and reception, you could go into the next studio and watch yourself finish your dance. I was possibly the first dancer to appear on television anywhere in the world, and was certainly one of the first to see himself dance. But unlike today's videos it was not very helpful, as one appeared almost as a shadow against the flickering light, and when dancing in the studio you could see nothing except the thirty lines that made up the picture, and they kept changing and flickering in front of your eyes; you could not even see the walls of the room — it was rather frightening.''

When the series of performances of ''Job'' finished Travis again went back to his cabaret and then home to Nottingham for his summer holiday. While there he appeared in a ''Nignog'' concert, specially for children. It was during this holiday that he was taken by his mother to see a fortune teller who said to him:

''Well, I know you are a dancer but I can see you getting a job to do with water or surrounded by water, and I cannot understand it''. I couldn't understand it either unless I was going to get a job at the end of a pier, and I forgot all about it until some days later when I received a letter from de Valois asking me to go and see her at Sadlers Wells, and I went to see her at Sadlers Wells and the penny dropped. I mean, Sadlers Wells had an aquatic history and right next door to it was one of the biggest departments of the Water Board. I was asked if I would like to become a permanent member of the company. I would not have a permanent salary but would be paid a pound per ballet performance and ten shillings for an opera performance, and I said ''Yes I would like it very much'' and I started. The first month went past and I was doing really rather well, raking in about three pounds a week, and at the end of the first month I was asked to go into the office, de Valois was there and Lilian Baylis was there; Lilian Baylis said ''Well Travis, you've been here now for several weeks and you are doing rather well, and we think that you would rather be on a much more stable basis than you are at present, so we are going to offer you a yearly contract and will pay you two pounds ten shillings a week.''

Although this meant a reduction of income Travis had no choice but to accept, and he was very conscious all his life of the honour of having been one of the first two male dancers to receive a permanent contract with the Sadlers Wells Ballet, which was in itself the first ballet company in England this century to give permanent employment.

Travis's mother now decided to come to London, and they rented a flat in Highbury. She began to make dance costumes and tutus, advertised in the *Dancing Times* and did very well.

The Nottingham papers continued to take an interest in Travis, often printing photographs of the Vic-Wells Ballet, in which for example, "Travis Kemp, the 17-year old Nottingham dancer, is seen standing in the centre of the group". The national press also began to mention Travis's performances, and *The Times*[2] gave special mention to his miming and that of Robert Helpmann in the Danse Chinoise in "Casse Noisette".

As well as dancing at the Old Vic and Sadlers Wells Theatres, Travis was also asked to perform with five other dancers in a play at the Lyric Hammersmith for which de Valois had arranged the dances: "The Fantasticks" by Edmond Rostand.

Travis danced with de Valois' company at the Old Vic in a series of ballet performances which began on September 24th 1931 and which were very well received. He performed in Ninette de Valois's new works, danced with Elizabeth Miller as Jack and Jill in "Nursery Suite", and partnered de Valois in "Fête Polonaise".

As is well known, Lilian Baylis was not only very careful with money, but was also a very moral person. Travis remembers her coming into class one day after the company had danced in the opera "Dido and Aeneas":

"The dancers were sailors and harlots, and at the end of a dance we lay down at the quay at the back of the stage; I don't know what we were doing but I think we were talking company scandal and giggling occasionally, and then suddenly remembering that we were harlots and sailors, and holding hands. The next morning Miss Baylis marched in and said in her very damning voice: 'I've had a complaint that last night your acting was a bit too realistic. CALM IT DOWN, WILL YOU, CALM IT DOWN'."

On another occasion, Travis was dancing in the opera "Tzar Saltan" with Claude Newman, Robert Helpmann and a boy called Tony Repetto. They had to lie on the stage throughout most of the act, and then get up and dance. As Travis said:

"It was one of those things that you think is bound to happen one day. Our music came and Claude jumped up and leapt about, and I jumped up and leapt about, and Bobby jumped up and leapt about, but no Tony. He remained fast asleep on the stage. We hopped around him, through him and over him. It was not until the curtain came down that we managed to kick him awake."

With his sense of humour, it is of course the amusing incidents which Travis remembers best. For example:

"De Valois would arrive at rehearsal with every bar counted out religiously, and you had to count religiously too, even Strauss waltzes. One day as we all walked out of the studio after a specially difficult rehearsal, we heard the forlorn voice of Stanley Judson, who was sitting in the corner, counting: "one thousand one hundred and forty two, one thousand one hundred and forty three. . ." In 'Douanes', Claude Newman, Guy Massey and I danced the part of Gendarmes. At one point we had to bring on a gangplank, and one day it caught on one of the flats and we brought the whole set down on top of us. On another night, at the end of a dance which finished in a lunge with our backs to the audience, Claude's trousers split from top to bottom. All de Valois said was "I'm glad you had a clean jockstrap on". She always had a sense of humour, and was in her youth a very effervescent person. She was not a bit like the image of the Madam who one feels she had to build, and in later years, the old Edris would come out occasionally, and she would giggle delightfully.

"At one time I became very annoyed because certain roles which had been promised to me, were given to Bobby [Robert] Helpmann, and I remember de Valois sitting almost in a washbasin trying to explain to me that Bobby was that much older than I was and much more mature.

"She was not a dictator but you were perfectly certain who was in charge. I remember one day coming to rehearsal late as I'd obviously misread the rehearsal list, and no sooner had I opened the door than there was a 'Travis, where have you been?'. I opened my mouth and said 'Well I thought. . .' and got no further. I was torn into very, very small bits, sort of rolled up and thrown out of the window. The next day the rehearsal list went up and underneath in large letters: 'WILL TRAVIS PLEASE NOT THINK'. She had the facility of making you want to work for her, and she really commanded a tremendous amount of loyalty. She really ruled by example more than anything else, as she didn't spare herself and she didn't expect us to spare ourselves either. We worked all hours God sent and we were happy to do so. Had there been a very strong union at that time, it is doubtful whether the ballet would have progressed the way it did.

"My first moment of sexual awareness was when my partner's bodice came down while we were dancing together. I clamped by hand firmly across her bosom so no-one should see it, and we continued to dance like that. I had great difficulty taking it away at the end, and much to her indignation held it there right up to the dressing room. I wonder if possibly the sexual awareness of dancers develops differently because we touch parts of the girls' anatomy which normally are prohibited until after marriage?"

When de Valois was building the Sadlers Wells Ballet, Marie Rambert had already begun what was to become the Ballet Rambert, and dancers from both companies often danced together for both de Valois and Rambert. Much has been written about Rambert's method of operating, and Travis had a theory that she worked like a permanent irritant and if they survived, drew out from her choreographers all they had to give, rather as a grain of sand constantly irritates an oyster until it either dies or produces a pearl.

Travis appeared with Rambert's Ballet Club during its 1932 – 33 season, dancing in Ashton's "Capriol Suite", Fokine's "Carnaval", and the role of the Umpire in Susan Salaman's "Le Cricket".

It was during this season that the company gave its hundredth performance which, according to the back page of the Ballet Club programme entitled 'OURSELVES: a subject for a back page', passed unnoticed. The announcement went on: "We apologise for failing to make it an occasion, and promise that the thousandth shall not be overlooked". The page gives information on developments and events at the Mercury:

> "After turning a parish hall into a theatre, we could not resist turning the dining room of the next house into an entrance lobby. Nobody has ever done it before, at least in Kensington, and it may never be done again.
>
> "It should be recorded that in a year's experience no one has attempted to leave the theatre by the doors marked EXIT. But they are always available for emergencies."

Travis remained with the Sadler's Wells for four years, appearing in the ever growing repertoire including Ashton's "Pomona" in the 1932 – 33 season. In the company's production of "Giselle" in January 1934, Travis danced the Peasant Pas de Deux with Ninette de Valois. The work was mounted with the help of Nicholas Sergeev, who had been a dancer and ballet master in Moscow; a rumour started by Stanley Judson went round the company at the time of this first performance, that when the ballet had been put on in Moscow, Sergeev had hidden in a dustbin on the side of the stage and had popped up and whenever possible to take notes; this accounted for certain gaps in his knowledge of the work. Constant Lambert conducted the performances, and at the dress rehearsal Sergeev was almost beside himself with fury to see him conducting with his head in the score, and kept shouting "He must watch the dancers, he must watch the dancers". De Valois tried to pacify him and assured him that at the performance Lambert would indeed do so, but Sergeev retorted "Maybe he will watch but he will never see".

The "permanent" contract was for nine months of the year, and although this was a wonderful advance on what dancers had been offered in the past and were still being offered elsewhere where it was the practice to pay per performance, it still left the dancers with three months in the summer with no income, and therefore towards the end of the contract it was not unusual for the dancers to look around for other work to see them through the summer.

And so it was that in the spring of 1934, Travis took a step which was to change the course of his whole life. He believes that:

"Looking back, you find your life has been in so many very definite little boxes, and if you go back sufficiently, you can find the actual moment when you change from one box to the other, and half the time, had there been a second's difference one way or the other your life would have taken a different form. One such moment happened that spring of 1934."

Pavlova Years

Far Eastern Tour

So many books have been written about Pavlova, the magic of her dancing, her repertoire and her tours, and so many of her former company members have spoken and written about life in her group, that this book will not try to deal with these issues, but will concentrate more on Molly's impressions, based on her diaries and notebooks and on conversations with her at the end of her life.

Molly joined Pavlova's company, consisting of nine men and nine women apart from Pavlova herself, for a tour of the Far East, which took them to Japan, China, Australia and many wonderful places which Molly thought she would otherwise never have seen, though in fact she revisited many of them twelve years later with Dandré's company. They set sail from Southampton on August 10th 1922 on the liner "Empress of Scotland" which took them to Quebec; from there they travelled by train across Canada for five days to Vancouver, where they stayed for two days before crossing on the "Empress of Canada" to Yokohama landing almost a month later on September 4th. Then came an hour's train journey to Tokyo where they were to give their first performance. Molly's mother wanted to go on the tour and, as Molly remembered

> "Father generously paid for her. She was the only mother to go along, but the other girls did not mind, and she kept out of the way. She did absolutely nothing at all. She couldn't even boil an egg. I carried her bag and everything. She didn't even sew my ribbons on. She said 'I'm not going to be known as Molly Lake's mother'. But she did watch some of the performances, and she was a very good critic. If I had nowhere to practise, she would take me into the bedroom, and although she did not know anything about it, she would make me do a barre."

Molly danced in the corps de ballet, and also in the Pas de Trois in "Snowflakes" and she played the role of "Oberon (dressed as a Hermit)" in "The Magic Flute", in which Pavlova was partnered by Alexander Volinine.

Molly never ceased to eulogise Pavlova's dancing, and many times during the ensuing years she recounted her memories of her. In one of her unpublished pieces she said:

> "Think of Pavlova. What was her salient characteristic? Vitality — an impatience of spirit and movement — (she was) an arrow — a flame — a devil, a generous and impulsive devil, but still more a devil than an angel. Her own amazing personality and vitality, her unrivalled gift for the actual movement of the dance, her speed and inner enjoyment of everything she did, made even her sorry repertoire something to be watched with bated breath. . . the most real, the most swift and vital, the most exciting dancer of the century."

Many years later Molly wrote an article entitled "I Remember Pavlova" for *Dance and Dancers*, in which she again tried to put into words the effect Pavlova's dancing had on her:

> "She was like some possessed thing — her incredible elan and speed — winged feet and mind darting through space — all the beautiful lines alive with the exhilaration of movement and sense of flight. Balance, and poise, (she would hold an arabesque on the point like a long sustained breath; it seemed impossible that she could remain there as long as she did), elevation, batterie, pirouettes — she had them all, but used them only as a means to an end, not as an end in themselves. . . She was the dance as you dream of it".[1]

Like so many of Pavlova's former dancers, Molly worshipped the ground she walked on and fifty-five years after Pavlova's death, she would still not hear a word against her; remembering how the whole company had been left on a station at three o'clock in the morning after travelling all night with no idea of where to go and no-one who could speak the language, while Pavlova and her entourage were taken to a hotel, Molly still insisted that Pavlova "never never" treated her dancers worse than herself, or expected any more from them than she did of herself.

She admired Pavlova's total dedication to dance, which she herself shared.

> "Being Pavlova didn't interest her. Dance was the only thing that did, and dancing was the most important thing in her life. For example, dancing in a temperature well below zero, with no heating in the theatre, the scenery door at the back open, because the lighting had failed and we had only the headlights of six cars to dance to: she wouldn't cancel the performance; she said 'You must dance here as you have never danced at Covent Garden, because here they have never seen dance'."

Molly thought Pavlova was the most beautiful creature she had ever seen. On one occasion she was summoned to Pavlova's dressing room after a performance because she had committed the unforgivable sin: she had brushed her hair from her face while on stage.

"She hurled every kind of abuse at me: She was so beautiful, without a stitch of clothing of any sort. She hadn't any lumps or muscle on her anywhere. But I never heard a word she said. Not one. She was so incredibly beautiful. The balance of her body was so right, and she had that wonderful bone-structure and terrific vitality."

Molly admired Pavlova's intelligence which was

"so terrifically quick. She could learn anything in about two seconds, was perceptive to a tremendous degree and could see things that nobody else could."

Molly felt that she had learnt most of her dancing from Pavlova, from watching her — "You saw her do something like the 'Autumn Bacchanale' and you wouldn't believe she was a living body at all" — and from the way Pavlova criticised and corrected her.

"She tore us to pieces, but it was not destructive: she took one outside oneself, to think what one must be looking like from outside."

Pavlova had a habit of wandering up and down the carriages on long train journeys to keep an eye on her young dancers and to see if they were reading suitable material and were appropriately dressed:

"She would not have liked us to go around scruffily dressed as many do nowadays, nor would we have been allowed to have our hair all over our faces. The face had to be open, always a small head.

"And then she'd suddenly point at a tree and she'd say 'What's that tree?', and you'd answer nervously 'It's a eucalyptus' and she'd go away; she'd come back half an hour later and pointing to another tree she'd say 'What's that tree?' and you'd say 'I don't know', and she'd say 'You fool, its the same type of tree'. She always got you."

Another example of how she 'got you' was when the dancers were in the wings while she danced. If they watched her she asked "Why don't you practise?", and if they practised, she said 'Why don't you watch?"

Molly was really happy and proud to be able to watch, and to be one of Pavlova's dancers:

"Think of it: all those performances, and class and rehearsal every day — eight performances a week, every week, and being able to watch Pavlova every night."

Pavlova occasionally gave them class and "It was absolutely the most terrifying thing on earth". Molly accepted their way of life as being the only way to live, never questioning or complaining, and years later she defended this point of view even more strongly:

> "Its the way to learn when you're young; it gives you strength; it's good experience; it's absolutely necessary, and if there'd been an Equity, we'd never have seen the places we saw."

Sometimes there was not even any time to eat after the show: they were just able to buy some bread from a baker on the way to the station

> "and that was our entire evening meal; and how much better it was. I think the welfare state has done more harm than it has done good. The dancers today don't know what hard work is, they've lost so much, and they don't even know it. The fun we got out of our lives! We felt we were doing something worthwhile, and the whole time it was: 'This is my life'."

Pavlova was very anxious that the dancers should see as much as they could of the countries they visited, and would give them time off wherever possible for sightseeing. They were allowed complete freedom as long as they behaved with decorum and did nothing which could impair the effect of the performances or bring a bad name to themselves or the company. For example, when they were in Western Australia, Dandré put up a notice which said "Piebald Sylphides will be fined" — they had been sunbathing too much!

Dandré was much loved by all the dancers; "He was considerate, cultured, interested, and a very benevolent person". On the interminable train journeys, he would help the girls with their Bridge which they played very badly, and Molly always felt she could go to him with her problems. Sometimes she felt sorry for him as on

> "a wonderful occasion when poor Dandré had changed the programme without telling Pavlova, because a girl had strained her foot. Pavlova had her dressing room up a little flight of stairs and when Dandré went up to tell her the programme had been changed, the most awful row ensued, which ended in Dandré being thrown down the stairs, with Pavlova shouting after him: 'If you can change the programme without me, you can do the performance without me'. It really was a shame, as he was such a nice person."

In spite of his benevolent presence, Molly found touring rather difficult:

> "I found Japan a disappointment at first. Tokyo with the rats running through the rubble of the last earthquake, the — to me — unpalatable food

— the crowning horror the raw fish cakes often given at tea parties accompanied by very pink ice cream — the agonising music at these parties, highly interesting national music that I now know it was, but to our very young and unintellectual ears, a series of excruciating squeaks, howls and groans; our hysterical desire to laugh, but Pavlova's eye was on us and no one was brave enough to commit such a breach of good manners."

Pavlova also found conditions difficult, as when on one occasion, she pointed out that the stage was too slippery and should be more sticky, and returned a few hours later to find that she had been misunderstood and that it had been spread with honey — the most sticky substance her hosts could think of.

They rehearsed in Tokyo for six days, and gave twenty consecutive performances, changing the programme every four days, in the Imperial Theatre where the dressing room contained no mirrors as it was the custom for Japanese actors to make up sitting on the floor holding their own handmirrors; luckily someone had bothered to put trestle tables in for the dancers for which they were very grateful. They had

"tiny little Japanese masseurs who used to run up and down our backbones. It was a most wonderful feeling."

They then travelled on to Yokohama, where they stayed in a comfortable though expensive hotel, and had in addition to spend money on transport to and from the theatre. An article published in 1923 under Molly's name described the theatre:

"The dressing rooms at the theatre were in Japanese style, paper walls and mat covered floors. They were small, and held only three of us. And how delighted we were to find that some thoughtful person had provided them with a table and chairs. The stage was very large, without a rake, and the front — as at most native theatres — was rounded like a concert platform. The auditorium was quite unusual to European eyes. Picture a gigantic chessboard raised about two and a half feet from the floor, and then imagine the cross lines of the squares made of polished wood some nine inches wide. Think of the squares as hollow and you have a number of little pens each containing a couple of cushions for the spectator to sit, or rather kneel upon. Each pen holds two spectators. To right and left, corresponding to the entrance aisles of a European theatre, there were two planks about three feet wide. The spectators walk along these to their places, and similarly the attendants cross the planks carrying small trays set with pots of tea which are passed on by the spectators to the persons requiring them."[2]

Molly told me

> "of course you couldn't make a sound in the dressing room because it could be heard all over the theatre. I don't know if they liked what we did, as they showed no great enthusiasm. Actually I don't think they were interested one way or the other, quite different from the Chinese, but they came, and it was always packed. When they liked something, they went 'ssss. .' It was terribly upsetting when you thought you were being hissed."

On October 4th they arrived at Nagoya at 3.00 in the afternoon, and encountered problems with accommodation which were to beset them throughout the tour and which, to middle class English girls, must have seemed very strange and burdensome. These too were recounted in detail in the *Dancing Times*.

> "There was one European hotel only, at which Madame Pavlova stayed, but which was too full up to take all of us. Hence we had our first experience of a Japanese hotel. We had to take off our shoes and were conducted in stockinged feet up precipitous flights of very narrow and highly polished stairs, without a guard rail, to our bedrooms. Here the walls were sliding paper panels, and the room was quite bare, except for a straw mat on the floor and a low narrow shelf at one end upon which was placed a dwarf tree set in a bowl. There was not a stick of furniture nor a single peg on which to hang one's clothes. The bed was formed by placing two or three futons, or quilts, on top of each other on the floor. The cover was a thickly padded futon. We did not essay the Japanese wooden pillows, for which we substituted our attache cases.
>
> "It was at this hotel that we met the Japanese bath. The door of the bathroom was transparent glass, and the wooden floor had tracks in it to drain off the running hot and cold water. In one corner of the room was a stone tub, like a well, containing water. This is the procedure: one kneels on the floor and soaps oneself all over, and then pours water over the body by means of wooden dippers, and finally as a great luxury one enters the stone tub for a short immersion. I should mention that it is considered the height of bad manners to allow a trace of soap to soil the water in the tub, which is changed at infrequent intervals. It is the Japanese custom for both sexes to wash together, and giggling nesans (maids) think little of watching one's ablutions, or, for that matter, of passing in and out of the room."

On to Osaka, where they gave six performances, then more travelling to Kobe where they stayed for six days, and then on again to Kyoto this time only two hours away and "a wonderful place. My idea of what Japan should be, an absolute fairyland which makes up for the disappointment that most of the rest of Japan has been." And in one of her notebooks:

> "most of all I remember the rushing rocky river, where long yards of brilliantly printed material held by boys, their kimonos rolled to their waists, were pulled, dipped and washed by the angry water — I take it that the dyes were being set, swirling sometimes under the water, sometimes on top, the gaudy colours were enchanting."

Conditions got on top of the dancers as on October 24th, when they arrived at Hiroshima

> "of course only a Japanese hotel and a bad one at that. No scenery, no decent shops, nothing. We were all late for the performance: we barely had time to get an unspeakable meal at the only restaurant in town. As a result of said meal I felt sick all the evening and went to my hard bed on the floor without any supper."

Hotels, food and travel expenses were very high and Molly continually complained bitterly to her diary. In Kyoto the dancers were so short of money that

> "after making a general collection I found that I had the equivalent of about 10d for my breakfast and that I had to walk to the station while mother went in a rickshaw with the bags. The only good thing about the place was the packed theatre absolutely full of the most stolid Japanese. I think they enjoyed it but most numbers went off without a hand."

Although it had its compensations later, October 25th started as a

> "truly awful day. We woke up in the theatre to a pouring wet morning, no restaurant to go to, and our train did not leave until 10.50 that night. We had no idea what to do, we wandered around and got very wet and then tried to eat a practically uneatable meal. We finally decided we'd have to go to a European hotel on an island 1½ hours away where all the "Royal Family" had gone the night before after the show. The train and boat were all right but when we got to the island we found there was a mile and half to walk in an absolute downpour. I think the scenery was the most beautiful I've ever seen. The island, in the Inland Sea (Miyajima), is an absolute dream. There are tame deer running loose everywhere. A strange thing though: as the island is a sacred one, neither birth nor death is allowed to take place there. . . . We left Miyajima at 10.30 in a motorboat which took us to the mainland. The rain had quite stopped and they took us down to the landing stage and through groves of trees with dimly seen shrines, and then along a narrow path overhanging the sea. It was like a dream procession. We were lit only by

coloured lanterns which we carried on sticks. I think everybody felt the unreal atmosphere because we were all silent. On the way across the water was faintly phosphorescent. I think the whole thing will always stay in my mind as a beautiful dream not a reality.

"Now we come to realities and very unpleasant ones too. We got on the train at 10.40 and nobody slept a wink, we were turned on to Shimenosehi station at 5 o'clock in the morning and had to take a ferry across to Moji. When we got on the boat, day was just beginning to show in the East, the harbour was indigo with darker indigo where the mountains were. The boats looked like vague ghosts gliding along and everything was coloured with the same intense sombre blue. It was only fifteen minutes to Moji but in that fifteen minutes the sun had risen and it was daylight. At Moji we got into another train and had another three hours to Hakata.

"In Hakata we had no interpreter with us as all the important people had stayed behind to rest at Shimonosehi. We went to the only Japanese hotel in the place where we stayed an hour and a half trying to find out the price of the rooms. We asked them in Japanese (about all we knew), but they either couldn't or wouldn't understand, and the whole household came up and giggled. Finally we left in despair and went to the theatre where luckily they found accommodation for us. By this time it was 11.30 and we'd had no sleep at all and no food since 7.30 the night before."(Notebook)

But Molly also had many happy memories of Japan:

"We saw Fujiyama; we saw the blaze of maple leaves in the autumn; we slept to the sound of a myriad cicadas; we saw the joy of the Shinto shrines; we heard the tap tap tap of the geitars, the lacquered sandals worn by men and women, something of a cross between a clog and a sandal...

"An enchanting sight was always a queue of men waiting for the bus, squatting on their haunches in their dull kimonos, crowned with an inevitable bowler hat, as a concession to education and advancement. The modern Japan has surely swallowed the Japan that we loved and hated — the beautiful, the sordid, the comic, what a dreadful word progress can be."(Notebook)

"The quaint streets with their wood and paper houses and their shops full of strange sweetmeats, brilliantly patterned materials or perhaps a window with a bowl of goldfish and a few oddments of bronze and ivory or lacquer. Each shop with its own sign lettered in black or blue or gold, in the beautiful Japanese characters and each one illuminated by a huge paper lantern. It makes one think rather of a toy town with its people also brightly dressed and the incessant wooden clatter of the clogs and the brilliantly coloured and lighted shops.

> "And then the Theatre Streets at night, thronged with resplendently plumaged humanity, the streets themselves narrow and lined with shop after shop, all with their goods displayed outside, materials of the most shimmering and gaudy hues, ribbons, lacquer clogs, hair ornaments, all hanging up outside and fluttering in the breeze. There is such a maze of colour and movement that one is absolutely dazed, even the theatres are more often than not painted red and hung with string after string of bright flags. Here and there you'll hear the peculiar and to me not unpleasant wail of the samesen and see two or three minute little geishas looking more like large humming birds or brilliant butterflies than human beings." (Diary, October 28th)

But with remarkable maturity for one so young, Molly realised that in many ways she had not really appreciated the wonderful sights and experiences, and on October 28th she wrote in her diary:

> "All this is Japan and seen from the point of view of a happy-go-lucky holiday maker it must be fairyland, but from our rushed and over-worked point of view so much of the fairy part of it has been lost in bare unpleasant realities and the impossibility to make anybody or anything hurry or even be punctual.
>
> "So much has been a disappointment but I feel there is so much more that is beautiful that we've missed. The circumstances have been too much against us, too much work and too little money have prejudiced us and have prevented us from doing and seeing the things we wanted to. We've been brought too much up against petty worries, the picturesqueness of the country has been spoiled for us by the fact that we probably can't get a decent meal or bed, that we're overtired and that we're short of money. I'm afraid too many glimpses of wonderful mountainous country, of blue sea and bluer sky have gone unnoticed.... I've many regrets and feel that I've wasted an opportunity, more or less unavoidably, of seeing and appreciating Japan as I feel it really is — a very wonderful beautiful country."

In December they made the short sea voyage to Shanghai. It was very rough, there was a terrible storm, and for the first time in her life Molly saw chain lightning.

> "The more serious on board, those who were not being sick, stayed on their knees praying, while the rickety little tub we were on, the 'Nillo Maru', thrashed, tossed, bucked, somersaulted, pitched, kicked and gasped her way into the pea soup yellow of the Yangtse river. What a relief that hideous yellow water was — it was calm.
>
> "I remember the Bubbling Well Road in Shanghai, with beautiful Chinese girls in their short bright jackets and black trousers, their long pigtails bound

with coloured silk, the hair cut in a short fringe on the forehead, jade bracelets on their very small wrists — like tulips or irises or tall, coloured daisies. I remember too the troupes of shivering rickshaw boys with nothing but ragged cotton to keep out the bitter cold, a miserable bowl of rice their only food — how I hated to be drawn along behind these panting labouring skeletons, and yet to refuse them was even more cruel.''(Notebook)

Molly remembered an incident which describes graphically the philosophy behind so many teachers and directors of the period, many of whom believed that a true artist could only be created through pain:

''I think that it was in Shanghai that I met my Waterloo in the shape of a private rehearsal with Pavlova. I was to dance the Lilac Fairy in her company's version of the Vision scene from 'Sleeping Beauty'. The rehearsal lasted from 12.00 pm to 3.00 pm. What happened during those three hours I squirm to think of even now. I was literally harrowed mentally, and physically turned inside out, and made to hate myself. Ending in furious exhausted tears, I shouted 'Take the beastly role away, I never want to dance again'. Immediately Pavlova was all sympathy: 'You are young, you must suffer, you can only learn through suffering. Now you will begin to dance.' Why she took so much trouble heaven alone knows. I wish that I could thank her — I hated her at the time.''(Notebook)

They stayed at the Burlington Hotel where, luckily, they only had to pay a maximum of £5 a day and where they were

''quite comfortable.... We gave 10 performances at the Olympic Theatre November 2nd to November 12th, and they were all a great success. We also met one or two very nice people who have promised to come and see us at home.... I think to stay in Shanghai for any length of time would be deadly; it's the most essentially artificial atmosphere I have ever experienced, and of course it gives one no idea of the real China.''

Molly was fascinated by the people and she commented:

''They're an absolute riddle from the meanest coolie to the most dignified mandarin. So much quieter and more impressive than the Japanese — one feels there is so much more behind them. Each Chinaman to me seems countless ages old with the knowledge of countless years behind his inscrutable eyes. I know that sounds rot, but I do feel it and I feel too that when they wake up to the realisation of their own power and to a resentment of the yoke of the white man (as the Japanese have done) that they will be the race to be reckoned with. At present they're all asleep and go along without any show or I think feeling of resentment at the abusive treatment which they receive from all sides.''(Diary, November 13th)

From Shanghai they passed Formosa where they saw the sun set

> "an indigo sea with a deep purple coast line in the distance, and a sky shading from palest apricot and turquoise to blood red. If it was put on a canvas, people would say how crude! How impossible! The only way to believe is to see it."(Diary, November 13th)

They passed through the Philippines, the beauty of which did not escape Molly:

> "We're just coming in to the Philippines; to our right is still the open sea, to our left a mountainous coastline wooded right down to the water. The higher parts of the island are still shrouded in cloud but where the woods meet the water they are touched with sunlight. The sea's a vague dull green until it gets close in to shore; there, between the soft green of the woods, growing right to the edge of the golden sandy shore and the dull green of the outer sea is a band of the most brilliantly blue water. It completely encircles the coast line like some great azure snake. The clouds now are beginning to lift from the crests of the mountains and the whole scene brings to mind all one has ever read of the golden strands and azure seas appertaining to the tropical islands of the novel."(Diary, November 18th)

In a boat which Molly found "so enervating that I feel I've not an atom of energy left", they arrived in Manila, "a cross between old Spain and a musical comedy tropical island".(Diary) The hotel was inexpensive although far from the theatre which was reached by rickshaw, and which was very large with a bad stage and dressing rooms. Molly complained to her diary that it was an impossible place to rest and that she never had more than five hours sleep each night; but she then admitted that it was partly her own fault as the manageress of the hotel had introduced them to many people, and they went out almost all the time:

> "either to afternoon bathing parties and tea dances, or after the show at night. Bathing here at sunset is the most wonderful thing in the world. We usually go with some people who have a house 2 or 3 miles outside, near the remains of some old wrecked Spanish battleships. I've never imagined anything so mysterious or beautiful as seeing the sun go down (supposed to be the most beautiful sunset in the world) and the moon come up. The only drawback is the jellyfish which are perfect devils and sting like the dickens, but still I have enjoyed myself here and shall be quite sorry to leave. It's the first time I've gadded about in my life and I think it's done me good"(Diary, November 24th)..."If we stayed here much longer I should become a nervous wreck and a dissipated one at that. I shall always keep very pleasant memories of its beauty, its hospitality, and some of its inhabitants. I'm afraid I am becoming a lover of luxury; sun and colour and beauty mean so much

'to me; it's going to be very difficult to go back to cold grey skies and cold colourless days.(Diary, December 1st)

"Discipline was slipping, and we were shipped back to Hong Kong just in time to prevent a complete relapse into comfortable complacency."(Notebook)

In Hong Kong, where Molly's mother rejoined the company after three weeks apart, life returned to normal with four evening performances and a matinee, ("I don't like this matinee habit"), and then afloat again on the way to Rangoon via Singapore. On December 8th Molly complained to her diary:

"This boat is pretty awful for us; they only took us on as a favour. We have no cabins, only two makeshift shelters with five of us in each, without washstands and furniture of any kind, except mattresses on trestles. Luckily the food is quite eatable but still five days with absolutely no privacy or comfort of any sort is rather awful. If it gets rough I don't know what will happen but I can imagine????"

That journey was so unpleasant that Molly enlarged on her memories in her notebook:

"Five days on a rusty old tramp, the 'Van Cloon'. We had no proper cabins and slept in some sort of curtained off space, on tables and camp beds — I had a camp bed which collapsed me in the night onto a floor covered with cockroaches. There was one wash tank in which was kept a lovely gold fish. I was always terrified that I might bale it out by mistake in the water scoop. Pavlova and her entourage were not in this boat. . . ."

They left Singapore on the S.S. Edarana, where they spent Christmas Day. Molly found it very depressing as:

"we none of us had any money to spare for presents, so we're not keeping it at all. It's rather a miserable sort of feeling, we're all rather forlorn especially as Lona, Joyce [Berry] and Sylvia are all ill and nobody seems to know what's the matter with them. Whatever it is it seems to be catching, and we're all waiting to get it."(Diary)

It was not until this miserable Christmas day that Molly realised that she had not recorded anything in her diary about work in Singapore:

"That shows how I'm changing: dancing to me is becoming a secondary consideration. Of course it's due to the atmosphere of the company and also because I've so little energy left, but still it's rather alarming: I don't think I mind any longer whether I go on dancing or not."

Molly did not like Rangoon "one of the saddest places I have ever been to", and she had few pleasant memories of it — Lona was left in hospital, and Beatrice [Griffiths] was ill with appendicitis — although she met one or two people who "did their best to give us a good time, and I shall always be grateful to two people in particular for helping me to think that the world is not such a bad place after all". They gave eight performances on an "unusually good stage" at the Excelsior, which were a great success, but Molly did not enjoy her stay there as much extra work was demanded of the dancers and there was "much grumbling and bad temper from the powers that be". As they sailed away she wrote:

> "Well goodbye Rangoon with your dust and glare and your myriad crows, birds of ill omen, your gilded pagodas and your motley citizens, you have sunk into the night now and your last light is only a vague blur in the distance. The moon is up and making a dream world with its silver light, a light that would give even Rangoon a beauty and peace."

What Molly remembered most about Calcutta was the dust that lay everywhere and even more so, the "hard glaring poverty as pitiless and hard as the sand and the dust". She did not enjoy

> "the Grand Hotel where the rats chased and squealed round the palm court and people chased rattled and squealed round the roller skating rink. I never got accustomed to the waiters treading on cockroaches with their bare feet especially when I was eating the eternal Grand Hotel bad curry. The rats were even more actively athletic in the theatre, lurking in our suitcases and running disdainfully over our feet. No ballet was safe from their speedy entrance and exit."

They spent one day in Delhi where they met the now recovered Joyce who together with some friends took Molly sightseeing, to an old Mogul Palace, to Agra, and the Taj Mahal. This made such an impression on Molly that she devoted over fourteen pages of her diary to describing what she had seen and fantasising about its past. Several days later she wrote:

> "Today has left me speechless, so satiated with beauty that to try and collect my thoughts and impressions seems impossible. I'd give a great deal to have just for this evening the gift of putting down what I really feel. Anything I can say seems so impossibly trite and commonplace compared to the reality."

Finally ten days in Bombay which Molly enjoyed much more than Calcutta. They gave fourteen performances there, eleven evening shows and three matinees, to most enthusiastic and packed audiences at the Excelsior Theatre. Molly was again "spoilt", and she felt very guilty at regretting leaving behind the

> "soft things of life. . . I had so much in Bombay and I'm afraid I've let myself get spoilt. Moonlight picnics on the palm grown beach of a tropical sea sound rot, but to me they're a wonderful and disturbing reality."

While they were in India the dancers were given classes in Indian dancing by Uday Shankar, and later much of what they learnt was incorporated into a short ballet called "Oriental Impressions"; as always Molly was full of admiration for Pavlova's performance:

> "How beautiful was Pavlova's slight sinuous body in her movements, how keen and quick her grasp of essential quality, how vast her enthusiasm."

There was also a Japanese section to this ballet, and Molly remembered how they had spent "an agonising time in Tokyo, learning the impossibly subtle intricacies of Japanese dance form. I am afraid that I was both stupid and unwilling."

They sailed back to England via Egypt, travelling second class as usual and being forbidden to "poke our noses into the first even after urgent and repeated invitations from the few first who are under the age of 90". They arrived in Port Said on February 19th, and performed in Cairo and Alexandria with great success, but by this time they were tired and cross.

> "Pavlova too was in her most difficult mood. One night before 'Autumn Leaves', her own rather beautiful composition, she kept the curtain down for ten minutes while she rehearsed a fall we had to do in this ballet. How many times we did it I do not know, but the floor cloth was a rough one, and by the time we did it to her liking, our knees and elbows were bleeding and our make up streaked with tears. Up went the curtain on this shambles. Next day there were some very puzzled comments in the papers."(Notebook)

Egypt did not impress Molly particularly and she wondered how she could have reacted to it if she had "come fresh to it and not with mind and eye impregnated with things that seem to be incomparably more beautiful".

On their way home they stopped off at Naples and visited Pompeii, so beautiful that "for a short while I managed to forget my longing for the East."(Diary, March 23rd)

By the end of the tour Molly realised that she had grown up a lot, and had gained a large amount of much-needed self confidence. On February 15th 1923, aboard the S.S. Kaisar-i-Hind, in the Red Sea, she confided to her diary:

> "I've met many delightful people who have made me feel that after all I didn't count for nothing, that I had charm and attraction like other girls. That all the lunches, dances, dinners, etc, that I have had have only been my common right and that theirs has been the honour to take me. I think it's a good thing I've realised this at last. Self deprecation is a hopeless obstacle in anyone's path. I'm not going to whine any more. If I've sufficient determination and strength of character I shall come back GW [God Willing]. I'm going to believe that it lies in my own hands and depends on my own strength or weakness."

Over and over again throughout her diary Molly repeated her determination to return to the Far East which she found so beautiful.

Throughout her travels Molly kept in touch with her beloved Cecchetti. They corresponded in French, and she lovingly kept every letter and every envelope. She wrote and told him everything about the work and travels and he in his turn wrote affectionately to her, sometimes complaining about the weather both in Paris and in London which caused him discomfort, always giving news of his students, and sending love to her colleagues many of whom had been his pupils, and particularly to Pavlova.

By December 1922 his letters were far from happy: many of his pupils left him when they found work, and although this pleased him "car le but d'un professeur, c'est de voir engagées ses élèves", he was very upset when Massine opened a school not far from his in London, and "ignoblement" lured his pupils away with promises of work in his company, and he was particularly hurt at the way in which this was done.

On June 19th 1923, Cecchetti thanked Molly for mentioning several of his pupils to Pavlova, and he himself also wrote recommending them.His health was deteriorating, and he took several months off from his school and students whom he missed very much, in order to recuperate. On May 24th, he wrote promising to be at the station to meet her when she returned from the tour.

Pavlova Years

American Tours

Molly was very happy to be invited to accompany Pavlova on both her tours of America. The first one lasted from September 1923 to April 1924, and was presented by Sol Hurok Inc. Pavlova was supported by Laurent Novikoff and Ivan Clustine (who was also the ballet master). Hilda Butsova, together with M. Pianovski (assistant ballet master), J. Zalewski, Fr. Vaginski and A. Oliveroff[3] were soloists. The corps de ballet comprised ten girls and seven men. The programme usually consisted of two one-act ballets or scenes from a three-act work, and a divertissement. There has been much discussion about the quality of the choreography of Pavlova's programmes, and Molly undoubtedly agreed with Arnold Haskell who wrote "People are wrong. . . when they call these dances trivial and unworthy of a great artist. . . . Pavlova does not merely show us Pavlova in a gay mood, she expresses gaiety itself'"[4]. Pavlova and her company were adored by audiences all over the world, and it was the accessibility of her ballets, the ability to reach those who were not balletomanes, which Molly learnt from Pavlova and was to remember for the rest of her life.

Molly's diary of the American tour, which took the dancers to every state except Florida was, in contrast to her other diaries, very brief — barely more than a list of towns and hotels. Simply reading the diary is exhausting, but Molly never complained about the fact that apart from a week in New York where they gave three matinees in addition to the evening performances and one complete week in Montreal, three days in Boston and two weeks in Chicago, they rarely stayed anywhere more than one night, always travelling on in a sleeper after the performance, and arriving in time to give one or sometimes two performances at the next venue. On one occasion, in Davenport, they did not even check in to a hotel but went directly to the theatre for a matinee and evening show and then went straight back to the train.

Her diary records an occasional break as on February 10th: "Free day, thank the Lord, saw the film 'The Light that Failed'", and at Christmas Pavlova managed, as she always tried to do, to give them several days off; she also gave them a holiday in Colorado Springs

> "which was so absolutely perfect that I can remember every moment of it. She gave us everything. We had told her that this was what we wanted and she gave us our full salary".

However, usually there was no free time at all or at the most only a couple of hours. She went out a few times with "Fuzzy Head". He drove her around in a very big car, often asking "Is anybody following us?" He never tried to touch her or to kiss her, and he took her home and introduced her to his mother. Two weeks after she left, Molly discovered that he was a bootlegger, and heard that he and his whole family had been shot by a rival gang. What a lucky escape!

On one of her rare days off, Molly saw the Niagara Falls, on another occasion she went riding, once she went to a cinema, and in San Francisco she spent half a day at the seaside, but on the whole she matter-of-factly reported what must have been a most gruelling tour. It is not surprising that by the time they reached Chicago on March 3rd, just before the end of the tour, she noted: "Bad tempers all round"; on March 4th: "Terrible rows, everyone fed up and dog tired"; March 5th: "More rows and everyone hopeless"; by March 6th when they had a dress rehearsal there was "comparative peace, but everyone down". But on March 11th "Abuse flared, and everyone came to a standstill"; however by the 12th there were only "small rows" and by the 13th there was "only general tension and nerves on edge". It is quite clear from her writings that Molly was aware that the rows stemmed from tiredness and never once blamed Pavlova for any of the "abuse". On March 14th the company was given an unexpected free day as the theatre was being used for other activities, and Molly went to see "The Ten Commandments".

It was not only Pavlova and the dancers who were tired and had rows, the wardrobe staff also had their problems. Once when they were in the far north of America the wardrobe mistress, Manya,

> "a lovely creature but temperamental as only Russians can be had had her boyfriend pinched by her younger assistant, and in a storm of tears and curses had thrown the keys of the still locked trunks out of the window on to the main road. The curtain was to go up in less than half an hour, and as usual it was raining. So out we went to retrieve the keys. Scrabbling in the mud was bad enough but dodging the traffic was almost lethal. Luckily nobody was killed and believe it or not, the curtain went up only five minutes late. It never struck us that we could do anything else; we belonged to the theatre, it was our responsibility to get that curtain up."(Notebook)

In October 1924 Molly performed with Pavlova's company at the Royal Opera House Covent Garden, dancing in the Pas de Trois in "Snowflakes", and fulfilling her usual parts in the corps de ballet. The following year, Pavlova went to Germany for three weeks taking with her only a few selected members of the company including Molly, who was very proud to be chosen, and after that they gave another season at Covent Garden.

In the winter of 1925 – 26, the company embarked on a second tour, this time to South America, and the contract which Molly signed on August 25th 1925 sets out in great detail the conditions of her employment. She gave her exclusive services for a total of nine performances per week — not eight as nowadays in Equity contracts. In addition she was required to attend as many rehearsals as requested without further compensation, unlike today's contracts which limit the total number of hours worked in any week. She agreed to dance in any ballet for which she was cast and to fulfil her duties to the utmost of her ability "and to the entire satisfaction of Mme Pavlova, under pain of cancellation of this agreement". She received $235 per month, out of which she was required to furnish her own silk tights and ballet shoes, and to keep them in proper repair at her own expense. In the event of illness, Mme Pavlova reserved the right to deduct a pro rata amount for each performance missed, and to dismiss her if the illness continued after two weeks. (Molly reported years later to a newspaper journalist how she had once been fined for arriving late at a rehearsal because of a bilious attack.) No payment was to be made for time at sea travelling to and from their destinations, and if there were no performances for the week before Christmas, only expenses totalling $4 per day were to be paid. If however, a few were given, she would receive pro rata for each performance. Equity has ensured that dancers' conditions of work are far easier today, although Molly would have argued that this is not necessarily a good thing.

On this tour also Pavlova won Molly's admiration for being willing to put up with the same hardships as those endured by her dancers: they arrived at Ann Arbor, a small town perched on top of a mountain, in mid-winter when all the roads leading up to it were iced up and impassable. The inhabitants made a human chain and pulled the dancers up one after the other, starting with Pavlova.

When they were in Mexico City, the company performed in a bull-ring and had to finish the performance even though it began to rain heavily. This was accepted as being perfectly normal: "It's raining, so what?". The dancers were often sick after a performance because it was so high up. "Nobody worried. You were sick and that was all." There were no oxygen bottles in those days.

Molly was still very young and well behaved: in Mexico City, some of the girls used to stay out after performances in order to see the town, and ever mindful of their moral and physical well-being, Dandré told them that they were no longer to do this. Molly "being a stupid fool and terribly righteous said 'But I haven't been doing it'". He looked at her and said "I didn't expect you to do anything as happy as that".

Pavlova's dancers were paid more than in other companies and on this tour living expenses were not too high. As a result, Molly felt very privileged and well-treated, and by the end of the tour was able to report with satisfaction that she had saved 260 dollars.

This was to be Molly's last tour with the company for while they were in Mexico City she met Norman King and took a step which she thought would take her away from ballet and would change her whole life: she agreed to marry him. She was attracted by his very lively mind, and succumbing to pressure from her parents who were anxious to see her "settled", she did not think about what would happen to her dancing.

Molly was still very young and Walter proved in Mac Street's [illegible] as one of the girls [illegible] performances in order to see the town [illegible] and physical [illegible]. [illegible] told them [illegible] they were [illegible] Mac Street's [illegible] stupid [illegible] and [illegible] said. [illegible]

[illegible] were glad [illegible] her [illegible] and on the [illegible] were [illegible] Molly then [illegible] the end of the tour was [illegible] with [illegible]

[illegible]

In the Wilderness

Norman King, later Sir Norman King, was the British Chargé d'Affaires in Mexico City. He had re-established diplomatic relations between Britain and Mexico after many years, and was highly respected by the diplomatic service. Molly was fascinated by him: she found him very interesting and kind, and her parents were happy that she would at last be settled. Norman King showed her many beautiful parts of Mexico, which he knew "backwards, sideways and upside down", and which Molly thoroughly enjoyed. They then returned to London where they were married in May 1926 and went on honeymoon to Venice.

Throughout her life Molly's big decisions were always determined by her unquenchable need to dance, often leading her along paths which made life much more difficult in the long run: her marriage did not last more than a few months as this urge once more took over her life. Molly confided years later that she had always known that she could not live without dancing and that she simply had not thought enough before marrying. It would have been difficult for a Consul's wife to have a full time dancing career, but on reflection Molly felt this might have been possible had she been a bit older and more determined, as Norman King was "such a kind person and would probably not have fought at all". Some time afterwards when Molly was dancing in a lunch time concert at the Marlowe Theatre Canterbury, her ex-husband was in the audience and sent her flowers, which Molly thought was "very forgiving".

The next few years were dreary and frustrating for Molly, for although Pavlova did not die until 1931, Molly never returned to her company. There was little or no ballet in England, she was tall — a disadvantage in those days for a classical dancer — and she did not always see eye to eye with those who might have helped her. "The cat that walked by itself is a dead loss for anybody who has a way to make on the stage, and a long cat even more hopeless". She taught a little when asked to fill in for other teachers, even at times taking classes for Lydia Kyasht and Tamara Karsavina, and she worked with Margaret Craske who had taken over Cecchetti's studio when he left England for Milan. Occasionally there was a performance as when, on February 12th 1934, she appeared in "Elijah" at the Albert Hall, with Alicia Markova.

Whenever possible, she gave recitals which were organised by an impresario named Albert. All that Molly remembered about him was that his sister, who lived with a prostitute in Carnaby Street, had a crush on her and that her father found this amusing. One such recital was at the Rudolph Steiner Hall on June 7th 1928, "supported by" Kathleen Crofton and Marie Nielson, and with two singers, Wendy Nash and Bernard Conett. The programme included a "Minuet", "Mexican Dance", "Danse Hindou", "Danse Russe", and many other short items. The "Referee" a few days later considered Molly's performance

> "an artistic and engaging entertainment. Gifted with a beautiful figure, a keen sense of rhythm, and evidently artistic perceptions which have been judiciously cultivated, her skill and grace were captivatingly exhibited in a series of dances remarkable for freshness and well designed costumes."[1]

She had worked at times for Ninette de Valois: in her ballet "The Arts of the Theatre" at the Sunshine Matinee at the Queen's Theatre on December 8th 1925, in "The Picnic" at the Old Vic in 1926, and in her choreography in the play "A Florentine Irony" at the Festival Theatre, Cambridge on November 28th 1927.

That same year she was invited by Ninette de Valois, who had high regard for her teaching ability which was based on having studied both the Italian and Russian schools, with Cecchetti and Astafieva respectively, to teach at her newly created Academy of Choreographic Art; she appeared with the students when they gave a series of performances at the Court Theatre in November 1928, when she danced in a pas de trois in "Scene de Ballet". Mary Clarke later described her as one of de Valois' chief helpers.[2] She based her classes, as she was to do for the rest of her life, on the teachings of Cecchetti, who she considered to be "the greatest teacher there has ever been in the world". She fervently believed that he "knew everything to make a dancer" and she admired his use of the floor and the way he helped dancers to project their line beyond themselves. She stressed this last point in every class she taught till the end of her life.

Molly remembered that Ninette de Valois was effervescent, with a great, sometimes naughty sense of humour, but that she lost this when she taught. However, she did not teach much at that time as Molly and Ursula Moreton undertook most of the tuition.

Molly's classes were greatly enjoyed by her students, but Molly knew that it was de Valois' "terrific strength of purpose — enormous" which had eventually built the Royal Ballet, and she greatly admired her for it, but her drive lay in a different direction: she had to dance, and once again she made a decision based on this alone: in spite of the fact that her students enjoyed her

Molly

Molly

Molly with Karsavina in "The Truth about the Russian Dancers"

Molly (The Marilyn Dancers)

Marie Nielsen, Frederick Ashton and Molly in cabaret

Molly

Molly in Fokine's "Carnival"

classes and benefited greatly from them, and the fact that she enjoyed teaching, she left to dance in a pantomime with some of her students, and felt that de Valois, who had planned her life and career so carefully, found it very hard indeed to understand why anyone would prefer to dance in a pantomime than to take part in the building of a new company. Years later Beatrice Appleyard, who had been one of Molly's students at that time, wrote that it was from Molly that she had gained her ''feeling'' for dance.

Molly returned to Paris where she studied with Egorova and Trefilova, and in the summer of 1930 she was given the opportunity to join Boris Kniasseff, whose small company had several really good dancers, including one who helped to finance it.

The repertoire consisted mainly of Kniasseff's own choreography which in Molly's opinion was ''drastically no good, as was his dancing''. However in contrast, a critic at the time described the programme, which consisted of eight ballets, as being ''d'une couleur et d'une lumière extraordinaire''.[3] Kniasseff was not easy to work with, and in fact Molly felt he was slightly mad: he would start rehearsing at eight o'clock in the evening and continue until about four o'clock in the morning — ''None of us objected at all. None of us said a word''. After rehearsing for several weeks, the company opened in Paris in July, following which it was taken to Rietti, a town in the mountains just outside Rome. Suddenly Kniasseff announced ''Company finished'' and disappeared. The dancers had of course not received any pay for rehearsals, as was the practice at that time — and in fact Molly was not paid at all that year — but they were not angry, in spite of the fact that their plight was caused by sheer incompetence. Their philosophy was simple. As Molly said years later:

> ''One sort of thought 'It may be good, it may be bad, you've got to take your chance. And if it's bad, tant pis'. It was really good for us. What Pavlova said is true: 'Suffer and you'll learn'. These spoilt creatures of today don't know what life is, they haven't even started, and what do they get as a result? Nothing''.[4]

The dancers were left to make their own way home as best they could. Luckily one of the men managed to arrange a contract for five of them with Grigoriev, who was collecting a small company to fulfil the end of the contract held by Diaghilev at Monte Carlo, and in the winter of 1929 Molly, Chamié, Chabelevsky, Blinova and Petrova managed to scrape together enough money for third class tickets to Monte Carlo, and embarked on a journey on uncomfortable seats which took over two days. They had no money for food, and were very grateful when some Spaniards in the train saw them eyeing their ''very smelly fish with bread'' and kindly gave them some. They arrived

> "triumphant and hungry and full of hope. What a season it was! Danilova Dubrovska, Tchernisheva, Chabelevsky, Yassinsky, and the remaining members of the corps de ballet of Diaghilev's company. Amongst the singers were Chaliapin, and Conchita Supervia. *Schéhérazade* and *Prince Igor* were given as operas with ballet, *Don Carlos* with Chaliapin, and *Carmen* with Conchita Supervia. What a revelation they both were — the only *Carmen* I have enjoyed since is *Carmen Jones*. Chaliapin, Supervia, Pavlova, they all three had something of the inspired devil that made their performances flash and burn — *never* to be forgotten."[5]

They appeared on 23rd January 1930 in the Monaco Fête in "Helen in Egypt" (R. Strauss) and in "Un Nuit à Venise" (J. Strauss). In 1931, they again performed in operas, and in several short ballets[6] — "What a season it was!".

In both seasons, although she was given a "few bits and pieces", Molly danced mainly in the corps de ballet, and her name therefore does not appear in the programmes which list only the soloists. The repertoire included a Glinka "Mazurka" which Molly had danced with Pavlova. In this dance two lines of dancers who were holding hands, had to cross each other, and much rehearsal time was spent in trying to remember how this was done. Molly suggested that while crossing they let go of hands, but she was rudely told that, as she was English, she knew nothing and should be quiet. Molly admired the superb dancing of the Russians very much, and felt that they had far more vitality and sense of rhythm than the English ones but she was very angry at the time and energy spent on the problem to which she had already provided the solution; finally one of the Russians suggested, as Molly had done, that they let go of hands. She often said that English dancers no longer have the vitality they used to have in Diaghilev's day, and talked about the English-born Lydia Sokolova who, she felt, danced as well as any Russian.

Molly thoroughly enjoyed her time with the company, although she found it very difficult: they worked too hard to be able to enjoy the sea or the weather very much, the dancers often quarrelled noisily, one "enjoyed herself" by "stealing" other women's husbands, and none was particularly friendly; the girls would watch her avidly as she stripped and washed in the basin in the dressing room, weighing her up and discussing her body.

Molly felt that Grigoriev was doing a very good job but she did not enjoy the classes given by his wife Tchernicheva, as she found her hard: "She had no softness in her, and yet she did some very soft dancing". In 1932, after the two seasons were finished, Molly was offered a contract to appear at the Pigalle Theatre in Paris, in performances which were to include opera, drama and ballet. Komisarjevsky, who was forming his own company, was responsible for the drama, and Kniasseff, who was now the ballet master at the Opéra Comique de Paris, for the ballet.

> ''Rehearsals drifted on. Prokofiev himself conducted rehearsals of his 'Symphonie Classique' which Kniasseff was choreographing — so much hope, so much excitement, quite nice fat contracts. Came the first night, or was it only the dress rehearsal, an atmosphere of disorder and disintegration. Next morning the theatre was closed, no explanation and of course no money. I stayed on in Paris for a short time, pawning my clothes in order to live. I don't think they were worth very much, probably all holes.''[7]

One of the dancers, Birger (nicknamed Billy) Bartholin, who later became a director in Finland, Norway, and his native Denmark, won some money on the Calcutta Sweep and used to sing snatches of ''Schéhérazade'' under the window of Molly and her room-mate at three o'clock in the morning to wake them up and give them food. Molly's mother came to Paris, retrieved her belongings from the pawn shop and took her home to England.

In 1929 the Cambridge Ballet Society was formed under the patronage of Molly, Lydia Lopokova, and Ninette de Valois. Its first ''meeting'' took place on May 5th. The programme consisted of three ballets: ''Primavera'' inspired by Botticelli's picture, with music by Richard Dabell; a Divertissement, and a ''Smorgasborg''. ''F.B.'', in the *Musical Times* was impressed by the high standard, considering that the dancers, Molly, Georgina Wright and a Mr Kei Kurasawa, an undergraduate of Trinity College

> ''attained to a standard of excellence entirely unexpected from dancers not 'under the direct supervision' of a Cecchetti or a Diaghilev''.[8]

In 1930 Molly joined a group which included ''Mdlles'' Sanova and Elsa D'Arcy, and ''Mons'' Slavinsky and Borowsky, and which called itself ''Russian Ballet''. They received good reviews wherever they performed. The *Brighton & Hove Herald* praised all the dancers, noting particularly the

> ''high development of technique and artistry [shown] by two dancers, Mlles D'Arcy and Lake. If, as one supposes they are English, then their dancing reveals a successful blend of the slav and the Saxon. They strike the modern note.''[9]

The company was praised not only by the local press but also in the *Daily Express* where Gordon Beccles described a performance he had seen at the King's Theatre Edinburgh as a ''pathetic evening — pathetic because it was so good''. He went on to explain that since Diaghilev had died and his company was no longer in existence, the group was carrying on a tradition whose "fount has already dried up — legionaries of Rome with Rome sacked and the Empire fallen".[10]

Molly then formed a double act with another girl, which they called "Marilyn and Jani". Sometimes the group was extended and Molly appeared with Kathleen Crofton and Anna Northcote or Marie Nielson as the "Marilyn Dancers". In her biography Peggy van Praagh mentions that she also worked with them for a time in 1932.[11] They danced classical duets on pointe in pantomimes, appearing in Leeds at Christmas 1930 and in cabaret at the Criterion. They were employed as dancers at the Windmill, where they performed a trio with the dancer Rollo Gamble. Molly commented: "I've never known such a respectable place in my life. In spite of its reputation for nudity and sex, the girls, having appeared in the nude, went home to cocoa with mother".

In 1932 Molly joined the "Anna Ludmilla Ballet" as a soloist. They performed a ballet named "To Vienna" in the Bath Pavilion in March 1932. The work was described in the programme as a "Phantasy in Rhythm" and a "Viennese Episode", and was "played by the Vienna Orchestra, Characters from the State Opera and the Composer". The dancers included Stanley Judson, and the performers danced and sang to a bevy of popular composers including Franz Léhar, Johann Strauss, and Ricardo Drigo.

Next, Molly toured Germany and other European countries with a Swedish dancer, Greta Baronius. They performed short dances in revues, one of which, in Munich, was called "Grüsse uns Alles". Molly was not particularly interested in politics, but could not help being aware in Germany of the fact that she and Greta were treated very badly because they did not belong to the master race, and Molly never forgot this experience. While they were performing in Paris, poor Greta died tragically: she was cleaning a costume with petrol, as so many dancers did at that time, when suddenly it caught fire and she was burnt to death.

Molly then gave ballet lessons to Marie Rambert, and danced for her occasionally over a period of three years at the newly acquired Mercury Theatre. Like so many of Rambert's ex-dancers, she remembered Rambert "tearing everybody to pieces" and also one of the dancers responding with matching insults. When Molly decided to leave, Rambert tried to persuade her to stay as she could not understand why Molly should want to go.

Molly then gathered together a small group of girls: Eileen Keegan, Vera Sevna, Audrey Valeska, Anna Northcote, and Kathleen Crofton, and together they went on a

> "disastrous cabaret tour in France, Belgium, Holland — our own group of pretty and respectable girls doing pretty and respectable dances. After the first impact of our prettiness had worn off the respectability was an insurmountable drawback, a disgrace in fact, and home we came with just enough to pay the fare."[12]

They had refused to remove their BBs (bust bodices, as bras were called in those days)! Together with these girls and her students who had danced with her in pantomime, Molly next began rehearsals for a dance film with Anton (Pat) Dolin, and it was during rehearsals in his studio in Chelsea that "a miracle happened": an offer came from Victor Dandré to join a company, consisting mainly of former Pavlova dancers, that he was taking to the far East. Molly was very keen to go, but felt extremely guilty about letting Dolin down. She went to him a day or so before the filming was to have taken place and said: "It's an awful thing to ask, Pat, but would you let me go?" and he said "Certainly you must go my dear". Most of the dancers who were rehearsing with Dolin at that time went on the tour, and the film was never made. Molly commented "Pat was very philosophical about these things. He was a wonderful person."[13]

They rehearsed for a month in Paris, and once again conditions were hard:

> "There was not much spare money for rehearsals and we lived not even on a shoe string but on half a shoe string. Our class was at 8.30 am, a long walk, no money for bus fares, lunch a roll and any embellishment we could afford; then back to rehearsal, when we were at last free in the evening, the great moment of the day arrived, the walk from Montmartre where we lived and worked, to Montparnasse, a long distance over the river and up the Luxembourg. There was a Russian restaurant "Knam". We bought books of tickets at reduced prices, and ate almost as much as we could, never quite as much, as there was not enough money. Stanley Judson and Travis Kemp were at this time still with the Sadler's Wells company and went back to London for certain performances. They invariably returned with large slabs of milk chocolate. I think that never in their lives have they been so popular.
>
> We rehearsed "Les Sylphides" with Michel Fokine. He told us that we should move through a light mist of our imagining, that we should appear to float, covering ground as intangible and fleeting bodies — the solos to be done with wide unbroken line, a continuity that only comes with complete control. Modern dancers and audiences find "Les Sylphides" boring, too apparently easy to challenge their strength. This attitude is I think both our loss and our gain, as because of it we rarely have to sit through the irritating nostalgia of longing for "Les Sylphides" as it was in retrospect; but what a pity that late twentieth century dancers can neither create nor understand the elusive atmosphere and hidden technique of this ballet. The lack is in their

> approach that leaves a blank side to romanticism, or rather a blank imitation of it; better to bury it decently.
>
> This small and happy company set off on a three month tour of South Africa which didn't end till fourteen months later.''[14]

Little did Molly know as she happily set out on the voyage that she had already met someone with whom she was to share the rest of her life.

A Moment in Time

The moment Travis's life changed from one box to another happened as

"The bus was pulling away from the kerb as I came through the stage door. I did a couple of jetés and a pas de chat and managed to catch it before it picked up speed. It was late March 1934, and I was coming to the end of my third season with the Vic-Wells Ballet.

"Staggering on to the top I saw Stanley Judson and lurched into the seat beside him. Stanley, so he told me, was going to see Pavlova's husband Victor Dandré who was going to take a company to South Africa for three months; it would just fit in with our summer break, and would I like to come?

"When Dandré was in London, he stayed at Anna Pruzina's house in Little Venice, and to there we went. We were to rehearse in Paris and would be paid X francs per week living allowance. I asked if I could live on X francs per week and Dandré without any discussion doubled it.

"As our final performances at Sadlers Wells clashed with the Paris rehearsals, it was agreed that Stanley and I should cross to England on the morning of each performance, returning to Paris immediately after the show. Our return was eagerly awaited as we always brought back masses of chocolate. Chocolate was very expensive in Paris.

"The company was headed by Nemchinova and Oboukhoff, and included Natasha Bojkovich (whom Stanley was to partner), Eleanora Marra, Algeranoff, Dmitri Rostoff, Leonid Katchurovsky and Molly Lake, who had brought with her her own group of dancers including Kathleen Crofton, Anna Northcote, Eileen Keegan and Christine Rosslyn. There was also a fascinating Bulgarian girl of fifteen, Juliana Enakieva, who could do literally anything from three hundred and thirty two fouettes upwards. Had she not lived in the hiatus between Diaghilev and de Basil she might well have become world famous. She was also a grubby little thing, and on many occasions Algy would spit on his handkerchief and try to clean her knees before she went on to the stage. We christened her 'The Bug'.

"The repertoire included three of Fokine's ballets, 'Les Sylphides', 'Carnaval' and 'Prince Igor'. We knew he was coming but not when, and when he did walk into the rather dreary studio in which we rehearsed there was a dead silence and the studio seemed to glow. The girls curtsied and the boys bowed. It had not been arranged that we should, but it seemed the natural thing to do.

"To be rehearsed by Fokine is something one will never forget. He would explain, for instance, that the last entrance in 'Les Sylphides' should look like a flock of white birds circling to land on a green lawn. He would dance every role in 'Carnaval', male and female; one forgot the rather quiet middle-aged man as each character was created before our eyes. The sudden burst of speed, the sudden, almost flight across the stage. The excitement he could put into a leap or a turn brought the Polovtsian Camp from "Prince Igor" to life in that rather depressing studio and made it throb and gleam with vital movement."

Molly remembered how

> "he made you feel what you should do, partly by his absolutely inspired way of putting things, and by casual movement he made you see what he wanted".[1]

Many years later she compared his work to that of Jiri Kilian whom she admired greatly. Travis recalled:

"We left for South Africa on April 27th. Lilian Baylis came to see us off at Victoria bringing large bouquets for Stanley and me. She was an amazing woman, very generous, and in many ways unassuming and innocent. It is hard to believe that almost all English opera, Shakespeare and ballet stems from her efforts at the Old Vic and Sadler's Wells. We sailed from Southampton on the "Kenilworth Castle", accompanied by the Motherwell football team, whose main recreation on the voyage was to put effervescent salts into the chamber pots, much to the alarm of those who used them when the pots bubbled and overflowed.

"The traditional 'Diner d'Adieu' on May 13th, the night before we arrived in Cape Town, was enormous and included such things as 'Braised Partridge on Buisson de Truffe' and 'Plum Pudding and Lemon Sauce'."

The company was billed as "The Russian Ballet" and was "Presented" by impresario M. Alexandre Levitoff in association with African Consolidated Theatres Ltd. Raya Kuznitsova and Elvira Rone from the USSR joined the group and Miss Kuznitsova later became a principal dancer with both the Blum and de Basil companies. Everywhere the company travelled, emigré White Russians collected round Dandré, and everyone was convinced that the two girls were spies who were reporting back to the Soviets on the activities of the White Russian communities.

The ballet master was Paul Petroff (not the man with the same name who later danced with the de Basil Ballet). He had been trained in Russia under Petipa, and had appeared at the Imperial Theatre in Petrograd before accompanying

Pavlova on several tours, first as a dancer and later as her ballet master. He was not very popular with the dancers. Alexandre Kitchine conducted the local orchestras.

The opening programme in Cape Town on Friday May 18th, 1934 included one act of Petipa's version of "La Fille Mal Gardée" "Le Lac Des Cygnes" (the second act), and a divertissement comprising "Pas des Fleurs" (no choreographer mentioned). In later performances, "Snegurotshka", choreography by "Miasin" and danced by Nemtchinova was given, as well as Fokine's "Polovtsian Dances" and "Carnaval". The spelling of the names of the artists varied from programme to programme and even on the same page. Molly shared the role of Florestine (Estrella) with Elvira (sic) Mara, in "Carnaval" and Travis danced Pierrot:

"I decided to do the portion where Pierrot tries to catch the Butterfly as comedy. There were horrified exclamations from the wings, but as the audience liked it and papers gave me good notices nothing more was said. I always felt rather guilty for using this method to get across."

The *Cape Argus* described his interpretation as "that brilliant piece of work done by Mr Travis Kemp in the Schumann ballet"[2] and the *Cape Times* critic wrote of him:

> "Travis Kemp, the young English dancer, made a striking impression last night in the role of Pierrot, a clownish part that demands sometimes simpleness, sometimes gaiety, and sometimes sadness. Pierrot is mainly interpreted in mime, and Kemp's success was so complete in this part that he very nearly stole the thunder."[3]

The company performed "Ballet Visions" (from "The Sleeping Beauty") "arranged" by Paul Petroff, "Carnaval" and a divertissement, and at "His Majesty's Theatre" in Johannesburg Molly was mentioned as a soloist for the first time. Two Souvenir Programmes from the Johannesburg season are more elaborate than those from other venues, containing photographs, biographies of the soloists, history of the company, as well as detailed descriptions of the works performed. On one occasion, the programme included "Magic Flute" "arranged" by P. Petroff to music by Drigo, "Les Sylphides" and a divertissement. On another, the programme consisted of "La Fille Mal Gardée", the second act of "Le Lac Des Cygnes", and a "Divertissement".

The divertissements consisted mainly of dances that Molly had brought into the company with her group. At the opening performance it included a "Suite from Coppélia'' comprising the Mazurka, Theme Slav, ''Cardach'' (Czardas) and Coda; this was followed by five dances which are not accredited to any choreographer: ''Wind'' to music by Rimsky Korsakov, ''Rondo Turque'' to that of Mozart, ''Dance Toreador'' to Julio Carsonôs, ''Waltz'' to that of Fetras, and ''Grand Pas, from Paquita'' to music by Minkus. A ''Polka'' which Molly had choreographed and performed before joining Dandré was also often included, and Travis was proud that

Molly had chosen me to dance her Polka (a dance we later did in every company we were with until we finally gave up dancing). In those early days I would placidly go through the motions, and I would get a thump on the back as Molly would hiss ''Dance, damn you, dance!'' It was quite a long while till I realised what she meant.''

It is interesting to note that every printed programme contained the ''Story'' of each ballet. In the case of those ballets which did not have a narrative, the programme note, under the heading ''Story'', simply outlined the work, referring to the music and decor, and suggesting to the audience what especially to look out for.

In a three column article in the *Cape Times* (illustrated with cartoons of several of the soloists including Travis as Pierrot), about that first performance at His Majesty's Theatre, 'H.D.H.' not only described and criticised the company, but compared at length the dancing of Pavlova with that of Levitoffs' Russian Ballet. He came to the conclusion that, while the Russian company obviously had strong technique and was ''the best thing of its kind that had been seen here, it... seems to me to stop short at, or at any rate, not to penetrate very far beyond, those whose knowledge renders them capable of appreciating technical ability''. Whereas Pavlova and her dancers brought something more to their art:

> ''Pavlova, and (through Pavlova) every member of her company, knew that, in order to be better than the best, they must touch some responsive emotion in the mind of every spectator, and particularly in the minds of those not technically interested in ballet work.''[4]

In those few sentences H.D.H. appears to have summed up the difference between what Molly and Travis strove after and achieved all their lives — to communicate through dance with their audiences — and the work of so many ballet companies to this day. It explains why, in the years that followed, their work was always popular with audiences, and sometimes less so with the ''V.I.P.'s'' of the ballet world. But the Dandré company was greatly appreciated by audiences and most critics, and Travis is convinced that it greatly influenced ballet in South Africa.

"South Africa at that time had no ballet company of its own, so it is possible that our visit created the impetus to form the numerous companies South Africa has today."

"Strip down to your underwear and put on these overalls". They were visiting a gold mine just outside Johannesburg, and were taken down to the gold seam to watch the men working. It was clean, but unbearably hot, there was no room to stand or even sit and the men lay on their sides as they drilled. From time to time small charges were set off, and the dancers were very much aware that if the ground were to move ever so slightly as a result, they would never get out again. They were very pleased to get back into the lifts and as they were raised up to the ground, they *"felt as if tons of earth were being lifted off our heads, which actually had been".*

They were then taken to the compounds where the workers lived. Each compound had its dance team, and a band whose instruments were composed of oil drums of various sizes, each one emitting a different tone. A dance performance was put on specially for the visiting dancers who thoroughly enjoyed it. The men executed strong rhythmical movements into the ground, almost making it shake and one of them, dressed as woman in a short skirt, made softer, seductive movements, luring them to greater efforts.

The company worked in South Africa for two months and when the tour finished in Johannesburg

"Levitoff, who was Dandré's impresario and travelled with us, told me that the company was going on to the Far East and Australia and asked me if I would come. I wanted to go to the Far East, but more importantly I had fallen in love with Molly and wanted to stay with her. I did the unforgivable, I wrote to The Wells to say that I was not coming back. My explanation was reported in 'The Old Vic and Sadlers Wells Magazine'

> "Stanley Judson, on his world tour, sends all good wishes from South Africa, where he is accompanied by Travis Kemp (who meant to come back to us but was prevented from doing to because he signed a contract in a foreign language without fully understanding its purport)."

"Having run a company myself I now understand what it must have been like to be let down by your two permanent male dancers. In those days one didn't think about it, but it took twenty years and a war until I was forgiven. I knew I was forgiven on the day de Valois said 'Look, Travis, it's high time you stopped calling me Miss de Valois and called me by my real name'.

"We were to give a performance in Lourenco Marques, then board a boat for Singapore. We arrived for the train call to find that Nemchinova and Oboukoff who had contracts

elsewhere had left, and that Levitoff and Kitchine had had a fight during the night, had been arrested and were in the local gaol.

"Leon Katcherovsky was also leaving, and at the station there was no Audrey (Valevska). Back to the hotel where we found her half naked on her bed, her belongings scattered round. 'She loved Leon — she couldn't go on without him — she was going to kill herself'. We bundled her into some clothes, piled her things into her case and back we went to the station. The train was still waiting. The guard had heard the story and had held the train. He kissed Audrey's hand and said he would do anything for a damsel in distress.

"Vladimir Launitz had been hastily flown out to replace Kitchine and somehow, with a company consisting of eight male dancers and sixteen girls, we got a performance on in Lourenco Marques. The programme in Portuguese and English announced that it was to be in aid of a new medical ward to be erected by the 'Asociacao dos Empregados do Comercio e Industria de Lourenco Marques'. Fortunately it was a great success, largely helped by 'The Bug' who not only danced magnificently, but failed to wear a B.B. under her rather diaphanous blouse.

"We sailed on the "Barenz", a small Dutch cargo ship, beautifully clean. Apart from a man with his family who was going out to govern one of England's smaller islands, we were the only passengers. On every ship in which we travelled there was always someone going to or coming from governing some portion of England's possessions, and I began to understand Kipling when he said 'What do they know of England, who only England know'."

"We were on the "Barenz" for six weeks, calling at Beira, Zanzibar, Mombasa and wonder of wonders Mahe in the Seychelles. Not the Mahe of today, just simple and beautiful. One short village street and a small French pension. We had a class every morning and a party every night. Class on a boat can be unnerving, either the deck comes up and hits you when you least expect it or it is not there when you want to land on it. The parties usually finished up with cooking eggs and bacon in the galley at midnight, the girls having been put under the shower in their evening dresses. They were usually sensible and wore washable ones, except one girl who one night wore a crepe dress and the hemline finished up round her bottom."

The company was travelling without Dandré and when it reached Beira

"a cable awaited Molly from Dandré, to the effect that when we docked in Beira Molly should collect cash from the local bank and pay the company. The stage director had the salary book. Molly and I collected the cash and the book safely and started to pay the company. I then realised why Molly had been chosen to do the paying: all the Russians swore they should have received far more money than they did. I learnt quite early the phrase. 'It's in the book, it can't be wrong'. Luckily, Dandré flew out and rejoined the company in Mombasa."

Dandré was much loved by both Molly and Travis; he was, in their words, "a bit odd, aristocratic, and innocent in worldly things", and Travis had many memories of his unworldliness and his innocence. One of them was when one of the girls made trouble for Travis because he had rejected her. *"Hell has no fury etc etc. Normally I had reached the age when I should have been only too willing to oblige, but Molly filled my entire vision and I didn't; as a result the girl, amongst other things, spread the rumour that every night Christine was put naked into my bed. When this news reached Dandré, he was deeply shocked, and held a court of enquiry on deck. Christine of course denied the incident, and I defended myself by saying I had had no one in my bed except some ants, which Molly had put there as a joke. I got to know and like Dandré well during this period. He was almost over profuse in his apologies when he finally found out the truth.*

"We were paid for the performances we gave and although all expenses including tips were covered, we received no fee while we travelled, but the cabins were comfortable and the food good and we enjoyed ourselves thoroughly. It was like a paid holiday.

"We were joined in Singapore by Olga Spessiva, Anatole Vilzak and Levitoff who had been let off with a caution. Spessiva was all one dreamed about; she had a definite fey quality, and her impeccable technique was always used, as it should be, to create and transmit whatever emotion was required. The intense heat, the concrete stage, the mass of mosquitos affected her not at all. Vilzak was equally wonderful, a very masculine dancer. A quiet person off the stage, on stage he had a tremendous vitality that carried the whole company with him. He was also a wonderful partner, the girls loved dancing with him and one was never conscious of any effort in his partnering.

"My mosquito bites came to fruition in Java where I was left behind with an attack of malaria. I spent three slightly delirious days talking to a large spider and a cockroach that had managed to get under my mosquito net. On the fourth day the fever went completely, so saying goodbye to the cockroach and the spider I decided to fly to Bandung and join the company there. I had never flown before. In those days a car was sent for each passenger. My driver asked if he could pick up another person, and I said, rather grandly, of course he could. We picked up a young man with the biggest hangover I had ever seen. He was completely green, he staggered into the car, collapsed in a heap in the corner and went to sleep . I felt I had to be sociable, so I said 'Have you ever flown before?' He opened one eye and said rather blearily 'I'm your pilot'.

"However he seemed to have completely recovered by the time we reached the airfield. He invited me into the cockpit. 'Had I seen the volcano?'. 'No'. 'Good, we'll fly over it'. 'Had I seen this feature or that feature?' 'No.' 'Good, we will make a short detour to fly over them'. Time and flight schedules did not seem to matter.

"Only on one other occasion did a similar thing happen. Molly and I were flying to South Africa. Suddenly the intercom crackled, and the pilot said 'Kilimanjaro has no cloud over

it, its the first time I have seen it, I'm going to fly round it'. And fly round it we did. Three times."

Travis was obliged to arrange and pay for his flight himself, receiving no help from the impresario Levitoff, who was becoming increasingly unpopular with the dancers.

The girls in the company, particularly Molly, missed Travis badly and were very upset at having to leave him behind. Molly wrote to him from a train on September 17th, remarking how 'inconsiderate' he was to get ill and leave her alone, and pointing out that it was now two days since he had asked her to marry him and threatening to propose to him instead. *("Needless to say she never did. It took a war to make her finally decide that she liked me enough to marry me")*. Vera wrote and told him how everyone had walked out of rehearsal in a very bad mood at 1.45 after having been there since 9.30 and doing 'almost nothing'. Travis arrived at the theatre in Bandung.

"just in time to help Spessiva to paint white rings round the holes in the stage that we could avoid them more easily.

"Performances started at ten o'clock at night to try and avoid the heat. Even so bodies and costumes became soaked. Bodies were slippery to lift and costumes stuck to all the places which they shouldn't.

"From Java the company sailed on to Brisbane on the "S.S. Nieuw Holland", stopping at Bali — a portion of paradise. The Dutch allowed no missionaries or tourist hotels. The people were beautiful, innocent and appeared happy. The Temple Dancers danced especially for us. I wonder what it is like now.

"Australia had seen no ballet since Pavlova had visited the country many years before, and the Borovansky Ballet was still in the future. However, there were a number of ballet schools and at their request Molly held examinations and initiated the formation of the Cecchetti Society of Australia."

The company opened in Brisbane at His Majesty's Theatre on October 10th, preceding by several months, according to the programme notes, the first visit of "the boy violinist" Yehudi Menuhin. The programme was similar to that presented previously, but on November 28th in Sydney, they danced a 'Suite from Coppélia", "Venusberg" from the opera "Tannhauser", choreographed by Paul Petroff, "Carnaval" and, as usual, a Divertissement. Molly and Travis had obviously been promoted for in this they danced for the first time an excerpt from "Ice Maiden". The divertissement also included "Abhinaya Nritya" choreographed and danced by Algeranoff to authentic

Indian music, and described in the programme as "Ancient Indian Sculpture, Translated in Rhythm and Pose". Algeranoff had

"visited museums and picture galleries and took from painting and statues many positions and welded them into a 'dance'. When this was later performed in Calcutta, there was great interest when the dance started, but as it progressed the theatre slowly empted. The next morning the papers said that they admired Algeranoff's initiative, but that he must remember that all the positions had meaning and at times his choice of positions had been unfortunate and the burghers of Calcutta would not let their wives stay and see them."

Molly was repeatedly praised for her interpretation of the role of the "Good (Lilac) Fairy". In Brisbane she was compared to the Jacaranda flower which has lilac coloured blossoms, and was then in bloom all over the town:

> "anyone who went to the Russian Ballet on Saturday night and saw Molly Lake dancing as the good fairy in the 'Visions' scene must have thought the spirit of the jacaranda...had stepped onto the stage herself. Even Natasha Bojkovich...suffered an eclipse for the time being."

The company spent Christmas in Melbourne, and the *Star* appreciated the fact that the programme was so entertaining: "The Russian Ballet is to be congratulated on its appreciation of 100% entertainment value in a Christmas programme".[7] Travis found Christmas in the southern hemisphere an unusual experience:

"It was odd to see all the shop windows decorated with snow scenes when outside it was almost too hot to breathe. The season of goodwill was marred by a rift between the English and the Russians because the English did not invite the Russians to their Christmas party. In addition, at about two a.m. on Christmas morning there was a tremendous noise outside my bedroom. Indignantly I flung open the door and was about to yell 'Shut up' when a bottle flew past my ear and broke against the back wall. I shut the door quickly and locked it. When I asked about it at breakfast I was told 'It was just the boys having fun'. The Australians are nothing if not uninhibited, perhaps that is why they have made such exciting and vital dancers.

"It was in Australia that the ballet master transferred his affections to me. He made life hell for Molly and took out all her divertissements including the Polka. Finally I went to Dandré. He was wonderful: all Molly's divertissements were put back and peace was restored, the ballet master looking for consolation elsewhere."

In a section of the programme in Perth, which they visited in 1935, called 'Jottings about the Russian Ballet Company', Molly was given a whole paragraph to herself:

> "Molly Lake is a young English dancer, and was for many years a member of Pavlova's Company. In addition to taking principal parts in the Russian Ballet Company, Miss Lake also composes many of her own dances."

They travelled on to India via Colombo in Ceylon, where the *Times of Ceylon* found "Etude Plastique" to music by Liszt, and danced by Molly, and Misses Sevna, Northcote, Keegan and Rosslyn, "breathtakingly beautiful".

"It was in Ceylon in a small village by the sea that we watched a man place a seed about the size of a chestnut on the ground, pile sand round it and cover it with a cloth. He muttered a few words and waved his hands over it. The cloth began to rise. He whipped the cloth away and there was a small tree about a foot high. He put the cloth back and made more passes, again the cloth rose and this time when he removed it the tree was three feet high. There was no doubting that the tree was anything but genuine, as Molly and I were each allowed to pluck a leaf from it. I still have mine today. The tree was left in place, it is possibly still there. I have never seen the Indian Rope Trick, but I have spoken to those who claim to have done so. After seeing a man make a tree grow in a few seconds out of virtually nothing, under circumstances that allow for no charlatanism, I am perfectly prepared to believe they saw what they claim to have seen, and I truly think that certain Asians and orientals have powers that we cannot understand.

"Following Pavlova's policy of educating her company by ensuring they saw all places of interest on their journeys, we were given a week off with full pay to see Delhi and Agra. We spent a night in the grounds of the Taj Mahal, seeing the sun set and the moon rise, then seeing the sun rise the following morning. One always doubted whether the Taj Mahal was as beautiful as it was reputed to be. For my part nothing that has been said or that I can say can really describe it. It is like Pavlova or Spessiva, to be fully appreciated they had to be seen; no words or pictures would ever bring them to life.

"In India we were invited to a number of Regimental Messes. One evening after dinner we were walking by the swimming pool when Audrey suddenly said 'How cool it looks' and in she went, her dress billowing round her and making her look like a large water lily. Most of the younger officers went in after her. There must have been large bills for the cleaning of dress uniforms the next day.

"On to Egypt aboard the "S.S. Moldavia" through the Suez Canal, where we were stuck for twenty four hours. One of my main memories of Egypt is of sitting in a horse drawn cab waiting for Molly. A rather furtive small boy sidled up to me and asked: 'You want dirty postcards?'. From the morality of my twenty years I said rather sharply: 'No, I don't'. The small boy spat and said: 'You bloody English, we'll soon have you out'. I still think we lost Egypt because I didn't like dirty postcards."

From Port Said, which they reached in March 1935, then on to Alexandria, where they opened at the Alhambra Theatre on 13th April. Again the critics were full of praise, and Travis and Molly were again singled out: ''M. Kemp notamment, a su camper un 'Pierrot' touchant'', and Molly ''charma de sa longue baguette et de son exquise grace non seulement le Prince mais aussi le public''.[9] At last they began their journey home.

''We sailed for England on the ''Moreton Bay''; she was overcrowded, rather dirty and generally uncomfortable. One little thought that her sister ship the ''Jarvis Bay'' would die so heroically, some seven years later. We were due home the day after King George V's Jubilee, but with a little persuasion from all aboard and by dint of nearly bursting the boilers we arrived the day before.

''We had been away rather more than a year, but it seemed nothing more than a moment in time.

''Life is odd. Had I missed the bus I might never have seen as much of the world as I have seen. I might never have met Molly, and I might still be associated with what is now the Royal Ballet, possibly sweeping the stage.''

Fish and Actors

"At the end of the tour, Dandré had said that he hoped to re-form the company and that he would contact us, but for the time being, we were again without work. 'Let's go to a lesson with Kyasht'. At that time she was teaching in a studio in St. John's Wood, and although we had danced in several of her productions, we had never been to one of her classes. So we went. At the end of the lesson Kyasht told us 'Markova and Dolin are taking out a company, and your names have been mentioned in association with it. Why don't you go and see Van Damm and find out more about it?'. When we got outside we all, Molly and I and all the dancers from Dandré's company who were waiting for him to restart as he had promised, got into a huddle, and finally decided not to go: we had been attending classes given by Legat in his Baron's Court studio which had a stage at one end and, as Molly remembered

> "some of us decided to try our luck as a dance group. We scraped together costumes, music and odd (very odd) bits of scenery and actually succeeded in getting some drapes, I am afraid as odd as our scenery, barely enough money to pay our digs or eat, stages and dressing rooms and theatres of the most primitive. Puffing and panting our way through the quick change after quick change from one home made costume to the next, back to the 'digs' to split up the last potato, then hungry to bed — a fine time. We all enjoyed it."[1]

The group which performed under the name "New Dance Group" and which included Algeranov, Stanley Judson, Peggy van Praagh, Kathleen Crofton and Mary Skeaping, gave several performances in October 1935 of varied programmes which included works by Stanley Judson and Molly, as well as by Elsa Brunelleschi and Aubrey Hitchins.

At the same time as he was working with the "New Dance Group", Travis returned to the Ballet Club appearing for a short season with the Rambert dancers at the Royal Opera House in the opera ballet which was choreographed by Antony Tudor. He was also earning very well in cabaret, at the Hungaria Restaurant in the Haymarket, with Raya Kuznitsova and a Russian Balalaika orchestra. He was replacing the Russian dancer Dimitri Rostov who had left to join the de Basil company. One day he backed into a table as he danced and spilt someone's coffee. He turned to apologise and found himself face to face with Ninette de Valois. She had come along because she had apparently been told that there was a reasonable male dancer at the Hungaria Restaurant. When she saw Travis she said "Oh, its you" and was not pleased to see him, as she had not forgiven him for having left her company the previous year.

In 1935 Alicia Markova and Dolin began to assemble dancers for a new company, which became the "Markova-Dolin Ballet". There were a number of good dancers in England who had been with Diaghilev and with Pavlova and who, since their deaths had had nowhere to dance, and Markova and Dolin were glad that they were able to offer these artists an outlet for their talents as well as a living. Many of them were now with the "New Group", and Markova and Dolin now approached them and gradually they all accepted, except for Molly and Travis. However, after receiving a letter from Dandré dated 16th May 1935 stating that in spite of his hopes for another season, he had "reluctantly been forced to the conclusion that in the immediate future the organisation of a new tour was not feasible", Molly and Travis went along to see Van Damm. He asked "What salary do you want?" It was the first time in their lives that they have ever been asked how much they wanted, and true to character they did not request very much. The other soloists in the company were not pleased, as they then received the same as Molly and Travis. A few weeks later Travis received a letter from the manager of the Hungaria Restaurant asking him to come back, as the boy who had replaced him was not as good as he. Naturally he did not do so.

A syndicate called "Vivian Van Damm Productions Ltd" was floated with Alicia Markova and Mr Van Damm as Directors. It was financed by Laura Henderson, who had been persuaded by Markova's sister who was dancing at the Windmill at the time, to subsidise the company. She was an elderly lady who quite innocently liked the company of good looking men, and she would invite them one by one for dinner at her house in Knightsbridge. Molly and Travis did not meet her until they were in the company.

The first rehearsals were at the Windmill Theatre, but thereafter, whenever they came back to London between tours, they would work in a big rehearsal room in the Kingsway Theatre. The company travelled all over England, often on Sundays in a "fish train". As Travis explained:

"Prior to the war no one travelled by train on Sundays if they could help it, as journeys took twice the normal time, owing to rail repair and maintenance which were always carried out on that day. However, few theatrical companies had their own transport and almost all travelled by rail, and as theatre at that time was exceedingly popular, the railway was quite crowded on Sundays with actors, singers, musicians and dancers of all kinds. It also appeared that fish usually travelled on Sundays. I remember waiting on a platform when another train rolled into the station. The driver of one train leaned out of his cab and yelled to the other; 'Morning Bill, what have you got aboard today?'. The reply came back; 'Usual Sunday load — fish and actors'. I noticed he put fish first."

The company performed for audiences who had never seen ballet before. In spite of its foreign name and that of its principals, it was the first English ballet company of any size to undertake lengthy provincial tours. As well as its London seasons which included Golders Green and Streatham, the company visited Manchester, Liverpool, Birmingham, Bradford, Edinburgh, Glasgow, Bristol, Brighton, Eastbourne, Stratford-on-Avon, "and any other town you can think of". It was a large company, comprising many dancers, a wide repertoire, and an orchestra of thirty conducted by Leighton Lucas. He had started as a dancer and Molly remembered that as a result he

> "had an innate understanding of ballet rhythm as opposed to a purely musical approach, but conducting the second act of 'Giselle' was his despair. To follow Markova's endless change of tempo was beyond even him. He habitually wore a white carnation in the lapel of his tail coat but he remarked sadly that was there such a thing as a black carnation, he would always wear it on 'Giselle nights'. When the impossible happened and every tempo had been perfect, he was caught executing a very nimble entrechat six as the curtain went up on one of the many calls."[2]

Molly and Travis were impressed that Markova's weight, like Pavlova's was directly over her feet, and she was so perfectly placed that she almost did not need to practise. They found the experience of working in the company very exciting and very stimulating. Travis reminisced:

"Working with dancers like Markova and Dolin is the best way to learn, watching and seeing what they're doing, see why they can do a thing and you can't, trying and trying and trying until you do it. If you were not rehearsing and you had space, you never sat down. You were always trying to do something in a corner: if one boy did four pirouettes, then everybody else tried to do five, and if one did five, then everybody else tried to do six and so on, and you did it and you worked until you did it or fell flat on your face. One of the greatest things you can have is the desire to learn, and you can educate yourself. However, when we were working with Bronislava Nijinska, everybody had to watch a rehearsal, and the girl dancers who watched were not allowed to even cross their legs when sitting down, and everybody had to be constantly right up on their toes, the discipline was enormous."

Markova and Dolin were very anxious that their dancers should have interesting work, and should have the experience of working with those artists who had links with the tradition and schooling of the past. They were very happy therefore, that Bronislava Nijinska agreed to be the company's "Maitresse de Ballet". She came with her husband and daughter, and remained for about a year. After she left Victor Gsovsky became their teacher.

"Nijinska was very masculine in appearance, very strong in her movements, and knew what she wanted. She always wore blue slacks, a blue sort of sweatshirt with sleeves rolled

up the whole time and long white gloves, and she held a long cigarette holder with a half-smoked cigarette. It was very interesting to work with her because of what she knew and what she had done. She explained to me rather wonderfully how her brother had danced 'Les Sylphides', and what his reactions to dancing it had been and that helped me enormously. She said: 'Your arms should be moved as if they are the same material as the chiffon of your blouse' and in the pas de deux he was definitely not just a partner: they were two people of equal importance dancing together, and their movements would merge. A lift should not be a lift, a carry, and a put down, but should appear as if the girl was floating in front of you of her own volition. Your jumps must appear in the same way: there must be no effort, they just come off the ground and merge into it again. The dance never stops from the moment it starts until the end, everything merges into the other. You virtually fall into a movement. She gave me a completely different view of dance, and that was the first time I began to realise that it was not the steps, it was the way you do them."

Nijinska also mounted two of her own works, one of which was "The Beloved One", to music by Schubert and Liszt arranged by Milhaud. The costumes were designed by George Kirsta (Molly's was of "ravishing copper"[3]) and the scenario was by Benois; the ballet told of a Poet who with his music, evoked memories of his past. One of these was the Lioness, danced by Molly. Her partner was Keith Lester, and she remembered that he had "a very good sense of how he had to show himself off". An amusing incident she never forgot was when

> "Pat was supposed to be playing the piano with all the sort of feeling for it, and one day Keith leaned over it, and Pat said 'Get off the bloody piano, the leg's coming off.'"[4]

The work was always very well received, and the *Glasgow Herald* described it as being "genuinely vital, and the sequence of episodes that makes this ballet a kind of emotional suite was shown once more to have been well ordered and effectively varied".[5]

They opened in Newcastle on November 12th 1935 with the pas de deux from "Casse Noisette", "Carnaval", and the first performance of "David" by Keith Lester, in which Travis danced one of the four sons of Jesse. It had a scenario by Poppaea Vanda, a descendant of George Eliot, with costumes and decor by Joseph Meninsky, to music by Maurice Jacobson. "The most adroit discords that any modern student could desire, and in one or two episodes it did not seem to help in realising what was occurring" said the *Nottingham Journal*.[6] Several dancers were mentioned as being "outstanding in varied types of dancing, especially Travis Kemp's interpretation of Pierrot", and the *Liverpool Daily Post* felt that while "the corps de ballet seemed heavy in their movements, Molly Lake was admirable as the Queen of the Wilis."[7]

The company came to London on December 23rd 1935, and *The Times* praised the "smoothness that rehearsal alone can give".[8] The opening programme consisted of the second act of "Swan Lake" and the third act of "Casse Noisette", both produced by Sergeeff with, according to *The Times*, splendid decor and costumes by Hedley Briggs and William Chappell respectively, and a new ballet about circus life by Susan Salaman called "Show Folk". As always the reviewer could not find fault with the dancing of Markova and Dolin, and he also extended praise to other dancers: 'Guy Massey and Travis Kemp in the Chinese Tea Dance call for commendation".[9]

The Glasgow *Daily Record and Mail* felt that the Spanish Dance from "Casse Noisette", performed by Guy Massey and Molly "had rare rhythmic verve extended to its performance",[10] and the *Newcastle Chronicle* reported that Travis Kemp and Molly Lake "danced the Spanish Dance with rare feeling".[11]

Travis was occasionally lucky enough to dance with Markova, and the first role in which he ever partnered her was "Les Sylphides".

"I danced that on many occasions with her but the first time I ever danced 'Giselle' was when Dolin hurt his knee during a matinee and 'Giselle' was in the evening. I had a half an hour's rehearsal with Markova between the two shows and I went on. She really was amazing in the help that she gave and so was Dolin; he was tremendously generous in all things, and lent me his dressing room, his dresser, everything he could possibly do; he stood in the wings to prompt me when necessary. Markova did everything she could to help and she was terribly light and easy to work with, as she was dead on her balance, so that when she did a pirouette she went round, round, round, as many times as she wanted. Doing that kind of thing is a method of learning, it gives you confidence in yourself to try things again and again. That was another case where one was thrown in the deep end. Really it was the way anybody got their chance: if someone was off and someone else knew the role, they said 'I know it, I know it' or something like that, and if you didn't know a thing you never got a chance to do it."

The *Yorkshire Post* reported the incident "of disappointments and triumphs... which allowed Mr Travis Kemp to achieve a distinct success... which earned him a tribute from Mr Dolin at the close".[12] *The Telegraph and Argus* reported that Travis "undertook the part at very brief notice, and filled it with credit to himself and pleasure to the audience"; and *The Yorkshire Evening Post* was also full of praise: "He achieved his success by the confidence, thoroughness and sincerity with which he tackled it. The audience gave him a warm reception."

Another example of Dolin's kindness was when they were dancing their "Polka"

"We started off stage, and we went on without music, got to the centre to meet and then downstage centre to stand together, and then the music started. We normally had a quick change, and we used to have Pat's 'Hymn to the Sun' to change in, and we always had a rush: 'Don't keep the stage waiting, don't keep the stage waiting' had been so instilled in us; so as soon as Pat's applause stopped, we counted 1,2,3,4 2,2,3,4 and on we went. There was Pat in the middle preparing to do an encore. There was a burst of laughter, we counted 3,2,3,4, and off we shot. He was wonderful, he never made any fuss about it."

But things did not usually go wrong, and the critics continued to enjoy the varied programmes. "Hungaria", arranged by Derra de Moroda to Hungarian folk tunes was felt by the reporter of Edinburgh's *Evening Dispatch* to be an "outstanding piece" with the part of the evil gypsy girl being "admirably danced and mimed with real insight by Molly Lake".[13] Travis was "outstanding as the jilted lover", and the reviewer went on to discuss the divertissement, the most successful of which "was certainly the Beethoven suite arranged by Molly Lake, with its clean-cut choreography, its sense of design, and its hint of rustic humour of Teutonic flavour."[14]

Molly's performance of the Queen of the Wilis in "Giselle" where she "sustained the phantom-like atmosphere"[15] was frequently commented on. The opening performance of the company at the Prince of Wales Theatre Cardiff on October 5th 1937, attended by the Lord Mayor and Lady Mayoress, received a particularly sensitive review which highlighted Travis's explanation for the wide popularity of ballet compared with the post-war years: the fact that as well as being an "art form" it was always entertaining.

"The Markova-Dolin Company is real entertainment, marking a combination of the arts of the theatre with the spice of humour to relieve the severe classic rhythm and the poetry of fairyland."[16]

Markova was anxious that Molly and the other soloists should have something beautiful to dance, and when Cyril Beaumont told her that he had discovered in the British Museum the music of the famous Romantic "Pas de Quatre", originally danced by Talioni and her contemporaries, and suggested that the Markova-Dolin company mount a revival of the work, Markova readily agreed: "I felt it was my tribute to Molly. She had the training — it has to be used". Beaumont and Keith Lester researched the ballet, and Leighton Lucas orchestrated it. Molly danced Taglioni's part, Kathleen Crofton that of Cerrito, Prudence Hyman — Grisi, and Diana Gould — Grahn. The work always received high praise from audiences and press alike.

Molly was greatly respected by Markova and Dolin for her classical training, which had direct links with the best of the traditions of the past — both the

Molly as Taglioni with Beatrice Appleyard, Prudence Hyman and Maud Lloyd in Keith Lester's "Pas de Quatre"

Molly in Keith Lester's "Pas de Quatre"

Molly and Anton Dolin in Nijinska's "The Beloved One"

Molly in her "Polka"

Travis in Fokine's "Carnival"

Travis in Fokine's "Les Sylphides"

Travis and Prudence Hyman in Fokine's "Les Sylphides"

Molly in Derra de Moroda's "Hungaria"

Travis and Diana Gould in Nijinska's "Les Biches"

Anton Dolin, Travis and Guy Massey in Nijinska's "Les Biches"

Italian and the Russian schools, and it was "a little bit of a shock", as Markova remembered, for the company to find that she could also dance comedy roles very well indeed.

She was also attracting good notices for her choreography as well as for her dancing. The *Manchester Evening News* described her as "the dancer with a twinkle in her eye", and quoted her contention that it was "important that comedy in ballet should be carefully considered and designed".[17] As a result she gained the label "comic choreographist".

Her "Polka" was often mentioned favourably by the press; for example, *The Leeds Mercury* ended a very good review in which the critic praised the production of Fokine's "Carnaval" when Travis played Pierrot, with a special mention of the "very jolly Polka to music by Linter, danced by Molly Lake and Travis Kemp".[18] The *Birmingham Post* praised her

> "Can-Can, in the style of the eighteen nineties, given by Molly Lake, Diana Gould and Wendy Toye. In flashing skirts of orange and purple, the trio gave an impression of the high-kicking front-liners who were more concerned with tactics than with technique. The result was as amusing as it was original."[19]

On another occasion, in Liverpool, the audience insisted on an encore

> "of a saucy little burlesque — the sort of Can-Can I can imagine the girls of the *Folies Bergère* dancing after a champagne supper. Molly Lake, Diana Gould and Wendy Toye were the triumphant trio of merry maidens whose skittish gyrations and pretty pouts brought the house down."

The *Bristol Evening World* also reported that this dance was so popular that it was repeated as an encore. The dancing of the corps de ballet had obviously improved by this time, as the paper commented on "some of the most brilliant dancing Bristol people have seen for some years".[20]

When the company returned to Southsea in March 1937, they brought with them a revival of Nijinska's "Les Biches", now called "House Party", with reproductions of the original costumes and decor by Laurencin. The *Evening News* regarded the work as "in many ways an animated and ultra-sophisticated Watteau canvas" and praised "the fine, masculine dancing of Dolin, with Guy Massey, and Travis Kemp, to a brazen theme of Poulenc's, (which) was an excellent example of powerful artistry".[21] The *Manchester Guardian* went into more detail in its praise of the performance:

> "Its three brawny young men mock their own dignity as they move; Guy Massey and Travis Kemp, in particular, carry on amatory skirmishes with, at moments a fantastic gawkishness of gait."[22]

Travis remembers how he had had a row with Nijinska about that "gait", had lost his temper and had shouted at her. He later went to apologise, and was surprised when she said that it was far better to shout about it and to get it right than to be indifferent.

Many newspapers referred specifically to the music of Poulenc, relating how he had been one of "les Six" who had gathered round Jean Cocteau in Paris just after the First World War, and several commented very favourably on the admirable conducting of Leighton Lucas.

The *Nottingham Journal* also praised the dancing mentioning proudly in passing that Travis was a "dancer born and bred in Nottingham".[23] On the same day the *Nottingham Guardian* expressed the opinion that in "Les Sylphides" Travis gave "a performance which earned well-deserved recognition, and there was captivating dancing by Kathleen Crofton, Christine Rosslyn, Molly Lake and the corps de ballet".[24]

While they were at the Shakespeare Memorial Theatre Stratford in December 1936 they were very moved as they listened to King Edward VIII's abdication speech in the interval as it was broadcast into the theatre.

Every review the company received was unanimous in its praise of the dancing of Markova and Dolin and also of all the principals and, after the first few months, increasingly of the corps de ballet; whether they were making their first visit to a venue introducing new audiences to ballet, or returning a second or third time, audiences were undividedly enthusiastic. Miss Mary Davison, the company's theatrical publicity agent and at that time the youngest in the country, gave what was probably the explanation for this success when she told the *Bristol Evening World*:

> "I do wish people would realise that ballet is not an entertainment solely for highbrows.... It is not necessary to understand the technique to enjoy ballet.... It helps, of course, but there are plenty of beautiful things which can be enjoyed by everyone — marvellous movement and gorgeous pageantry."[25]

She went on to mention not only the entertainment value of ballet, which was widely accepted but its educational importance, an opinion not seriously taken up by the ballet world until more than forty-five years later:

> "Another point which is not sufficiently realised is that ballet is the ideal entertainment for children. It develops their sense of colour and music, and they can follow it easily.... Really, it appeals to them tremendously."

When the company folded after three years, Molly and Travis were "desolate".

Interlude

Ballet Intime

Molly and Travis were again in a situation where they did not know what to do. Finally, they decided to form their own company and managed, with a capital of less than £20, to get together a small group of twelve dancers, consisting of soloists from the Markova-Dolin and the Blum companies. Madame Pruzina was kind enough to lend them her studio in her house in Little Venice for rehearsals, and one day Molly and Travis invited Dandré who was staying there, to watch, although they did not have any particular request in mind. Afterwards he took Travis aside and asked him if he would like to join the de Basil Company, of which he was a Director. Molly was not invited because, as happens so often even today, male dancers were in greater demand.

The incident highlights the problem which faces so many dancers: if a girl marries a man who is not a dancer, it becomes difficult for her to carry on dancing especially if her work involves touring. If she marries a dancer, it is usually only possible to continue if they are both in the same company, for as so many dancing couples know to their cost, separation puts an almost impossible strain on the relationship. Although they were not yet married, Travis was wise enough to refuse the offer.

A small opera group ''Intimate Opera'' was performing at that time, and Molly and Travis felt that ''Intimate Ballet'' would be a suitable name for this small band of soloists without corps de ballet, performing chamber works. However, this name did not ''roll off the tongue'', so they decided to change it to ''Ballet Intime''. But this also caused problems because, in order to keep the company together they sometimes accepted dates in pantomimes, in music hall (where they topped the bill), and in theatres for audiences new to ballet. Here the French name was not understood, and they were called ''Ballet In Time''; so ''New English Ballet'' was therefore used instead when appropriate. In fact, they opened under this name when they gave a private performance at the Legat studio on March 12th, 1938, before embarking on a tour of the provinces.

Reporting on the launch in the *Observer*, Horace Horsnell felt that the format of the programmes, consisting as they did mainly of divertissements, was suitable for their ''mobile purpose'' and that although not all the dancers were of equally high standard, the performance had ''speed and variety''.[1] *What's On* reported with satisfaction the birth of a company whose aim was to ''put British ballet on the map'' both in England and on the continent. It concluded

> ''By the time the company returns to these shores it hopes to have established the quality of English ballet abroad, and it will then be left to us to appreciate our home-product. Good luck to them.''[2]

They had a varied repertoire which included Molly's ''Beethoven Suite'', a traditional Mexican Dance, and ''Olympic Antics'' choreographed by Molly to music by Offenbach; this was a humorous ballet about inconstancy on Mount Olympus, in which the characters wore the fashions of the 1890s, and it had its first performance at the De La Warr Pavilion in Bexhill during the Whit weekend. After the interval a divertissement was performed which was made up of about nine or ten short items, most of which were choreographed by Molly. Some were created by Keith Lester, for example: ''Valse Fantaisie'' to music by Glinka, and ''Titania and the Tar'' with music by Mendelssohn, about the love of a sailor for a beautiful immortal girl. His lovely ''Pas de Quartre'' was of course a jewel in the crown of the repertoire.

The press were enthusiastic, in Bexhill congratulating the company on their ''extremely attractive character''.[3] When they appeared in Guernsey, they received a long review in the *Evening Press* which described their programmes as ''One of the most charming entertainments Guernsey has seen for many a long day'' and proclaimed that ''the slogan on their poster is a true one: 'Classical, gay and artistic''' and that the men ''can do the most intriguing things which almost take one's breath away by their rapidity and apparent ease''. The reviewer noted the girls' ''perfect movement, pretty faces and quite delightful dresses'', showing that as always Molly and Travis knew how to entertain those not very familiar with ballet, and several paragraphs were devoted to Molly and to the fact that she had toured with Pavlova, and remarking that she found it easier to dance in ''the warmth of the tropics where less practice is necessary''.[4]

The population of Clacton was urged on October 8th 1938 not to miss the opportunity of seeing

> ''the first ballet ever to visit Clacton and...the most beautiful and charming entertainment...this year.... With delicacy of touch and true artistry the dancers at the West Cliff give the impress of every mood gay or sad, serious and frivolous that the heart can feel. Not the least enjoyable items in their repertoire are their delightfully shrewd burlesques which are refinements of comedy.''[5]

In *The Granta*, a journal written and edited by Cambridge undergraduates, Thomas Browne felt that Travis

> ''came to the fore as a demi-charactere [sic] of great virtuosity and skill as the strong man of Olympus, namely, Hercules''.[6]

and that his performance in ''Herbert Skates'' demonstrated that he was obviously a ''very clever actor''. However, Mr Browne though full of encouragement, thought that the company, though good individually were not yet a team and that the corps de ballet needed more rehearsal; also that the quartet should be replaced by two pianos and percussion. This was an opinion which was often expressed, and in fact Molly and Travis agreed with it, preferring to have only two pianos, but often the theatre managers insisted on an orchestra, which was often too small as funds were not great enough for a large one.

The company performed at Toynbee Hall in February 1939, and at the Rudolf Steiner Hall, and also toured. Patrons of an open-air performance in Cranbrook included several Ladies, a Viscount and Viscountess, a Marquis, and the King of Siam.

As the engagements of the company were still very sparse, Travis accepted invitations to dance elsewhere (always ''with the kind permission of 'Ballet Intime'''). In June and July 1939 he returned to the Ballet Rambert for two short seasons, appearing at the Mercury and on tour in Birmingham in a variety of roles including the Prince in ''Swan Lake'' Act II which he danced in August with Nina Golovina. He was lucky to have danced in a rich repertoire which comprised works by some of the best choreographers that Britain has ever produced: Ashton, Tudor, Howard, de Valois, Gore and Staff, as well as dancing in the Diaghilev (for example, Fokine's *Carnaval*) and classical repertoire.

That same summer he appeared in Kingston with the pupils of the Margaret Barnes School of Dancing, and the local paper of June 21st picked out ''a ballet number'' which he danced with one of the pupils as being ''an outstanding turn'', and extolled ''the exquisite grace and beauty of the dancing which captured the hearts of the audience, who would have liked more''. When Travis partnered the Sheffield ballerina, Joy Robson, in Adagio numbers in Sheffield City Hall's pageant production of *Faust*, two columns of twelve inches were devoted to a description of him and his career, and to his opinion that ballet was enjoying an increase in popularity.

Then, in September 1939, came the war. Molly and Travis sat in their flat in Great Portland Street and heard Chamberlain's famous speech which announced that Britain was now officially at war with Germany. And then the sirens started.

The beginning of the war brought hard times. Many theatres were closed, but Travis was much in demand. He danced occasionally on TV, and appeared with the Ballet Rambert during its second season at the Duchess Theatre from November 21st to December 23rd. Molly was left alone to try and carry on her life as dancer and director of her own company as best she could. The war news was confusing and depressing and almost every day Molly's diary reported it, often coloured by her own very perceptive opinions. On hearing that Russia had signed a truce with Germany, she opined:

> "More trouble for us. I said always that Nazism and Bolshevism were the same thing in a different covering".

and on September 18th:

> "Poland is a bleeding corpse with the vultures growing hungry and Russia waiting to pick her bones".

The uncertainty in the war situation was creating conflicts for Molly. She vacillated between fears that her dancing life was over, and determination to keep going somehow. On September 6th she wrote:

> "I went past some of my old haunts. It made me realise how completely my career, indeed my whole life, has gone. . . I do miss my dancing so".

She started practising again but it was hard to find a studio, and difficult to summon sufficient energy as she was always tired, and she wondered if she was getting too old to dance. She persevered but was riddled with doubts, and on September 11th, she:

> "practised for an hour. . . I wonder, is it silly to try and keep it up? I hate to think of the ballets and dances we have danced for the last time."

She continued to work, sometimes by herself, at other times with friends and students, until finally she expressed that cri de coeur, articulated by so many dancers when they are, or think they are, on the point of having to stop dancing, that feeling that one has finally mastered the intricacies of the technique, but too late:

> "Pity I have to get almost to the sere and yellow before I can dance decently. I really understand it now — from years of struggling to improve I have

learnt far more than I could have done from a teacher, every weakness of mine has been something to find a cure for, and now when it is too late, to a great extent, I have done it. I know how to husband every atom of strength, to dance with the minimum of force, to drain the weight of my body from my legs so that I feel buoyed and without weight — to leave my body supple and relaxed so that its rhythm should guide my legs and feet instead of being a heavy hindrance to them — all this for what?"

Sometimes the doubts turned to despair, as on September 17th:

> "I wish there was a way of escape out of the world other than dying — Paul Robeson singing 'Steal away, steal away, steal away, steal away to Jesus — steal away home'. I wish I could."

The practical problems also added to the difficulty of trying to carry on, though Molly's sense of humour never entirely deserted her:

> "Bought a pair of English ballet shoes; by their build they should be bomb-proof, sound-proof and dance proof. My feet looked at them askance and shied badly on being asked to try them on."

Molly tried to continue teaching, but many people were away or doing other work, and sometimes she did not even cover the cost of a pianist. Gradually a few opportunities for dancing arose: the annual Christmas pantomime, some concert parties, and a performance at Great Ormond Street Children's Hospital in which Travis also took part. Molly and Eileen Dolamore made up and put on their tights in Travis's flat, and made their way by taxi to the hospital through the blackout. Unfortunately they did not know where in the hospital they would be performing, but after wandering around the building and being taken to the casualty ward, they finally found the nurse's home where they were eagerly awaited, and all was well.

They danced the "Polka", the pas de deux from "The Three Graces" (a ballet based on the "Judgement of Paris") by Keith Lester, and Molly's "Can-Can". As usual, the Polka was "the success of the show", as the doctor stage manager told them.

Molly was thrilled about the possibility of four matinees at the Embassy Theatre with Keith Lester, but was very worried that they would not be financially viable. They had to be postponed for a week because Keith was on air-raid warden duty, and when Molly tried to get the company together again, she reported sadly that it was "dissolving": one girl was working in an office, another in a hospital, but there were "several hopes and one certainty". Then things began to look up and rehearsals began. The "one certainty'' was Peggy van Praagh, but after a week of rehearsals, Molly heard that the London Ballet, which had been run by Antony Tudor, was to be revived and that Peggy was to be in charge of it; she would therefore not have time to dance with Molly and Keith. As Molly reported sadly; ''A week's rehearsal wasted''.

It was Molly's understanding of human nature and her positive outlook which helped her through the hard times. After describing one of her dancers who was very ''grim'' and ''stupid'', she commented:

> ''As long as we can remember that most of the bad things that happen to us are our own fault, we're all right, otherwise we're sunk and sunk fathoms deep too, in a sea of bitterness, resentfulness and self-pity''.

She never lost her love of nature and throughout her diary she repeatedly describes scenes which moved her and which she found beautiful. In her last years this admiration and love of nature was translated into stunningly beautiful photographs, which she took with a Leica camera bought with £100 left to her by the mother of Monique Boam, one of her dancers. This was stolen several years later when she was in Amsterdam, but was very soon replaced. At the beginning of October she recounted how she:

> ''saw a lovely sunset sky tonight, — a delicate old lady's sky, I thought it at first — gentle, pale grey clouds, in long slender streaks, with a sort of lace knitwork of pale rosy pink brightest pale blue; such a gentle sky, and to make it more perfect a clump of silver birch trees, their frail skeletons outlined in every detail. It had been raining all day and it smelt so good.''

And at the end of October:

> ''Such a lovely misty autumn morning — the sun coming through on to the yellow leaves and the most enchanting pearly spiders' webs. Shaggy flaunting dahlias, michaelmas daisies, looking startling with mauve, crimson virginia creepers, and that delicious smokey smell of autumn.''

Molly's love of nature extended also to animals, and in the midst of all her anxieties about work, she found time to relate how she saw a calf in a farm cart in Watford

> ''for the butcher I suppose. The ugliness of life! Why does one's God allow a baby thing like that to feel that blind horror that is fear, go to an ugly sordid death. I had visions of it gambolling ridiculously and beautifully round its own particular green field — I couldn't hurt a thing like that, imagine having to kill it! Reduce that happiness and grace, that zest for life, that loveliness to a hideous mass of bleeding flesh and bedraggled fur, poor baby!''

Molly's mother was a constant source of worry and guilt. The family decided that she should not live in London because of the bombs, and she was not happy where she was staying in Purley with friends. Molly's father no longer lived with her, and she was ageing, depressed and incapable of thinking or acting for herself. Finally, in October Molly saw her off to Bournemouth:

> "Poor Mother, who can help her!. . . I can't give my life up completely and I'm not strong minded enough to go calmly and kindly my own way. I become resentful because my conscience nags me if I don't give way to her and allow myself to be a child again to please her. I can't allow her to dominate me, our outlook, our sense of values, our whole ideas and make up are so entirely different — if only she had some outside interest."

Life continued somehow. It was hard to travel around, and Molly was cold, tired and depressed. Travis came home when he could, but not often enough for Molly who commented:

> "I miss him too much. War in the summer is bad; war in the winter is unbearable."

Towards the end of October an enquiry came as to whether Molly would be willing to go to France in a concert party. "Would I be? My goodness and how!!!???". But it never materialised.

It became increasingly difficult to run the company, as both Travis and Keith, as well as several of the dancers were also working with the London Ballet, which had moved to the Arts Theatre from Toynbee Hall, and they were often required to rehearse for both companies at the same time. At one point Keith was asked to run London Ballet which would have meant his leaving "Ballet Intime", but luckily that did not happen. Travis also danced sometimes with the Ballet Club at the Mercury Theatre, and so was not only unavailable for rehearsals, but could not help Molly with any of the administration, publicity, or any other arrangements. Molly complained:

> "It seems a pity to let so good a small company disintegrate but how can I hold it alone?"

And on November 2nd, she recorded:

> "It is difficult to retain one's sanity in these conditions."

But of course she did, maybe mainly because she still had her main preoccupation — that of dancing herself.

> "Learnt the rest of my solo, lovely, but so hard, needs to be done almost in slow motion — a prolonged sigh resting on the air — that is how I should like to dance it."

She and the dancers sewed costumes, Travis and other dancers hammered scenery, and two artists they had found came and painted the scenery — all in Molly's flat.

The hardships of day-to-day living in the blackout affected Molly and her dancers in their own particular way: not only did they have to cook in a dark kitchen which had not been sufficiently blacked out, but they could not rehearse beyond 5.30 pm for the same reason. And when they finished, they had to

> "grope for our clothes and get dressed as best we could".

Preparations for the pantomime continued, and so did the problems, as almost at the last minute several of the dancers declared that they did not want to go because the pay was insufficient.

Molly was always cold and tired, and refers to this over and over:

> "I was so cold and hungry. . . too tired to eat at all. . . . Can't cope with it all, I'm too tired. . . cried all through supper. . . I was weak and bad. . . I was so cold that to move was painful. . . . I'm so tired I want to sleep but I have too much to do."

The London Ballet, now run by Peggy van Praagh, continued to cause problems for Molly, repeatedly taking her dancers by virtue of being able to pay them higher wages and to offer them more permanent employment, while Molly continued to struggle with debts which she was paying off a few shillings at a time, with no money for publicity or regular salaries and the constant fear of losing more dancers. Again she was near despair.

> "I don't know which way to turn — I wonder is it possible to succeed without backing or help of any sort".

However, there were the occasional moments of relaxation, with visits to the cinema — accompanied by feelings of guilt: "such dissipation" — and work continued unrelentingly on preparations for performances, together with the attendant difficulties:

> "The troubles and trials of home costume making for an ambitious small ballet company are getting too much. One of the two, comparatively

expensive, pink nymph frocks from the new Arethusa ballet has mysteriously disappeared — dropped in the blackout by the owner of the second pink frock — she must have picked up two instead of one when taking her own home to paint and without realising have dropped it on the way. Our poor flat — a 50 foot backcloth being painted in the lower hall — the pantry turned into a carpenter's shop — my room littered with half made costumes, pins, pieces of material and washing — the kitchen, a cross between a bargain basement and an old clothes shop!!!.... The material for the lost frock has been sold out and cannot be matched — what do we do now?"

But luck was not always against them, and Molly reported that Mrs Wilton, the mother of one of the dancers, was giving her the Giselle dresses, which she had originally paid for. As if the problems of work and the cold and the war were not enough, Molly's mother returned.

"Mother comes back on December 1st. I'm frightened! Does it mean the end of my freer life, my friends and my general happy-go-lucky existence? Wish I had a little money...She'll never put up with the loneliness and inconvenience of the flat...I'm afraid to have the old strain and repressed atmosphere back. Will it mean no more friends and no more freedom?...I shall find it hard to accustom myself to her complete domination again."

Another constant worry was lack of money, and Molly complained to her diary about not even being able to buy a pair of stockings or a tube of toothpaste.

Molly travelled to Peterborough to make arrangements about the pantomime, and had lunch at the local Ritz Hotel. She described the meal which far from met with her approval:

"The lunch was the usual incredibly unimaginative tasteless but eminently wholesome fare of the English Country Hotel, personally I could do with a little more imagination and a little less wholesomeness — what is pork without crackling? What are roast potatoes without the sticky brown bits on the corners! and tell me this, what is English pastry anyhow!"

She watched some children's classes given by a friend, which she enjoyed, but with her usual modesty

"did hate my temporary synthetic importance and the fact that I had to 'say a few words'".

At last the time came for Molly and her company to go up to Stockton for the pantomime, and travel in England at that time was far from pleasant; there was no heating on the train, and no refreshments; they had to change twice, and arrived cold and exhausted.

Molly did not like pantomimes and only did them as a way of keeping her company together and in work. And hard work it was — Equity would not have approved!

> "What an unattractive life a third rate theatrical one is. We rehearsed from 10 – 1, 2.30 – 5.15, and 6 – 10, came home and had a very insufficient supper...rehearsals...dreary but no strain mental or otherwise...utterly inane movements...utterly bored."

As anyone who ever performed in pantomime at that time, or even until the 1950s will remember, it was often bitterly cold, both at the digs and in the theatre, and Molly's diary refers constantly to the extreme discomfort, often caused by the 'commercials', the commercial travellers to whom landladies always seemed to give preference. They could not be disturbed by the dancers' baths late at night, and they were always given the best rooms and the more efficient heaters. Molly's description of the dress rehearsal may sound familiar to many:

> "We started dress rehearsal at 5 and finished at 4 am. What an evening — falling scenery, unrehearsed blackouts, orchestra at sixes and sevens, comedians gagging endlessly, poor children almost asleep, surly stage hands, swearing producer, listless chorus girls, draughty stone stairs, unheated stage."

The references to the cold continued and became more desperate.

> "depressed and old, wondering if I can ever cope with the company and the teaching again.... The heating gave out at night and the cold was almost unbearable...our teeth rattled over the orchestra; one girl fainted from sheer cold...the stage was so cold that it was impossible not to shiver — hands were purple and faces were grey with cold. Hands are so cold even sitting in front of a fire that I can't hold my pen."

In addition, Molly felt that her work was not valued: when a pantomime is too long, the producer often decides that it is the dances which must be cut, and this infuriates the dancers and choreographer who have worked so hard on their short section of dance in a show in which they are so often required to spend much of their time walking on. This pantomime was no different, and Molly reported "rows, rows, rows".

And then the letter from Keith arrived.

Ballet and Bombs

The letter which Molly received from Keith on New Year's Day 1940 was the best New Year's present she could have wished for, and it gave her hope for her professional future: she and Travis were invited to join the Arts Theatre Ballet directed by Keith Lester at a salary for Travis and her of £8 per week each. The invitation extended to two of her dancers, and she was to be first dancer, artistic adviser and "something else I can't remember". She of course accepted and also asked for more of her dancers from "Ballet Intime" to be made room for. She was a great help to Keith Lester who was delighted to be able to delegate much of the burden of running the company to her, and he remembers her as having been a lovely dancer with a sense of period, who "danced because she loved dancing, and the audience knew this", a wonderful interpreter, a very good teacher and a very hard worker.

> "what a joy! It'll be lovely to be free of financial troubles for a little while — I am so thankful, grateful too".

The Arts Theatre Club was set up by Harold Rubin at the Arts Theatre in Great Newport Street as a

> "Social and Creative Clubhouse and Theatre for BALLET, for BALLETLOVERS, for BALLETDANCERS and for all interested in the arts of the theatre".[1]

Three companies, the Ballet Rambert, The London Ballet, and the Arts Theatre Ballet all accompanied by the Arts Theatre Chamber Orchestra, appeared in rotation, and went on tour while the other two companies had their London season. (In 1940 Ballet Rambert amalgamated with the London Ballet, and from June 1940 to September 1941, the joint company was sometimes known as the Rambert London Ballet). Arnold Haskell wrote of the Arts Theatre Club in the *Bystander*

> "Ballet needs the small theatre movement. . . . All this is of definite national value".[2]

Meanwhile the pantomime season in Peterborough still had to be finished, and Molly's interest in the world around her and her compassion for others never abated; she discovered that real acrobats were almost extinct as there appeared to be no longer boys tough enough or keen enough to stand it. She also commented "it's bad for the people here to live in so much ugliness".

In the meantime, her dancing was developing and she reported that she had done an unsupported quadruple pirouette on stage for the first time "whoopee!!!". Wartime conditions were becoming a matter of course: there was blackout and rationing, luxury articles difficult to obtain, and even "women bus conductors here and there", and of course the difficult travel conditions.

At last the pantomine was over and on January 21st they all returned to London, on trains which were delayed and cold, to the different problems of living in London. For Molly the first obstacle was her mother who was becoming impossible to live with, and was so unpleasant to Molly's friends that she felt she could no longer invite them to the house.

Life in the new job also had its difficulties: the atmosphere at first was not very friendly and Molly found the dancers "a bit blasés". To make things worse, Molly's position as artistic adviser had not been made clear and she felt that members of the company were being asked to pass judgement on her ballets, which she was contributing free of charge together with costumes and scenery, although they had not even seen them. Molly was very bitter about this and questioned why she should give her ballets and her hard earned experience for "such cavalier treatment" and the same salary as the other soloists. Everything was in a muddle and the company's prospects did not look too good.

The Arts Theatre Ballet, composed mainly of former principal dancers from the Markova-Dolin Company, included Molly, Diana Gould, Kyra Strakhova, Prudence Hyman, Helene Wolska, Walter Gore, Travis Kemp, Keith Lester, Guy Massey, Alexis Rassine and Harold Turner as soloists, and Joan Kent, Vera Lavrova, Lydia Vernon, Thea Wilmer, Angela Hellas, Beryl Kaye, Sara Luzita, George Gerhardt, Igor Barszinski, and John Pygram.

Much of the repertoire was also from the Markova-Dolin Company: Keith Lester's "Pas de Quatre", "Bach Suite in B Minor" and "De Profundis", Molly's popular "Polka" now called "Polka 1845" and "Flora and Fauns". The programme always contained a Grand Divertissement which comprised excerpts from the classics as well as short original works by Keith Lester, Molly, Walter Gore and others. Longer sections from the classics: Giselle Act II (reproduced by Molly), Swan Lake Act II, Casse Noisette Act II, and parts of The Sleeping Princess, were also performed. The company was lucky enough to have Leighton Lucas as their conductor.

The best designers of the day worked with the company: Sophie Fedorovitch (Lester's "Concerto"), Hugh Stevenson, who painted the sets himself ("Giselle", "Swan Lake", "Casse Noisette"), Guy Sheppard ("May Collin"); and the music of a wide variety of composers was used: Mozart, Tchaikovsky, Mendelssohn, Bax, Wolf, Fauré, Bach, Beethoven, etc, all played on the two pianos to which war-time audiences had become accustomed, or occasionally the Arts Theatre Chamber Orchestra.

The aims of the dancers were set out in programme notes:

> "To keep alive the arts, to divert and amuse those whose days are spent in the support and defence of their country, as well as to employ themselves in their own profession, is their object."

They pointed out that as well as dancing, the dancers found time for voluntary work. For example: Prudence Hyman became a nurse, and Keith Lester worked in an A.R.P. depot. They all

> "came with the new company, new ballets, and a new spirit to fight the darkness of the moment".[3]

The programmes also included a few quotations from press reactions. For example:

> "Keith Lester is one of the few choreographers who can express themselves fluently in the classical idiom."
> *News Chronicle*

> "The Grand Divertissement that completes the well-danced programme displays the talents of the company."
> *Observer*

> "Molly Lake is certainly talented as a choreographer, showing a wide range of understanding."
> *Cambridge Gownsman*.[4]

The conditions under which they had to work were very difficult. On weekdays they gave two performances each of one hour, the first at 1.0 o'clock, the second directly after it, and on Saturdays they performed four times, beginning at 1.0 o'clock, and ending at 6.0. On Sundays there were three performances.

The winter of 1939/40 was one of the coldest on record, and travelling around at night without a torch was a daunting experience, landing Molly many times knee deep in drifts of snow. As usual her pity was not reserved for herself "poor soldiers, poor birds and beasts, poor us, poor world".

When they were not in London they toured the country, appearing in Nottingham, Southsea, Eastbourne, Cardiff, and Hastings twice. It was while they were in Hastings in May that an incident occurred which made a great impression on Travis and which for him symbolised the end of an era and the beginning of the war. He described it as follows:

"In the spring the Arts Theatre Ballet was appearing at the White Rock Pavilion in Hastings. Between rehearsals we were having coffee on the terrace overlooking the sea. As we sat there a small boat pulled alongside the pier, disembarked about 60 French soldiers and immediately put to sea again. The soldiers looked tired and worn but they formed up smartly enough and marched off into the town, watched in silence by those on the terrace and in the silence we could just hear the guns of Dunkirk.

"The silence was broken by a loud explosion and a section of pier disappeared into the sea. We learnt later that all piers along that part of the coast had been treated in the same way to prevent them being used for an expected German landing.

"There were two elderly ladies at the next table; they were speechless for a while then one said: 'Maud, I see the Military have taken over the pier. I wonder why?' Maud thought for a moment then replied 'Isn't it the anniversary of dear Queen Victoria's birthday?'. We couldn't help smiling, but as I looked at the pier again and thought what it implied, it never entered my head that three years later I should have to get a 3-ton gun across that gap. The next day I went to sign on with my age group and was told to return two days later for a medical."

By June 7th Molly was able to report that the company of which she had hoped so much had grown in strength and merit and was on its way to becoming an established part of the dance world. She felt so lucky to have a well paid job that she was happy in, to have the opportunity to dance good parts, to be able to produce and to have a say in the running of the company; Harold Rubin was grateful to her for her "guidance", the "value of your influence", and her dancing in "Giselle"; reviews were unfailingly complimentary and there was goodwill and a pleasant atmosphere in the group. Her lessons were appreciated, she could see the dancers improving every day thanks to her efforts, and she felt she was building something worthwhile. She was very grateful and thankful.

Molly's reporting of the company's successes was always balanced by the war news, and she never seemed to lose her sense of proportion. Recording happily the great success of Giselle, she said "so trivial compared to the appalling tragedy of the war", and her loathing of the Nazi horrors was almost prophetic:

> "The brutality of the Nazis passes human understanding — the hordes of Attila were gentle in comparison: an endless list of degrading cruelty will go down in history".

She shared the country's sadness at what was happening to France and its determination not to let it happen to England.

> "If France goes, then it will be our turn. I love my country. I love its green lanes and fields, its peace and its quiet beauty but I would rather see it a smouldering heap of ruins to arise free for a new generation than to see it in Nazi hands. . . . How long before it is our turn?"

And again the balance between her life and the horrors of the war.

> "The war deepens in horror. Tonight at 6.00 Italy announced to France and Britain that as from tomorrow she joins Germany against us — will it never end? I sat this evening in a little park, just a green circle in the midst of peaceful Georgian houses, shady with old trees and full of the scent of flowers, and so few miles away France is fighting for her life — millions of men killing each other with the help of every ghastly weapon man's mind can invent — the sounds, the sights, the odours of horror — such a thin partition between the little flower scented park and that horror in France.
>
> "The Germans are in Paris. A lot of us went to the swimming pool this afternoon, playing and laughing in the sun and all the time Paris has fallen, a dead and shattered Paris with the alien barbarian in its deserted streets — the core of France — the centre of civilisation lost to the French, it seems too cruel. France devastated, France without a capital — we must win, but how?
>
> "'God's in his heaven, All's right with the world'; either God is not in his heaven or Browning didn't know what he was talking about."

The dramas of a ballet company continued. It irritated Travis that

"Helene was leaving. Helene was always leaving. I don't think she ever had any intention of really leaving, but always enjoyed being persuaded to come back. It seemed to have a stimulating effect on her: she always gave a better performance after one of these upsets."

Molly and Keith wanted to let Helene go, but Rubin took her back, apologising for going against the wishes of the directors of the company. He said he did not want to see his lovely company disintegrate.

There were other tensions: a quarrel with Harold Turner who wanted to rehearse in the studio in which Molly was teaching resulted in a fight recollected by Molly with humour

"Travis and Harold came to blows during rehearsal this morning and had to be pulled apart both blind with fury, Harold apoplectically purple, Travis green as his shirt, very undignified but quite funny."

Travis also remembered the incident years later:

"It was on the same day that Harold made a disparaging remark about Molly. I flew at him. We met in the middle of the stage with a thud, Harold looking like a boiled turkey cock and I looking a greenish black, rather the colour of the shirt I was wearing. For a short time we staggered about clasped in each others' arms until we were pulled apart both looking rather relieved as I don't think either of us knew where to go from there. The rehearsal continued peacefully but at the end a group of ladies from a local women's organisation who had been watching came up and said how much they had enjoyed it, especially the fight scene which was most realistic".

Of course, simply trying to get on with life was enough to increase tension for everyone, as there were continual air raids. When these first occurred during a performance, the curtain had to be lowered, to allow the audience to leave if they wanted to, which they rarely did. The dancers used to bribe the stage manager if they were in the middle of a difficult solo not to bring it down until they had finished, otherwise they would have had to start all over again. But one day there was a very loud bang and the audience began nervously to get up. Travis quickly put on a Hitler-style moustache, poked his head out under the curtain and said "Heil Hitler. Das ist meine Luftwaffe", and the audience laughed and sat down again. Later on, performances were not stopped: a sign was lit up announcing that an air raid was in progress, thus giving the audience the opportunity of leaving if they wanted to.

In the middle of June Molly received a message that her father was ill and she rushed down to her mother in Sevenoaks, only to learn that he was in hospital in Hertford. So she had to travel all the way back through London to see him, and for probably the first time in her life she missed a performance. His death on June 25th left Molly with financial worries, as he had left hardly any money, and Molly suddenly found that her meagre salary had to support both herself and her mother. On June 28th, she attended her father's cremation in the morning, and in the afternoon went to the wedding of Otto to Thea Wilmer, one of her dancers:

"white satin, choir boys, tulle veil and Mendelssohn's wedding march all complete, so different and yet so grimly like the ceremony of the morning. I have seen nothing today that has made me like the human attitude towards marriage and death better than I did before."

Poor Thea, within a few weeks, Otto's ship disappeared into a Japanese smokescreen and was never seen again.

On July 2nd the company opened at the Arts Theatre with two works choreographed by Keith Lester, "Perseus", and "The Glen" in which Molly and Travis danced the parts of the Demon Queen and King. Molly felt she had danced quite well, but she had a rather low opinion of "Perseus", in fact she thought it had "not had the abuse hurled at it that to my mind it deserves"; however, a press review in Harrogate praised both the repertoire and the dancing:

> "programmes splendidly proportioned... blending fantasy, drama and comedy. This last quality is important because it offers a friendly introduction to the art to the unversed, and in addition provides the necessary diversion in long sessions of pure ballet.... A virile Prince Albrecht was given by Travis Kemp. Molly Lake... was an inspired Myrtha."[5]

The viewpoints of dancers and choreographers, and that of critics, when determining the quality of programmes is obviously very different, particularly when the performances are attempting an introduction to ballet for those with no previous experience of it. The aim of the dancer and choreographer must be primarily to entertain, while the critic has other priorities. It is this conflict which is often at the root of much controversy over pioneering work.

While the company was in Harrogate Travis received his call-up papers giving him only three days notice. For Molly who loved him, had just agreed to marry him (which she later did, in 1942), and was frightened at being left alone, the last day of performance was "hell", while Travis was "gallant and casual. I wonder what I should have felt when I saw my costume folded up for the last time." They danced "Arethusa", "Giselle" and "Casse Noisette" at the matinee, and in the evening "Concerto", "The Glen", and a Divertissement which included the Polka that Molly had created for herself and Travis while they were with Dandré, which they had taken with them to Ballet Intime, and which would go with them to Ballet Guild. Travis joined up on July 29th, and Molly was left with the "futile and irritating vision of his red velvet polka jacket before my eyes". She saw Dandré briefly that day and was saddened at how old, sad and ill he looked, and she commented on the hardness of having to outlive one's work, friends and health.

A few weeks later Travis came home on leave, looking very fit but with blisters on his feet from the army boots. Molly felt sorry for him, but did not dare show it as he was so full of stories of his army life. They sat in the park and ate buns, and Molly later sent him two soft pairs of socks, and wrote to him ''This is your first day as a Capitalist'': she had bought him £41 worth of savings certificates as well as some for herself, bringing her own total to £220.

In mid-August Molly took a few days off for what she thought would be a quiet holiday, but this was not to be for she went to Selsey which is not far from Portsmouth, and she saw and heard many bombings, dog-fights, and planes being shot down. On one occasion she was very frightened indeed: she saw a German plane turn inland and head straight for her and her companions who were out for a walk.

> ''I flung myself down under a hedge, the elderly woman clutching my skirt and wailing that she 'didn't like it'. Incidentally I wasn't too keen myself. I felt that bullets must be raining down and that every moment was my last one. I pulled myself free of the woman who had by this time almost pulled my dress off.''

Molly returned to London and to the Blitz, to people she knew being killed and familiar buildings destroyed to ''listening for the drone of a plane, anticipating the whine of a bomb'' and wondering if this time it would fall on her — ''No, its not you this time but someone has been destroyed'' — to sleepless nights in a cupboard under the stairs and the resulting tiredness. Fear became her ''constant companion'', and the world became ''a cage with no way out but death''. In addition there were the worries of running the company: Helene ''left'' again, another girl demanded more money, and the men were gradually being called up. She longed for ''a sympathetic shoulder to weep on and a friendly ear to my sorrows'' and she wished she were braver.

Like most others at that time, Molly and her colleagues tried to carry on as normal. One day towards the end of August she was teaching in West Street when the air raid warning sounded. She and her seven pupils continued, but were interrupted by a message from the air raid shelter below the studio saying that the sound of jumping was making the people underneath nervous as they thought it was bombs. Keith Lester who was in class said ''There are children here who don't appear nervous'' and they completed the lesson.

Travis came back for a few hours, and Molly gave him a class at the Arts Theatre. He was delighted that he could still dance and Molly was happy for him, though with deep understanding and foresight she recorded:

> ''He has got guts, never a wail, not even a mild grumble; he has lost his career and his hopes, and his finances are 1/- per day; he has the

> uncomplaining patience of an animal and the gentleness and courage of real goodness — poor Tabby! He deserves so much more than he will ever get in this world."

On one of his short leaves, he danced in "Giselle". He had

"sort of ambitions of going up to the cross and falling flat on my face in a rather grand gesture, but regrettably I hit the cross as I did it, and the whole of the scenery came down on top of me".

At the end of August Keith Lester told the company about the proposed formation of a limited liability company. They would be subsidised to the tune of £3000 a year which would enable them to run a smaller group giving each person a guarantee of £2 per week for the year whether or not they worked, and leaving a small margin for fares, wardrobe expenses and new productions. Apart from the £2 each, they would run on percentages. Everyone was very pleased and Molly felt they were very lucky, but unfortunately the wonderful conditions never materialised.

The raids intensified and the days were spent dreading coming home knowing that once again the nights would be spent under the stairs. By September 10th almost all the theatres were closed, the streets were empty, restaurants almost deserted and their choice of menu non-existent. Food was becoming scarce as railways were hit, and cooking was difficult when gas mains were bombed. Telephones were for military use only, and telegrams took twenty four hours to arrive. There was also the constant fear of invasion, and Molly confessed to Travis in a letter of September 11th: "I am very frightened. I feel quite desperate as dusk comes on and that awful eight or nine hours in a cellar has to be faced... I do wish you were here with me, Tabby. I probably shouldn't be so scared. I wonder, shall we ever be together and happy?... Anyhow, its very good for me to have to look after myself entirely."

Molly was not alone in her fear: the mothers of several of the dancers were so "panicky", insisting that their daughters leave London, that Keith Lester arranged for the company to go to Norwich, and on September 13th, after not having had her clothes off for over a week, Molly slept in her nightdress. But life there was not much easier. There were raids and bombs, and one morning the dancers arrived at the theatre to find it had been roped off as a time bomb had fallen nearby. Rehearsals were cancelled and then the matinee. When they were finally allowed into the theatre there was no electric light until 6.15, giving them just enough time to make up before the show. It was Guy's last performance before being called up, and Molly was very upset. She danced the Polka with him that night, the first time in seven years that she had danced it with anyone but Travis. However the productions were going well, and they "seemed to be building up a ballet audience in rustic agricultural Norwich" — again the pioneering, educational aspect to their work. They developed this when they returned to London in February 1941, and presented a series of programmes with a specific educational slant.

As well as appearing at the Arts Theatre, the company performed at other London venues, as when they gave "Lunch Ballet" and "After-Lunch Ballet" at the Ambassador's Theatre at 2.15 and 3.15 on Saturday 22nd February 1941. On Monday 24th they gave a "Lunch Ballet", which lasted one hour and included "Blue Danube", the second act of "Swan Lake", and "Serenade", which was choreographed by Harold Turner to music by Hugo Wolf, with costumes and decor by Diana Gould who also devised the work. This performance was followed by an "After-Lunch Ballet" at 2.15 p.m., and consisted of Molly's "Beethoven Suite", "Pavane", "Ecossaise", a solo choreographed by Euphan MacLaren for Helene Wolska, and many other short items. They were paid only as for four full performances, but as Molly wrote to Travis: "Still, we'll be lucky to be alive to give them". By now they were "minus you and Guy, Kyra, Lisa and Angela".

The Arts Theatre Ballet was very successful, but Rubin obviously was not getting what he wanted from it, and in April 1941 he decided to withdraw his support.

When the company had been set up, Molly had brought with her from Ballet Intime several of her own ballets as well as the costumes, and when in 1941 Rubin disbanded the Arts Theatre Ballet, she naturally expected to get them back, but Rubin was reluctant to release them, and only did so after much argument. The company finished with a small amount of money in the bank, which Molly hoped would be used to help create Ballet Guild, a new group which would grow out of the ashes of the old, and which would take over where the Arts Theatre Ballet had left off. But the money was divided among the dancers, and once again Molly entered on a new venture on a shoestring.

While Molly had been struggling with company problems, Travis had been experiencing a very different life in the army.

"'You Are About To Become A Soldier'"

Travis takes up the story:

"We were dancing in Harrogate. There I received a rather sinister looking envelope marked O.H.M.S. Inside was a photograph of George VI saluting and underneath in large letters the words 'YOU ARE ABOUT TO BECOME A SOLDIER', and in lesser lettering 'You will report to Uxbridge Depot on the 29th July 1940 at 11.00 hours'. Rubin wanted me to apply for exemption which I could have got on the grounds of being essential to the Company, but had I done so I should have had difficulty living with myself in the future.

"At that time Mother and I had a flat in Blandford Street just off Baker Street, and at 9.30 on the 29th I left as I usually did when going to rehearsal, calling goodbye to Mother as I walked through the front door, but Mother, possibly with memories of 1914/18 when the average life of a soldier in the trenches was four weeks, rushed after me, burst into tears saying, 'Aren't you going to kiss me goodbye'.

"I arrived at Uxbridge station 15 minute early and went into the buffet thinking I would have my last civilian cup of coffee. I had only just been served when a stocky soldier with two stripes on his arm marched in, glared round the room and said 'Anyone here for the 75th'. I said rather diffidently that I was, he concentrated his glare on me and said 'Get outside at the bloody double and CALL ME BOMBARDIER'. Rather sheepishly I did.

"I lined up with about 10 unhappy looking youths all like me carrying a small suitcase. The suitcases were to be used to send home one's civilian clothing after uniforms had been issued. I often wondered what wives and mothers felt on receiving these last pathetic remnants of their loved ones' civilian lives.

"At the depot which was just a field covered by numerous tents we were issued with uniforms and other bits and pieces considered necessary for a soldier's life. When it came to identity discs one youth asked rather tentatively 'Why have we got two Sarge?' The reply came back in a growl 'One's sent 'ome to yer next o' kin, the other's buried wiv yer'.

"We were also issued with a little ticket with a tent number, told to change, pack our civilian things in our suitcases and give them to the Quartermasters Store. I went to give in my suitcase.

"On my return there was another man in the tent; I told him to get out. However, on comparing tent numbers we found we were both in the tent, so having divided the tent

meticulously into two I went with him to hand in his suitcase. When we returned there were 18 other men in the tent!

"In battle dresses which fitted only where they touched, P.T. shorts which finished well below the knees, and boots which rubbed our feet raw we were doubled up and down the field until it was a sea of mud. However, there is quite a lot of theatricality in the army so I didn't do too badly. P.T. I found fairly easy, though I was always referred to rather scathingly by the Instructors as 'That bloody ballet dancer'.

"Scathingly until one day I decided during a break in P.T. to do coupe jetés round the field finishing up with a series of turns in the air. Even the Instructors became a little dissatisfied with their ups and downs and rounds and throughs and wanted to do turns in the air. It was suggested that I transferred to the Physical Training Corps., but I thought better of it and said no.

"At the end of the month we were all sorted out, those who were to stay with the 75th and those who were to be posted elsewhere. I was one of those chosen to stay. I was also told I was to be recommended for a Commission.

"The 75th Searchlight Regiment had nothing whatsoever to do with searchlights, it was recruited mainly from former technicians of Pinewood Film Studios plus those selected for their 'binaural' qualities. This was the ability to centralise a sound, to determine exactly the direction from which it was coming, by using both ears equally, and we were trained to operate what was then known as the 'Fixed Azimuth System' which, it was hoped, would help to stop the bombing of London.

"There were two rings of sound locators around the Capital, each sited accurately in relation to the others. A plane passing between two locators in the outer ring could be accurately pinpointed — call this point A. In the same manner it could be pinpointed as it passed through the inner ring — say point B. Theoretically, if it took so long to get from point 'A' to point 'B', one could forecast the exact moment it would reach point 'C', and at the forecast time a box barrage would be put up at point 'C'. All this co-ordinated and controlled from the Knightsbridge Underground Station.

"However, this forecast could only be accurate if, and it was a big 'if', the plane flew on a constant course and at a constant speed between points 'A' and 'C'.

"After some weeks of frustration it was discovered that seldom if ever did planes fly on a constant course and at a constant speed for the time required so, as radar was just entering the scene, the locator sites were dismantled and the regiment assembled in a Manor House in Shenley.

"At Shenley I mainly remember 'Gargle Parades: 5.00 am, shirt sleeve order, mugs filled with a ferocious disinfectant. It was a bit like 'Dad's Army'.

'Drink, 2, 3,
Gargle, 2, 3,
Spit, 2, 3,
Wait, 2, 3'.

"It was rather a messy business, the ground became a quagmire, the blokes behind you inevitably spat down the back of your neck, and I am sure that more men got sore throats than the gargle cured.

"While I was at Shenley I went to my first Commission interview. The Major who interviewed me was Nigel Balchin the film director. We both decided that it would be better if I gained some experience as an N.C.O. before I went to Officer Cadet Training Unit (O.C.T.U.), and some days later I received my first stripe and, as Kipling puts it, became 'arf o' nothing': a Lance Bombardier.

"In the Spring of 1943 the regiment moved to Blandford to train on Bofors Guns. The Bofors Gun was primarily an anti-aircraft gun, but it could also be used in an anti-tank role. It could put up 120 2-pound shells in a minute and was then so much ahead of its time that even today it is not completely obsolete.

"I enjoyed gun drill: it can be very theatrical and bringing a gun into action is like an intriguing piece of choreography. Also, I found the discipline of the dance helped greatly with that of the army. I also found the gun mechanism intriguing and became very mechanically minded. At Blandford I received my second stripe and became a full Bombardier.

"During all this period, whenever I could get leave I danced with the Company. First when it was the Arts Theatre Ballet and later when it became the Ballet Guild. It was wonderful to get back into the theatre, but I did get a little worried when during a performance of 'Giselle', owing I think to army food, a large tyre appeared between the top of my strap and the bottom of my tunic. The press was amazingly helpful and produced long articles comparing army boots with ballet shoes. I must confess that during the first few weeks in the army I never thought I should ever be able to run in army boots, but at the end of the war when I said goodbye to them for good, I missed them.

"Training at Blandford having finished, the regiment moved out to gunsites round the Middle Wallop Aerodrome. Middle Wallop was a night fighter drome and included amongst its pilots a man who later became famous as Cats Eye Cunningham.

"It seemed that when dawn broke after a night operation there was always one plane on its nose at the end of the runway. Rumour went round amongst the men that these planes had been flown by Cunningham and he had to shoot down at least two enemy planes per night to make up for those he messed up when landing.

"About a month after arriving at Middle Wallop I was given my Sergeants stripes and took over command of the detachment. At that period equipment was still short and we had no small arms on site; a War Office Order came down explaining, with diagrams, how to make clubs with barbed wire wrapped round heavy sticks. At that time these clubs seemed to us hilariously funny. I erected a highly ornate rack in the gun pit for them, each club marked with its owner's name and number and I put up in large letters Standing Orders for their use which, as far as I can remember ran something like this:

Clubs, Soldiers, for the use of:

A. Approach parachutist before fully recovered from fall.
B. Remove his helmet.
C. Hit on head with club.
D. Replace helmet.

"Thank heaven we never had to use those clubs.

"The father of Thea Wilmer, one of Molly's dancers was a Brigadier stationed at the Gunnery School in Larkhill, and when he heard that I was in the neighbourhood he very kindly invited me down for the weekend. On the Monday he asked if I would like to see the trials of a new gun; of course I said yes. On arrival I was introduced to three other fierce-eyed Brigadiers to whom I gave my best theatrical salute and settled down to watch the trials. It was an interesting gun mounted on the back of what looked like a 30 hundred weight chassis. It could be brought into action virtually instantly and could be entirely controlled and fired by one man. However, I always mistrusted anything that was too automatic: a piece of shrapnel in the wrong place and it was completely useless. It looked very high off the ground and very vulnerable. It had a curved trajectory which usually meant a low muzzle velocity and a short range. The trials ended and I turned to find the piercing eyes of all four Generals on me, and one said 'And what do you think of it Sergeant?' It was like having a bad attack of stage fright, but I managed to come out with 'I think the muzzle velocity is too low, and its range is too short for its vulnerability'. I was then asked the muzzle velocity of the Bofors which fortunately I knew. I never learnt the outcome of the trials, but I never saw the gun anywhere in action.

"The following week I had my second interview for a Commission. Rather terrifyingly ferocious looking Officers throwing questions at you. Nothing to do with the army. 'What did you do in civil life, where have you been, what books did you read, what were your interests in life?' and so on. As time passed they became more friendly saying that I would hear the result through the normal channels but (in rather conspiratorial tones) not to worry. They succeeded in boosting my morale enormously. I duly received notification that I had been recommended for Officers' Training and at the end of 1941 was posted to the O.C.T.U. at Shrivenham. O.C.T.U. initially rather frightened me. My past life had taught me to be able to cope, more or less, with meeting all kinds of people socially, but I

had never been thrown in with so many young men of the so-called 'educated classes', and on an educational basis. I began to feel my lack of schooling, especially when one of my papers was returned with about twenty words heavily underlined in red and at the foot of the paper also in red the words 'Wot spelling'. It all gave me a rather bad R.T.U. (return to unit) complex. However, as the course progressed I found my experience as a Sergeant invaluable. From personal experience I knew more about the guns than most both of their use in action, and from the mechanical point of view.

"One thing pleased me during the latter part of the course. We were to be taken out to see what we were told was one of the best run sites in the area. When we arrived I found it was my old site at Middle Wallop with all my Orders still up and being used.

"I was commissioned in February 1942 and found rather to my amusement that my status as a newly commissioned Second Lieutenant was far below the status of the Sergeant I had just been.

"Since I first met Molly in 1934 I asked her daily to marry me, always being tactfully turned down on the grounds that she was too old for me. However on my post O.C.T.U. leave I got fed up with the whole business, I made all arrangements to be married at the Marylebone Registry Office, took Molly down there and we were married almost before she realised what had happened. I had told mother and mother brought Noreen with her, otherwise no one knew we were to be married. I really remember only four things: 1. that Noreen was carrying a large bouquet of lilies of the valley; 2. We hadn't got a ring so I took one from one of Molly's other fingers, turned it round so that it appeared to be a gold band and used that; 3. Molly whispering to me through the longest part of the Service: 'Do wish he would hurry, I am giving a lesson in half an hour'; and 4. at the end of the service I said to Molly 'Well, if I am killed now you at least get a pension'.

Nissen Huts and Aeroplane Hangars

Molly's new venture was the Ballet Guild. This was the brain child of Deryck Lynham who became its director, and Christmas Humphreys who was its Chairman. Molly was appointed "Maître de Ballet". It began performing in April 1941, although it was officially set up one month later, on May 10th.

The Ballet Guild, based at 44a Loudoun Road in St John's Wood, where it had a rehearsal studio which was also used for children's classes, offices and a storeroom, was a non-profit making organisation set up to "encourage and develop the ballet". It was an ambitious venture, encompassing not only performances and lessons, but educational and academic facilities as well. The pamphlet published on its formation explained that

> "There are ballet schools and Ballet Companies in England, but until the formation of the Ballet Guild there was no permanent organisation free from State control which provided not only a Ballet School, a Library, and lectures and publications on the Ballet, but also a Ballet Company."

Now, in the 1990s there can be little doubt that the Arts Council enjoys a certain control of the companies it subsidises and by omission also of the ones it does not, and the words "free from State control" demonstrate a remarkable foresight and awareness of the dangers of state or official interference of any kind. Molly's and Travis's view on this never changed, and on her retirement, she refused to apply for accreditation of the school which she and Travis set up, preferring to keep her independence.

While membershp of the Ballet Guild was limited to one hundred and was granted only to those "who work in some capacity for the advancement of the Ballet", it had "no barriers" and members of all companies were welcome at its headquarters. However, this was obviously found to be too exclusive, and on February 15th 1942, the Ballet Guild Club was formed "to provide a means whereby members of the audience and other lovers of the Ballet" could give their support to the Ballet Guild.

The Club provided lectures and performances; it gave a platform to such eminent speakers as Cyril Beaumont, Ninette de Valois and Joan Lawson, and recitals were given by Molly, Gerd Larsen, Florence Read and others. It had a library which on its formation already contained over three hundred books on dance, music, costumes and decor. It also had a museum of photographs, designs and "other relics of the ballet". This collection, which included programmes, photography and press cuttings lodged by Molly and Travis, passed to the London Archives of the Dance in 1945, and was later handed over the Victoria and Albert Museum. Molly and Travis subsequently took back the material which they had donated, because they felt it was not being taken care of as they would have wished.

Membership of the Ballet Guild Club was open to all who were interested in ballet, and the subscription was £1 for full membership, although for those who lived more than twenty miles from Charing Cross, it was reduced to 10/- per year. Dancers and students could be admitted for 10/- subscription. Theatre membership, at 2/6 per annum gave the right to purchase tickets for Sunday shows.

Writing in the *Picture Post*, Arnold Haskell expressed the view that while the popularity of the Russian ballet companies in the 1930s had been described as a "boom" which would disappear, on the contrary "ballet both as an indigenous art and a popular entertainment has come to stay, a taste we share with our Soviet ally". Again the question arises: why, in contrast, has ballet in this country come to be regarded by some as an "elitist" art? Haskell praised the work of the Guild's school and rehearsal class which encouraged the amateur who

> "badly needs to temper his applause with knowledge and a sense of proportion. Ballet depends for its quality on an enlightened audience."[1]

Once again we are confronted with the fact that Molly and Travis were involved throughout their lives in pioneering work, successfully introducing new audiences to ballet, as were other small companies at that time.

When the company first started, all the dancers were girls and the repertoire was chosen accordingly, although they drew on outside dancers and guest artists whenever possible. Molly frequently wrote to Travis, begging him to try to get a week's leave, so that they could accept an engagement in Wolverhampton or Norwich, or some other larger venue. He was usually unable to do so, and in September 1941 they "lost Wolverhampton to the Poles" [Anglo-Polish Ballet], to whom Molly was occasionally asked to give class.

The company performed whenever it could, sometimes appearing for one evening only at theatres, at others for a week's season (when they were able to find a male dancer and could present "Giselle" or "Swan Lake" Act II). They appeared at the Rudolph Steiner Hall, Toynbee Hall, the Garrick

Theatre, Wyndham's Theatre, "Q" Theatre, Arts Theatre and the Wulfrum Hall in Wolverhampton. Ticket prices usually ranged from 7/6 to 2/6 with unreserved seats at 1/6, but performances at the Garrick Theatre which were given on Sunday evenings were a social event for which tickets were more expensive than at other theatres. In contrast prices for those at the People's Palace in the Mile End Road in 1944, were organised and presumably subsidised by Stepney Borough Council under the Holidays at Home Scheme were only 3/-, 2/- and unreserved 1/-.

The programmes, which were accompanied by the Ballet Guild Quintet, were changed daily when the company appeared at the same theatre for several days, presenting up to eleven works during the course of a week — something which today's companies would rarely dream of doing, and included traditional, classical and romantic ballets such as "Swan Lake" Act II, "Giselle", and "Les Sylphides". A popular piece in the company's repertoire was Keith Lester's "The Dark Mirror", which was premiered in Bath on April 15th, 1941. The Bath and Wilts Chronicle described it as "An intense human interest story vividly and convincingly portrayed.... The five scenes are powerfully mimed."[2]

Many of Molly's ballets were also performed; these included "The Nymphenburg Garden" (Mozart), "La Valse" (Ravel), "Beethoven Suite", "La Petite Fadette" (Fauré, arranged Tunnard, book Lynham, based on a story by Georges Sand). This last was in two scenes, and the programme note outlines the story of how an outcast in the village is befriended by one of the villagers who falls in love with and marries her. Travis danced the lead when he was on leave, and a lithograph of him and Gillian Lynne in this work was included in "Ballet in England, a book of Lithographs" by Sheila Jackson, as was the company's production of "Les Sylphides". Years later, in an article in *Dance Magazine* in July 1988, Gillian Lynne was quoted as saying "Molly Lake was the best teacher I ever had. She was phenomenal, and I just blossomed".[3] Molly was constantly praised by the press for her performances; for example:

> "Molly Lake as Queen of the Wilis...combined good technical work with good characterisation...
> Molly Lake [in Lester's 'The Dark Mirror']...understood how to characterise a love-lorn maiden by means of dance and mime."[4]

However, in contrast to a review praising the "well-balanced" programme of the Arts Theatre Ballet, on this occasion the performance was criticised for a "superfluity of divertissements". The question arises whether the criteria of a ballet magazine which was read mainly by balletomanes and those knowledgeable about ballet, were relevant to this company which was appealing so successfully to new audiences. The fact that they were indeed doing so becomes obvious when reading the reviews of the company as they toured the provinces. For example, the "Weston Gazette" reported that it was impossible to buy a seat as all were sold well in advance and that

> "the whole company in solo or team work was brilliant and provided us with a series of wordless poems and colourful stage patterns that will be remembered as a refreshing glimpse of beauty in an ugly war".[5]

(The paper also commented in passing on the fact that as most of the male dancers had been called up, it had only been possible to present single acts from the classics. It also mentioned that every member of the orchestra — conducted by Leighton Lucas — and the back stage staff were women, for the same reason).

The *Yorkshire Post* took up the same theme: it felt that while ballet was commonly supposed to be an aristocratic art, the Ballet Guild in contrast was a "democratic" company touring the provinces as it did under difficult conditions, "rubbing up against a new reality", and meeting the challenge of new audiences by presenting works which they could relate to and enjoy. The reviewer considered "The Dark Mirror" to be "the sort of thing a touring ballet, meeting new audiences should do". Readers were told how rehearsals were made difficult by bomb blasts throwing the needle off the gramophone, and how most of the male dancers had been called up.[6]

The critic of the *Harrogate Herald* began his long and enthusiastic description of the company's work by equating ballet with entertainment:

> "Every one is agreed upon the necessity of artistic entertainment in these times, so there is no need to dwell upon the value of ballet."[7]

He went on to list the problems that had been encountered in getting together an orchestra to accompany the dancers and recounted how several soldiers had been allowed leave of absence at the last minute to come and play for the performances. He continued by saying how lucky the inhabitants of Harrogate had been to have seen many dance performances by different companies, and by praising the performances of "Ballet Guild": Helene Wolska who "magnificently" danced the title role in "Giselle", Keith Lester's "expressive" Prince Albrecht, of course Molly's Queen of the Wilis, and some "excellent comedy" in the divertissement.

Many performances were given in aid of charities. For example, the Five Arts Gift Fund for Comforts for the Red Army, the Tavistock Clinic, and Malta.

Under the heading "Ballet helps Malta" the *Evening News* devoted a 5-inch column to the Ballet Guild describing the Guild and its aims.[8]

The programme of a Sunday afternoon performance at Wyndhams Theatre comprises "La Petite Fadette". Tudor's "Soirée Musicale", and three divertissements. The cast included Molly, Sally Gilmour, Peggy Van Praagh, Gerd Larsen, Walter Gore, David Paltenghi and Travis. In the *Queen* magazine there was a whole page on the Ballet Guild with four photographs, a brief outline of its aims and charity work, and a mention of a forthcoming performance for Lady Cripps' United Aid to China Fund, in the presence of Sir Stafford Cripps who was scheduled to make a speech from the stage.[9]

In addition to Molly, the company included at various times, Gillian Lynne, Diana Gould, Keith Lester, Gerd Larsen, and others amounting to about twenty dancers at any one time. Travis danced with the company whenever he was at home.

One such occasion was June 28th 1941, when he received forty eight hours leave in order to dance the part of Albrecht in a performance of "Giselle" which was given at the Rudolf Steiner Hall to celebrate the ballet's centenary. It started at 7.00 pm and included Grand Divertissement which consisted of twelve short dances. The performance was very successful, and "Giselle" received fourteen curtain calls. Travis set off for barracks immediately afterwards.

The programme which cost 1/- showed a reproduction of a print of Carlotta Grisi the first Giselle, and photographs of Anna Pavlova and Olga Spessivtseva in the title role, the original cast list from the programme of 1841, two pages of historical notes on the origin and creation of the work which stressed the dramatic demands of the main parts; it included a synopsis and a quotation from the "Moniteur des Theatres" of June 20th 1841 on Perrot's contribution to the choreography.

The rehearsals, performances and teaching continued during the day, as did the raids by night, and Molly wrote to Travis about how frightened she had been when bombs were dropped in Hampstead while she was on fire watch: "I wish I was one of those fearless superwomen, think what a lot of wear and tear one would be saved". But her love of nature restored her sense of balance as it always did.

> "I took Tam [her dog] up to Hampstead this morning, it was as mild as summer, one of those lovely still, golden days that you get sometimes in late autumn — so still that you are afraid to speak in case a leaf should fall — faintly misty and full of colours".

On August 28th 1941 the Ballet Guild signed the first of several contracts with the Entertainment National Service Association (ENSA) for whom they gave sporadic performances in England until the end of the war. One of the conditions of the contract was reminiscent of those of Music Hall: it stipulated that the company was

> "not to give expression to any vulgarity, or words having double meaning, nor to use any objectionable gesture".

ENSA was one of the largest organisations set up during the Second World War for promotion of the arts, and it ran an entertainment and performing arts programme on a larger scale than anybody has since attempted in Britain, employing such "stars" as John Gielgud, James Mason, Eva Turner and Noel Coward. It was, as John Pick reminds us:

> "All fatally entertaining, presented without that conscious desire to elevate and improve which, in the upper cavities of the British mind, has become the hallmark of true art."[10]

Other organisations, more attuned to the promotion of "Art" were therefore set up, among them the Committee for the Encouragement of Music and the Arts (CEMA), and it is interesting to note that the tours of England which the Ballet Guild undertook during those war years, and those of the Sadlers Wells Ballet, Ballet Rambert, the Anglo-Polish Ballet, the International Ballet and such smaller groups as the Three Arts Ballet were almost all organised by ENSA rather than by CEMA. When some of these companies worked in Europe after the war, their performances for the troops were also organised by ENSA (while those for the civilians were arranged by the British Council). In other words, ballet at that time was considered to be a form of entertainment which could be enjoyed by all, rather than "Art". Molly also was obviously aware of the importance of the entertainment element, and the reception of a new ballet "Phantom Procession" which received its first performance in December 1944 surprised her: "I thought it would be a complete flop as far as an ENSA audience was concerned: it's pretty high brow". However, it seems that Ballet Guild also met the requirements of CEMA, for Molly reported to Travis that a representative came to inspect the company in November 1944, and that she "appeared staggered at the improvement and was most complementary.... She thought it a very good show."

For Molly it was a continual struggle to put on performances; finding and keeping dancers was always a problem, and she lost a very good one when the Home Office decided that the girl should work in a factory instead of dancing. She had a male dancer who had been blown up in the army and had been ill ever since; unfortunately, he was often too sick to dance.

In addition to running the company, Molly continued to choreograph and to dance herself, although a leg injury gave her a lot of pain and kept her from performing from time to time. Travel conditions were "a bit tough", as when they had to travel two and a half hours before and after a show in a bus which had insufficient seats, and in which the "odd chairs" which had been put in fell over at every turn.

In November 1944 she managed to put on a performance of "Giselle" in Folkestone, where the stage was large but had a very bad surface. Molly herself was dancing the part of Giselle; "Whenever I give myself something big to dance, I always wish that I hadn't". The dancers did not always do their best without a certain amount of encouragement and driving: "'Swan Lake' Act II looked well groomed and well trained, competent and pretty, but danced without a vestige of atmosphere or feeling — they got Hell this morning".

That month they gave a performance for the

> "rowdiest audience of sailors and dock hands we have ever had. We were scared stiff; it was like being thrown to the lions, but we soon got used to it, and we were a great success — it was my proudest moment."

At the beginning of December, the company performed at a Mosquito and Spitfire drome, and Molly admired the organisation and precision with which they took off. The one Spitfire among them "seemed to run up into the sky almost vertically. It was all so orderly and laden in drama, it was hard to believe that some of those planes might never come back." If they returned with wounded aboard they dropped red flares, which the dancers could see from the dressing room windows during the performance. In the mess afterwards, while the officers were doing their best to be polite, Molly always sensed that they were waiting for the planes, and when these did start to return it was obvious that everyone had started to count.

Molly missed Travis more and more. In July she wrote "The last piece of solid, very solid, familiar ground seemed to slip from under my feet when you left", and in December: "I'm getting so old and I do so grudge the waste of time". After keeping it from her for three months, Travis finally admitted that he had been sent to France. Molly had already guessed and was, of course, very worried about him. She wrote, "Don't get your feet wet, and wear wool next to your skin, you mean rather an unpleasant amount to me."

While running the Ballet Guild, Molly was also arranging the dances in several pantomimes including Wolverhampton and Hereford, and here too she had problems: she found it hard to engage enough dancers, and was unable to sign any contracts with the managements till she knew how many she would have, in case she committed herself to more than she could provide.

In spite of all the problems, the Ballet Guild shows were going down well at R.A.F. stations, and there was some recognition of their work, as when Cyril Beaumont gave Molly £10 towards the cost of the new production of "Giselle". She gave the money back: "I can't take money from Beaumont". Kay Ambrose offered to do a series of drawings of the camp shows, and told Molly that she was doing real pioneering work and that it should be recognised. "What a hope!".

In January 1945 the Ballet Guild appeared at the Garrison Theatre in Taunton where they played for three days for the American army, and although the audience was "vetted, combed out with a tooth comb as audience. . . nothing can stop the whoopee! element". The manager suggested that they start the performance with the American and British national anthems, for which the soldiers would have to stand for four minutes, which would "knock them out for about half an hour, and by that time they are used to it". When they performed for the U.S. wounded, the manager brought in two rows of village children "in front to form a sort of breakwater". Molly was very surprised to have a personal success with the American soldiers: "I don't know what did it — I look pretty awful these days, so it must either have been my lovely dancing or my lovely nature".

The strain of continual touring under difficult conditions was telling on the company: they were continually bursting into tears in class and even, on one occasion, on stage:

> "The other night in 'Les Sylphides', I was in the wings and heard someone crying very loudly. I went and looked in all the dressing rooms but they were all empty. It was one of the girls *on the stage*: her feet hurt!!! Seventeen years old, well bred and a first class education. What is the answer to that?"

The dancers were late for class, were slack about costumes and grooming on stage, and there was a universal lack of courtesy and consideration. Molly had to "read the riot act with a vengeance". She made a set of rules, failure to adhere to which were punishable by fines to the Red Cross, and finally by dismissal. She hated doing it — "It pushes me into a very lonely position, but seems to be the only way to run a company". Some of the men in particular, were sometimes a problem, as the soldiers at the bases occasionally derided them for being dancers and for not being in the army. At a base in King's Lynn, two men in the company refused to do class or to rehearse. Molly was ready to sack them and to carry on without them, but she decided to ask the opinion of other members of the company, and in the end only one left.

The travel conditions and the dancers were not Molly's only problems: by the time they were in their twentieth week of the ENSA tour, she and the Guild council were no longer in total agreement. She was receiving only £7 per week, in spite of the fact that she was "ballet mistress, choreographer, teacher, principal dancer and general company director and stooge". In addition, a number of the costumes, most of the music, and most of the ballets also belonged to her and Travis. She felt that it was due to her efforts that the company was successful, and she hoped that she would be allowed to continue to run it. However, at a meeting in January 1945, she gained the impression that the council felt that it was they who were alone responsible for the Ballet Guild's success, and that they had decided that the company would cease to exist after the end of the ENSA contract the following March. Also, although Molly and Travis had been paying one third of all expenses, they would not then be allowed the use of the studio. Molly was very angry and most upset: she felt that the management was incompetent (for example, they had had no violinist for six weeks), and in view of the fact that she was being so very badly underpaid, she wondered where the income from the performances was going. In February she was asked to spend two thirds of her time teaching at the Guild's school, and this made her even angrier as she knew that the company would cease to improve without her, and she did not want to teach when she did not gain financially from it. Finally at the end of February she had a meeting with the management council and threatened to leave unless she received more loyalty and co-operation from them. She laid out plans for the future of the company, which included finding new young talent, and also interesting an agent or an impresario who would take on the company after the war.

She heard that ENSA would not renew their contract beyond March, and that Army Welfare did not want ballet. (In the event, ENSA did engage them again, and sent them to Europe.) She expected Travis to return in about June, and was in despair as to how to keep the company going until then. Mr Jackson, who had been helping to run the company, offered to manage it in its new form. He later suggested that they try to be taken over by CEMA, and Molly wrote to Travis: "CEMA, or rather the Arts Council as it calls itself now, will I think be the power of the future".

Running the company for those last few months proved to be increasingly difficult. The health of the dancers was bad, as they were all run down, the healthier ones doing extra work "with the result that no one is very fit". The conditions in the ENSA hostels were often hard, but Molly was "ashamed to grumble when I think what these men are doing and how little comfort they have; it consoles me to think perhaps I can feel a very small bit of your discomfort''. Occasionally though, life was easier, as when they were put in to a beautiful eighteenth century house with plenty of hot water, where Molly was able to wash every item of clothing she had: ''I literally stank''. They finally were given two weeks away from ENSA, one of which was spent doing odd dates for themselves, and the second was at last a much-needed holiday.

Molly's concern for animals showed itself once more on a journey from Exeter to Salisbury; she found a lost dog on Exeter station with a Plymouth address on her collar. She could find no-one who would do anything about it, so she took the dog with her on the train in order to contact her owners herself. Luckily the compere of the show was wearing his pyjama trousers under his ordinary ones because of the severe cold, and he gallantly lent Molly the cord to use as a lead. She commented ''I don't think he's very comfortable now''.

Molly and Travis decided to have the house they had bought in Springfield Road decorated so that they could let it, and in March she wrote: ''It's a damn nice house; I don't really feel that I should live in such a ''classy'' looking establishment until I look a little more ''classy'' myself. She asked Travis to bring back some bulbs from Holland for the garden.

Throughout March they continued to tour Britain, performing for soldiers, the R.A.F. and munitions workers. In Beith where there was a stone stage (''My poor feet!''), and where there were ''not many in the audience but those that were, were very quiet and enthusiastic''. They played at an army depot on the Clyde where the audience was:

> ''Sub-human is the only word — they didn't laugh or cat call they just sat and stared without a shadow of life or expression on their faces — it was a full house too''.

In Greenock, where ''the inhabitants are not (on the surface anyhow), as tough as their reputations make them out to be'', they danced in an old and very large theatre.

> ''The house was packed with sailors from the ships in the river — it was a nerve racking afternoon, but we emerged in one piece, and quite enjoyed ourselves. Ballet on Clydeside is something of an achievement, and to keep an audience of that type friendly was a pretty good effort I think.''

Molly thoroughly enjoyed a performance which they gave at a naval centre near the Forth Bridge, and where they had a good stage with very adequate lighting and a full house. The show was attended by some officers from a Russian cruiser, and after chatting to them afterwards in the Mess, Molly was:

> ''distinctly shattered when one who had attached himself to me for the evening embraced me so enthusiastically on saying good night, that I was almost knocked into the flower bed — I shall never live it down in the company''.

On March 28th they performed in Cupar, and were thrilled to find a most appreciative audience:

> ''A good many had seen a lot of ballet, and the rest made up for their lack of knowledge by their enthusiasm. I collected two or three Guild members''.

In Catterick, where the theatre was good and where the houses were about three quarters full ''and quite ballet minded'', Molly distinguished herself by

> ''going down a wonderful wallop in the Beethoven — slap between two men and right on the note — choreographically a masterpiece but biologically very painful''.

They found dancing at a Canadian Air Force camp in Northallerton rather tough going, as the wrong posters had been put up, and the audience was expecting a variety bill, but in Ripon, where they performed Giselle for a ''very ballet minded R.A.F.'', they were a great success, so great that they did not leave the Mess until 2.00 am, ''after having done all the 'Knees Up Mother Browns', sung every stupid song, and sad to relate in one or two cases drunk every beastly drink''. Molly was pursued by two officers, one of whom

> ''would talk 'lights out' with elaborate allusions to my 'marvellous understanding of it' — the other would sing and present me every few minutes with another drink, none of which I drank — all I wanted was a good solid meal. Neither art, nor song, nor wine moved me half as much as a fried egg would have done; lucky they did not know to what ends I would have gone for a meal!''.

They travelled through beautiful countryside which Molly always described in detail, even after she ''promised I wouldn't inflict scenery on you again'' and when they moved on to Stirling where they stayed in a miners' hostel, Molly said: ''We may be poor, but we do see life''.

The situation with the management of the Guild did not seem to be improving, and Molly wrote despairingly to Travis about how, although the company was still without a violinist after eleven weeks, the administration in London were unable to spend the time trying to obtain deferment for their eighteen year old cellist, and had insisted that he himself travel down to London to arrange it himself, thereby missing at least two performances.

Molly missed Travis and like everyone else, was tired of the war.

> "Life for the last six years seems to have been nothing more than a series of shadowy pictures, nothing clear, or certain anywhere. The Lady of Shalott said that she was 'half sick of shadows'; I say that I am wholly sick of shadows. I feel unreal and find it hard to believe that I am really myself at all. Still I suppose that I am, and that somewhere a long way beyond this mist and these mountains you too are pursuing your shadowy existence — a nice solid cheerful shadow, I hope."

Molly went to see the Jooss Ballet while she was in Inverness and thought they were very good, although she was very annoyed to hear that they were to have a thirty piece orchestra, "being enemy aliens", while her company had to struggle with barely adequate accompaniment; "I wish we were Germans or Japanese and someone would back us at once!".

By the time they reached Perth at the end of March, the company had travelled 1,700 miles through Scotland, and although Molly was enjoying the tour, she was very anxious to work abroad, and so she volunteered to take the company to the Outer Hebrides (ENSA would only accept volunteers as the work was very difficult, and the sea journeys long and hard).

And then at last, in May, the war was over and Germany defeated, and Churchill's speech

> "made me almost burst with pride at being British. I think that after all we have been tremendously lucky to live in such an era. I know it has been foul in fact, but now that the greatness and the grandness has commenced to slip away and fundamental pettiness has begun to re-assert itself, I feel like despairingly clutching at the vanishing grandeurs of what seemed in 1940 or 1944 to be ordinary things of life, and asking why, if we could reach such heights in those horrors, we cannot reach even higher ones in peace. Churchill might get us there, but I think that a great many people are ready and willing to turn on him. I am so afraid we shall have a labour government which is merely labour because it wants something somebody else has got and the American way as our standard of living. I think then darling that we had better pool our assets and go and live in Mahé?"

At last the Ballet Guild was sent by ENSA to perform in Europe, and Molly kept detailed diaries of their adventures.

Camp Followers

On September 24th 1945 Molly woke early and struggled into her army uniform ("coping with collar and tie at that hour nearly ruined me") and made her way to Victoria where she met the rest of the company and boarded a train to take them to Newhaven. Conditions were not easy: they queued for an hour and a half for lunch, then learnt that the sea was too rough to cross, and had to spend the night on board in the saloon with about sixty other people. The next morning they rose at six, queued again for an hour and a half for breakfast, were ordered to disembark, and had to go through customs for a second time. In Dieppe, which they reached at three in the afternoon, they found that no seats had been reserved for them on the train taking them to Paris, and they had to squeeze into a crowded compartment. They finally arrived in Paris at midnight and were met and taken to a hostel near the Opéra Comique which was very comfortable: Molly even had a bedroom and private bathroom to herself, and with her usual modesty, she wondered whether

> "it was offended at having so unexalted a personage in it, after all the Edith Evans and Margot Fonteyns who had dreamt their illustrious dreams therein".

They were to dance at the Marigny Theatre and Molly was very apprehensive, and hung around the theatre all day "my heart in my boots". The French stage manager did not help her confidence as he kept telling her that the Vic Wells Ballet, which had performed at the theatre recently, was a large company and had scenery and a large repertoire, whereas Molly knew that the Ballet Guild had no scenery, only sixteen dancers "mostly raw", and only two men: Jak Carter and Alex Thompson. In addition, the English ballet world, according to Molly's diary had "spared no pains to let the company know what a poor and cheap little affair it is — why did we come?" The evening arrived and the curtain rose on "Les Sylphides" before a packed house. By the time the last notes faded away they realised that in spite of having been looked down on at home, they were a success with the sophisticated ballet audience of Paris, and they went through the rest of the programme "in a daze of happiness". They gave four performances to packed houses and by the end people were being turned away.

Molly was upset by the corruption everywhere, the black market, the fact that while luxury goods were obtainable at fantastic prices, necessities could not be found, and she felt ashamed at being well fed and secure. On September 30th they travelled overnight to Brussels, and were taken to their hostel, again a hotel, luxurious by the standards they had been used to in England where five of them had shared a room in NAAFI huts. Molly again had her own room, and was surprised to find that Brussels was a city of plenty: sugar, butter, fruit, cakes and sweets — goods which were unavailable in England.

This time the company was to perform in a large music hall for a more typical ENSA audience consisting mainly of soldiers rather than civilians, but again they did well and Molly enjoyed being warm and able to buy small luxuries that she had not seen for so long.

On October 7th they moved on again, this time to Germany via Holland, where they were to give an average of eight performances per week, usually one-night stands. In spite of the continual travelling in very difficult conditions, Molly insisted on a class and rehearsal every day, as without them she felt the group would have ''gone to pieces completely''.

As they travelled through Belgium the people they passed seemed well fed and prosperous, but once over the Dutch border they saw desolation and poverty everywhere, and as they went deeper into Germany conditions deteriorated and they found whole villages in ruins and peoples' expressions ''sullen and obstinate''. They had to go round the town of Wesel because it was just a heap of rubble with no road through it; yet well dressed people still lived there. As they passed through the Ruhr the damage was appalling, the ground pitted with bomb craters, piles of debris, and shells of houses, and as always Molly remarked on the animals, ''skeletal horses dying on their legs''. Their destination was a little town near Essen, and here the theatre was dilapidated and smelly; the curtains were threadbare, the lighting was insufficient, and the huge auditorium was always three quarters empty as there were not many troops in the district and little transport for those who wanted to come from further afield. But those who did come were interested and appreciative.

Destruction was everywhere, the local people were cold and hostile and once again Molly remarked on their treatment of a horse

> ''dying of starvation and exhaustion on the cobbles, a crowd of the inhuman people, trying to pull it up by the mouth so that it could serve them for another few hours of misery''.

and then

> "a very blind, skeleton of a horse crept painfully down a hill, he twitched one poor shabby old ear forward to sense the way he couldn't see — sentimentality over a horse!".

Molly was almost tempted to feel sorry for the people

> "then I think of what their kind have done to other peoples and I know that Essen is justice — is it though? I wish I knew. *Next day:* Yes it is."

On October 18th they thankfully left the Ruhr and made their way through beautiful coutryside towards Berlin, stopping off for lunch at the Officers' Club at Salzuflun "a sort of super Cheltenham Spa" where they had excellent food in sumptuous surroundings and where "nothing so vulgarly realistic as war damage or enemy hostility obtruded itself". Then on through wooded hills and green valleys of Westphalia to Minden, where they stayed and from where they were taken to dance at an R.A.F. Station at Buckeburg, nine miles away. Molly loved the journey through the autumn countryside where the colours seemed more brilliant and varied than at home, and the villagers could be seen in their peasant costumes with long bright red or magenta skirts and kerchiefs on their heads.

The company took a very varied light repertoire, which comprised the can-can which had been so well received whenever it was performed, several comedy items including "Olympic Antics", and short classical dances, though "nothing as ambitious as Swan Lake". While in Buckeburg they put on a new work, "Mid Summer Day Dream". The cast had suffered many injuries but Molly felt the repertoire needed the new work.

At last they left for Berlin, in an uncomfortable truck with only a couple of "nasty sandwiches", a journey of two hundred and fifty miles, one hundred of which were through the Russian zone, where they saw "chatty little notices" in Russian saying "Give thanks to Stalin", and "Praise to our Glorious Red Army". They also saw a horse drawn Russian convoy, healthy stout horses which "did my heart good". They passed village women on their way to church wearing their national costume, this time brown velvet tight jacket bodices and very full skirts elaborately embroidered in black and with a dark green silk apron. In another village the older women all wore long black silk cloaks.

When they finally arrived in Berlin on October 21st and were installed in a villa in Charlottenburg, Molly could hardly believe it. Since 1939 Berlin had seemed "as distant and unattainable as the moon, impregnable, evil, fantastic Nazi Berlin". Her bedroom was decorated in cream with windows right down one wall, the carpet and furniture very modern and well made, all opulent and in good condition. Only later did she notice a hole through the wall by the window, the shattered bathroom door and strips of cardboard covering bare bricks and cracks in ceiling and walls. Most of the buildings were in bad condition, including the Chancellery where Hitler had had his office. The interior consisted mainly of one long marble hall after another, one of which,

> "a quite hideous hall in red and gold mosaic, is a cross between a Roman villa in Pompeii and the marble hall in the Holborn restaurant".

Molly had expected to

> "sense an atmosphere of evil, to feel something more than curiosity in this dead heart of Nazism — but I didn't, to me it was just a cold, empty shell and the lavatory had blue tiles!".

Coming home late one night from a dance after the show Molly was astonished to see lights in many of the skeletal houses and realised with horror that people were living in them. Many of the Germans Molly spoke to did not believe that Hitler was dead, but Molly felt that "if Hitler is not dead, Berlin most certainly is". They went to lunch at the British club in Wilhelmsdorf which was "not unlike Cecil Beaton's setting for 'Lady Windermere's Fan'".

From Berlin they moved on to Gutersloh, a ten hour drive from Berlin. The hostel where they were installed was "not exactly up to standard": it was cramped, with no hot water and not enough basins to wash in. The theatre was even more depressing and Molly could not decide which was worse — the lighting or the lavatory. To make things worse one of the girls, Shirley, was in bed with asthma and looked like being there for several days. While they were at class one morning there was a fire in the hostel; Shirley's room was the worst hit, and she and her belongings had to be carried out of the building. Luckily no one lost any of their possessions.

Two days later, on November 1st, they arrived at Warendorf after a journey of only an hour and were installed in

> "a fantastically fusty and unbeautiful hostel — I don't know whether it's German Early Victorian, or German Edwardian; whichever it is, it is frightful!"

There was no bath, and Molly could only hope that

> "the adage 'a rolling stone gathers no moss' holds good and that the amount of 'rolling' I do will prevent my gathering many far more unpleasant things than moss".

Their audiences consisted of both local citizens and soldiers. Although there had been some ballet in Europe before the war — for example, the Berlin Opera had a ballet company attached to it, the predominant form of dance in Germany had been Expressionist modern dance, and both the people and the soldiers were unfamiliar with ballet. At their first performance, it became obvious to the dancers of the Ballet Guild, that their audience was also new to theatre-going for as the curtain came down on the first ballet there was a deadly silence, and not a hand clapped. However, when it rose again and the dancers bowed embarrassedly, then the audience applauded with great enthusiasm. It was, as Molly said, a "pioneering show".

On another occasion, an officer came to see Molly after a performance, and apologetically explained that, as he and his men had never seen ballet before, they did not know if they were supposed to applaud or not; but now they they had seen the show they knew that ballet was something to be enjoyed, and they were grateful to Molly and the company for their first introduction. Many people came to Molly with the same tale, and the theatre correspondent of *The Polar Bear News*, the army newspaper published in Neheim, wrote on the same theme. He devoted over 18 inches to the company under the heading "I See the Ballet — and Praise Everybody". It began

> "When I knew that the Ballet Guild were coming over from England to entertain the troops here I must confess that I was apprehensive. Ballet is not every man's cup of tea and I was of the opinion that the audience would be so small that it would not be worth E.N.S.A.'s time and trouble to continue. But I need not have worried. When I saw the company in Paris two months ago the houses were packed each night with very appreciative audiences... and it has been the same throughout the tour.
> These youngsters are doing more to popularise ballet than anybody has done since Nijinsky left the art. I spoke to quite a few members of the Monday audiences who had never seen ballet before, and were doubtful about whether they would like it or not. And these same people were there on Tuesday and Wednesday, and would be there every night of the week if the ballet was still running."[1]

Molly constantly felt guilty that, in spite of the physical hardships of her existence she was so much better off than the local inhabitants. For example, she went to a piano recital given by a young German, and felt that she would have liked to give him a meal as he looked so thin. She always felt embarrassed about eating, knowing that "hungry German eyes are watching", and she also ''squirmed'' when she saw a British officer breaking a beautiful chair in front of the Germans.

While they were in Iserlohn, one of the dancers left as she was pregnant — she had signed the contract knowing that she would not be able to fulfil it because she wanted to go to Paris with the company. It would appear that, as she had no intention of staying, she did not always behave very well, and Molly wrote:

> ''The temptation to give the rear portion of her fat anatomy a hearty kick has at times been almost shatteringly strong — thank heaven the temptation is now removed.''

She was replaced by Angela Bayley who Molly at once realised would be an asset to the team both as a dancer and as a person.

Travis managed to spend a day with the company, and Molly showed him the new work ''Berners''. She was relieved that he liked it, although he felt that it was still under rehearsed, and that the floor patterns were not yet always clear.

They had some company photos taken by a ''pallid and grumbling photographer who did nothing but bewail his fate and the treatment he received in general''. Molly advised: ''Bung him into the Russian zone and he'll change his tune''.

On November 13th it snowed and Molly awoke to a beautiful view. However, the stove was out and there was only icy cold water to wash in; Molly would ''Willingly have swapped the view for a fire and some hot water''.

On to Neheim where in contrast Molly had her own stove in her room and chrysanthemums on the table. She felt ''private and peaceful''.

The theatre was ''a bit of a problem'' with curtains which remained closed when they should have been open, or open when they should have shut, the dressing rooms colder than the street, and the sanitary conditions primitive. Molly commented ''It's hard to keep up standards in such conditions, but obviously we have got to.'' Luckily, their audiences responded well.

They returned to Iserlohn after waiting for over three hours in an unheated room for their transport which turned out to be a luggage truck, with open sides and back, and wooden benches to sit on. Even so, this was ''paradise compared to the morning''. Their audience was appreciative but very small, and Molly felt disheartened to ''play to so few after such a long and hard day''.

The tour continued to Ludenscheid, where the small audience gave them a very warm welcome. Indeed throughout the tour the soldiers had been very appreciative and enthusiastic, yet the dancers were constantly being given to understand that ballet, however good, did not have a general appeal and that the company was not really useful. The effect was very depressing, but when they returned to Warendorf (where Molly reported "I nearly froze in my bed"), their morale was lifted when the General asked them to do some additional performances.

> "A feather in our cap, a very small feather I know, but if you are not a fashionable company, feathers are hard to come by, and those we get from our novice ballet audiences are treasured."

They were continually invited to "honour such and such a mess with their presence for lunch, tea or supper, or failing that, for a bath or perhaps the loan of a car". The problem became one of not being "killed with kindness". Molly related years later that an added reason for their popularity was that they were "the only ENSA company who've been out here who haven't stolen our net curtains".

The officers often made passes at the dancers, but usually were relieved when they were rebuffed, and instead were able to ask the girls' advice about presents for their wives and girl friends. On one occasion when they had been invited to a mess after a performance, the girls noticed with horror and embarassment that one of the male dancers had taken off his shoes and socks and was sitting with his dirty feet up on the fender — definitely not mess behaviour!

While they were in Warendorf accepting hospitality from the 51st Highland Division, Molly was most surprised one evening at dinner, for which everyone dressed as it was always very formal, when the General suddenly insisted on taking off his shirt in order to show her an example of the string vests which the Division had invented and developed. Travis came to spend a few days with her and they relaxed together and bought a couple of watercolours which Molly had seen

> "some days ago, a wintery bit of wood, the foreground half under water, a grey sky and a pallid sun half showing through the clouds. It fascinated me by its loneliness, and I went to look at it every day and finally contacted the artist. After being told that it was not for sale, I finally bought it for 400 marks — there is nothing in Germany that cannot be bought."

Only too soon Travis had to return to Gogh, leaving Molly feeling very sorry for herself, staying in a noisy hostel with two other touring groups and the usual company problems. They began to travel back home, passing through such beautiful scenery that Molly realised that ''those Christmas cards are not impossible''. In Celle, they danced in a warm theatre with excellent lighting and a cyclorama ''to use it on''.

Molly found time to do some sightseeing and went to the Schloss. She found the room beautiful but

> ''so disfigured by a super exuberance of Teutonic bad taste in decoration, that I still feel as though I were suffering from glare stroke. The first room was red, not bloody, not crimson, not scarlet, just red: the carpet was speckled red, the walls red silk, the furniture red velvet, the curtains red satin, the chandelier was not red but it obviously should have been.''

On to Peine, a ''stinking hole'', with a hostel which was ''dirty, entirely unheated, without a bath or a drop of hot water, scanty and almost uneatable food, and an all pervading smell of stale cabbage and bad sanitation''. Molly would have put up with it without complaining but felt that now that there was peace, it was not necessary and was simply the result of slackness and lack of organisation. Molly complained:

> ''Oh! for a manager who knew how to look after us. How it is possible to keep up standards in the performances, when we are too cold to move, let alone dance.''

However, to Molly's great surprise and delight, the theatre was attractive with an adequate stage, wing space and ''wonder of wonders, running hot water, the first we have met out here''. Naturally Molly spent all her spare time in the theatre.

Then to Hildesheim, where Molly was given a room in what had been the quarters of an officer of the Luftwaffe. The mobile, tiny rickety theatre was also on the station. It was unheated and to Molly's disgust, had not a single mirror. The food was excellent, but again the cold was appalling and there was

> ''No place where one can get even fairly warm; we dread getting up in the morning knowing that we shall not be warm again until we are in bed at night. I was so cold during the performance tonight that it was all I could do to keep tears from my eyes with the pain of my joints.''

Pointe shoes were running out though this did not worry Molly unduly:

> You were literally dancing on your toes, which sounded much better, and your feet got stronger. In the Pavlova company you got fined for making a

> noise in a white ballet — you had to dance on your own feet and if your weight is in the right place, you can. Well, look at the Azerbaijans: they dance on pointe in their boots.''

The company was now three girls short, with one in bed, Shirley in hospital with asthma, and another girl going in with tooth trouble. Molly did not know how she would carry on.

It took them twelve hours to travel 200 miles to Wilhelmshaven, after waiting around for over an hour while the driver tried to persuade the frozen truck to go. Even with a large number of blankets which a kind-hearted officer gave the dancers — ''a very hush hush present'' — they were blue with cold and their breath almost froze. The countryside was dull, with only the sight of some enchanting children playing in the snow to lift the spirits.

Wilhelmshaven, which they reached on December 12th was bitterly cold, and the theatre, ''fifteen frozen minutes walk away'' was far from satisfactory; the only entrance was through the auditorium, the only way onto the stage was through the men's dressing room, and the only lavatory was in the front of the house. The stage itself consisted of some rickety boards with some dusty black material insecurely pinned up for drapes, a curtain which did not pull, and the lights comprising only four spots. However, the audience which was small because the performance had not been adequately advertised, was enthusiastic and the dancers put on a good show.

They spent a miserable night travelling in the pouring rain in a leaking truck which had been left out all night and which was ''awash''. They surrounded themselves with blankets and raincoats, which did not provide much protection from the continual dripping. They finally arrived at Luneburg at 3.45 p.m. ''almost drowned''. The next morning they discovered that no-one had really expected them, and that a German company was playing in the theatre and so they did not perform that night. They were pushed ''from pillar to post as though we were not only unnecessary but a complete nuisance''. Molly found this ''cavalier treatment'' which was the result of a row between Army Welfare and ENSA very hard to understand in view of the fact that they were always being told about the scarcity of entertainment and how necessary it was. In the end they gave two performances in the beautiful state theatre which, as the event had not been publicised, was almost empty. On three consecutive occasions the same thing occurred: they arrived at a town only to find that their performance had not been advertised, and indeed they were not even expected. Molly wrote to ENSA H.Q. on December 16th, that over the eighteen months in which the Ballet Guild had worked for ENSA they had found

> "a small but enthusiastic audience for ballet both here and in England. We have taken great pride in our work, and felt that we were doing a useful job. It seems a great pity that our present treatment is likely to damage both our spirit and our usefulness."

Molly was very taken with the children and was often guilty of "shameless 'fratting'", buying their friendship with sweets and biscuits. She felt there must have been a way of "persuading this almost universal charm and gentleness to remain after extreme youth".

On December 21st, they danced in Kiel, 23 miles from Rendsburg, and while driving to the theatre Molly was once again upset by the suffering of an animal: she saw a plump steer being led along with "a look of bewildered worry on his gentle face" obviously on his last journey. The audience was once again small but appreciative, and on the way back to Rendsburg they passed many German soldiers who eyed them sullenly. Molly mused

> "Would it be so difficult to hold up a busful of women? Was revenge sweet enough to be worth the retribution that would surely follow? The answer is sometimes yes — not often though."

Shortly after seeing the German soldiers the truck broke down, luckily near a Red Cross Unit, which supplied hot tea and a comparatively warm room where they waited till 2 am for alternative transport, returning to base at last at 3.00 in the morning.

Molly was very upset to learn that the authorities had decided to curtail the company's stay in Germany, and to send them back to finish the remaining three months of the six-month contract in England, after a week's holiday in Belgium. In spite of the physical conditions, Molly was enjoying the tour for Travis was stationed nearby and was able to meet her from time to time; she was also worried that the ballet world in England would assume incorrectly that the tour had not been a success. In addition Molly had engaged a man from a camp for Displaced Persons as violinist for the company, and he would have to return to the camp where the mother, father and son were all living and sleeping in one room. Molly went to Lubeck to try to obtain permission for the family to return to England with them, but she was unsuccessful.

On Christmas Day 1945 the company were invited to a rather dreary Christmas party at Flensburg near the Danish border where all the soldiers became too drunk to drive the dancers home. They were therefore obliged to stay and did not get to bed until 5 am but had to be up by 8 in the morning to go to a Carol Service at a nearby R.A.F. station. In the evening they had their

Christmas dinner and enjoyed food and drink which had been unobtainable or too expensive in England for over five years including turkey, goose, duck, fish, fruit salad, apples, oranges, champagne, cointreau, whisky, and gin, and later

> ''our Estonian violinist playing Beethoven's Sonata, his wife pretending that her nose is red because the day is cold and we have only a small paraffin stove to warm us. I want always to remember these moments — a small brown room, and erstwhile bar, dull wood floor, three small tables, three dingy plush settees, branches of fresh pine everywhere, the lighted Xmas tree, the oil stove, torn lace curtains at windows suggesting the dark cold emptiness of the street outside. The music — the Spring Sonata — the violinist stroking those lovely sounds, his wife watching him, in one corner a Polish soldier lost in his thoughts and no one else.''

As always in the midst of her enjoyment, Molly felt for others less fortunate than herself

> ''How many people without a country, without a home? — Lost families, lost parents, lost children seeking always each for the other, seeking security, warmth, any sort of stability. Insufficiency of food, loneliness, cold, darkness, ruin, devastation everywhere. All this mass of humanity driven like leaves before the gale.''

She remembered the Christmas of the previous year — the German push through the Ardennes, with Travis somewhere in Europe, and she felt that it did not have the ''unbearable sad quality'' of this one.

> ''Then the peace with its limitless possibilities was ahead, the magic of that word then — a goal for which no hardship was too much to dare in the hope of reaching it. We reached the goal, passed it and found it more death than war — and that death is in ourselves; the descent from a high hill so much more rapid than the ascent, the plains so much emptier than the high places — how can we be great enough in this peace?''

On Boxing Day the company gave a performance at Schleswig, followed by another party and more drinking, but Molly became increasingly sad as the time for their departure drew near. She spent a day in the ENSA hostel in Hamburg, where conditions were much more pleasant than the accommodation she had become used to on the army camps. Travis was given permission to ''swan around'', and he picked Molly up in the afternoon to take her to Mohn See to see the New Year in. On that day everything shut down and Travis was unable to get any petrol; but he had a very helpful driver who said ''leave it to me'' and returned a little later with a full tank. Travis never asked him where he obtained it, and they set off on their journey, travelling in the back of a freezing jeep, bundled in a sheepskin lined bag. At that time, young Germans used to call themselves "Werewolven", form into gangs and go onto bridges and over the autobahns where they would shoot at passing vehicles. Travis recalls:

"The sparks intrigued Molly who said "How nice, they are flashing lights at us", and she wondered why neither I nor the driver spoke, but she understood only too well when a lorry in front of us was hit and the driver had just time to get out before it burst into flames. We stopped to pick him up and took him to the next army post."

After seeing the New Year in, Travis took Molly back to Gogh, and then the company travelled to Klarfeld where it was to pick up the train which was to take them to Brussels. Travis, who was to remain in Germany, would travel with them as far as the border and then return to his regiment. The train did not arrive and could not be traced, until it was discovered that it had been in a collision and two carriages were blocking the line. Suddenly it arrived unannounced and they scrambled aboard, Molly segregated with the women's service, and Travis with the men's. The train started, and stopped again, this time for breakfast.

Brussels appeared even more luxurious than it had done three months earlier, "very pre-war and unbelievable". This time Molly was able to enjoy being there more than she had done on the previous occasion, as now she was on holiday, and she also made friends with a Belgian family who showed her around, and took her to the black market "La Rue des Radis" and the old "Marché aux Princes". Molly was struck by how crowded and noisy the market was in comparison with the other black markets she had seen which were furtive and secretive. She spent an evening at a Brussels Music Hall "L'Ancien Belgique", a large cafe with a platform at one end and the audience seated at large bare wooden tables. The show was of a much lower standard than in English provincial music-halls, and Molly found the audience far more interesting to observe: families with the mothers wearing large decorated hats, fathers nondescript, daughters plump with hair tied up in pigtails and bows, all completely absorbed in the "painfully substandard show". Molly also went to see a performance of "Tosca" at the Théâtre de la Monnaie: she liked the florid beauty of the building, with its plush, gilt, and crystal chandeliers, but found the production "barely adequate". It was followed by a performance of "Spectre de La Rose" which Molly found so "crashingly inadequate" that she described it in detail:

> "... a young lady in a very shiny white silk dress with a large hoop in it reaching to just below her knees, bare legs, very nice legs too, and a pair of

> brand new ballet shoes without ribbons, cantered coyly, if unsteadily round the stage executing God knows whose choreography and finally collapsing into a chair with such gusto that her hoop flew well over her head.... The only authentic part of the ballet was the music and the fact that the window and chair were in the usual place.... The audience applauded so loudly at the end that I almost came to the conclusion that the version of "Spectre" to which I was accustomed must be the wrong one."

The usual problems beset the company's journey from Brussels : delayed start, cold uncomfortable seats. They arrived in Calais after six and a half miserable hours and were taken to a hostel in Marquise, a village fourteen miles from the town. They went immediately to the theatre where they were to give a performance, and found a beautiful opera house which like so many provincial theatres Molly had seen, "shame our English West End ones".

While they were in France again, Molly though it worth trying to get a return date in Paris, but the red tape proved too much. First she phoned her contact there, and after many attempts finally reached him. He was very keen but said that Molly first had to obtain permission from HQ in Brussels. Again long waits and frustration while she tried to get through to Brussels. This permission was finally obtained, but only on condition that officials in Hamburg also formally agreed; and this proved the stumbling block: Molly simply could not get through to Hamburg. She was very disappointed, but glad that those in Paris had wanted the company to peform.

Illness continued to dog the company: one girl was left in hospital in Brussels with influenza, two more were in bed with sore throats and temperatures, and Shirley was still ill with a temperature of a hundred and three. Molly was also unable to get a message through to Travis and "generally speaking the future is a muddle".

On January 13th Molly and her company were taken to Ostend for their last week of performances before embarkation for England. It was a very pleasant week, during which their audiences built up gradually:

> "We collected an enthusiastic ballet audience, and by Saturday they were almost ballet fans".

They found it exhilarating to dance on a lovely stage with adequate sets for "Les Sylphides", "Giselle" and "Swan Lake" instead of the "drapes" and rickety platforms they had had to make do with for so long.

The end of the journey was a "crashing anticlimax": they were put in an ENSA hostel, in a room with nine beds, five of which were occupied by strangers, and Molly found this "gregarious slumber a severe strain on my not very Christian resignation, and an even more severe strain on my weary anatomy". They rose at four to be ready to sail at six on a troopship, without any food except for a couple of sandwiches. The journey which lasted six hours was followed by a two and a half hour shivering wait in customs in Tilbury, and continued with more shivering for an hour and a half in an ENSA bus which took them to London, and "dumped" them in Aldridges garage in Croydon.

They continued touring in England for ENSA until the end of March, putting on new ballets and reviving old ones. They spent the last two weeks in Bulford Camp, in Wiltshire where, although the surroundings were bleak and desolate, the theatre miles away, and audiences not very good, they at least had good food and Molly had a room to herself.

But then Molly's problems started to multiply. Some of her best dancers left her, as others had done before, to join the Sadlers Wells Ballet where conditions were easier and work more secure. Apart from the sadness at losing her dancers, Molly was sorry to see their dancing change in order to conform to the "Wells" style. Travis was still not demobilised, and he was concerned about how well he would be able to dance when he finally came home. Molly told him:

> "However bad the army is for your figure, its been good for your soul. However lacking you are in elevation, you've acquired something a damn sight more useful and satisfying. You'll be a good dancer Tabby, a better one than you ever were."

She begged him to train every day to get into practice so that he could dance leading roles and lift heavy girls as soon as he returned, but she was worried as to whether he could in fact do so after six years of "a more or less sedentary life".

The company pianist refused to play for rehearsals because he had joined the union "to prevent starving musicians being imposed on". This very much annoyed the dancers who decided to pull his leg, and they infuriated him by saying "we can't do this, and we can't do that, because our union won't allow us to". The pianist's action also caused difficulties in the mounting of a new ballet by Jak Carter; Molly considered asking him to play while she took the rehearsals, and then realised that probably the union would not approve of that either.

The Ballet Guild was then disbanded, its costumes and scenery were rented to Molly at £5 per annum, and the tab track (the curtain rail), was lent to her until it should be needed.

Meanwhile, Travis's military experiences had been very different.

"I Looked For You On The Beaches"

Travis continues the story of his life in the army:

"The day after our wedding I was posted to a Unit on the South Coast. The regiment, under A.A. Command, had gun sites along the coast from Littlehampton up to and including the Portsmouth Docks. Under A.A. Command, gun sites were static and the incoming unit took over such equipment as the previous one had left. Later when I was posted to a field regiment the guns belonged to the regiment and moved with it.

"I was interviewed by the Major to whose Battery I had been posted, his face seemed familiar and I liked him. I was walking back to my quarters when his car pulled up by me. He opened the door and said 'You were in the 45th Scouts in Nottingham, weren't you?' I replied yes. Then he said 'Don't you remember me, we were in the same patrol'. I then realised why his face seemed familiar. It was a good start to my life as an Officer.

"I was given command of the sites in the Portsmouth Docks. The equipment still seemed short, I had one almost obsolete multiple pompom and a number of First War Lewis guns. Small arms were almost unobtainable, the men still had barbed wire clubs and I had a .22 garden gun.

"The cruiser Manchester was in dock at the time and one of my Lewis guns was sited by her gang plank. I always felt a little foolish, the Cruiser's massive guns towering above and we were supposed to protect her from air attack with our pathetic little Lewis guns. I was checking the gun when the Manchester's Captain came down the gang plank. I gave him one of my best salutes, he looked at me, grinned and said 'If you have to fire that thing you will try not to hurt my ship, won't you'.

"A few days later the Manchester put to sea, the Marines lining the rails and the band playing. I often wondered what happened to her. Years later when I was reading of the defence of Malta I found out: She had been sunk in the tragic but heroic Malta convoy.

"Courses were the bane of young officer's lives. No one wanted to go on them so the newest recruit was always sent and as such I had to do my stint. However for me this turned out well: I came back with the highest grade of report, and on the strength of that was taken into Regimental Headquarters and made Regimental Training Officer. Initially this meant touring the regiments area and giving instruction on gunsites.

"It was generally considered unsatisfactory to send a newly commissioned officer to a unit in which he had been in the ranks, but the army was expanding rapidly, the three batteries

of an experienced regiment would be split up, each battery recruiting and training two others, so that shortly there would be three experienced regiments in the place of the original one, and I found that my old battery was the senior one in this newly constructed regiment. I found I knew most of the sergeants, knew their capabilities, and very capable they were. Incidentally some had turned down the offer of commissions preferring to remain N.C.Os.

"After touring the sites for a few weeks I was sent for by the Brigadier and asked to start a school to train the mass of new recruits pouring into the brigade. I could choose my own instructors, and I chose the sergeants I had known in my old battery. They were terrific.

"I was given a field just outside Chichester, a few huts and some tents. My sergeant and I worked like stink for three days and were open for business.

"The following day our first intake of 100 men arrived, we looked at them on parade; we had never seen so many men with two left feet before. All we wanted to do was crawl home and die.

"However we tried to make the guns, the bringing of them into action and the engaging of targets, live for them, rather than being a series of unrelated movements. I think that my sense of the theatrical helped in this. They responded wonderfully and soon made up by enthusiasm and hard work for what they initially lacked in dexterity.

"After two weeks we took them to firing practice in front of the Brigadier. At the end of the shoot he called us over and said 'I don't quite know what to say to you, I've just been complaining to Div. H.Q. about the poor standard of the men we are getting and you have turned them into some of the best gunners we have got'. We all went out and got drunk.

"Halfway through my third intake I was told that I had been recommended for a 'War Gunnery' course and I was to report to the gunnery school at Manorbier in South Wales. In peace time a war gunnery course takes three years, in war time it is crammed into three months. Rumour had it that on the previous course two young officers had committed suicide through the strain. I almost got to that stage myself.

"I could cope very well with the light guns; you see what you are shooting at and can make your adjustments accordingly, but with the heavy guns you were usually shooting at an unseen target, the adjustment made by predictor or worked out mathematically by the officer directing the shoot, and I hadn't even heard of logarithms. At completion I found I had been given an 'A' for the light guns but had failed the heavies.

"From Manorbier I was posted to the 126 Light Anti-Aircraft Regiment then stationed at Mablethorpe. The 126 had originally been the 9th Battalion of the Middlesex and we could wear the artillery cap badge or that of the Middlesex Regiment or, if we felt like it, both.

"The first word of the artillery motto is 'Ubique' meaning everywhere and we were, as the 2nd in command put it, not only ubique but unique. However, the C.O. laid down that we should wear the Middlesex cap badge and the scarlet and gold Middlesex shoulder flashes under the R.A. shoulder flashes.

"Even at that early date the regiment was preparing for the invasion, and my first job was to take the unit's 54 rather dilapidated gun towing tractors to an ordinance depot just outside Nottingham and draw new ones. Most of the old tractors broke down on the way but by dint of a little pushing, shoving, pulling and towing I managed to get them all there.

"The new tractors were magnificent and I suddenly realised that I was in a field unit preparing to invade Europe. There was no question of barbed wire clubs. Whatever we indented for we got: Bren guns, Sten guns, Piats, rifles, revolvers, hand grenades, the lot.

"In the spring of 1944 we were moved to Southampton. On our way we were deployed for a few days round a small airfield. Nothing seemed to happen there except that at odd times during the day a hangar door would swing open and out would come a small plane surrounded by security guards. The plane would take off, circle round for a short time and land. Immediately on landing it was again surrounded by security guards, hustled back into the hangar and the door was slammed shut.

"I examined the plane through field glasses and found to my surprise that it had no propeller. It was some time before I realised that we were watching the beginning of the 'jet age'.

"On arrival in the Southampton area our guns were sited along the beaches of the Solent. We were given a pep talk by the Brigadier and told that on no account must any German plane that flew over the area be allowed to get back. With the R.A.F., the heavy guns and us for low flying stuff, I don't think any did.

"In May we were pulled back into the New Forest for what was called Waterproofing — a few simple adjustments to all vehicles to prevent the engine stopping if they were driven off the landing craft into deeper water than was expected. Even then, I don't think we fully realised what we were preparing for.

"I went to one of the few still-occupied houses in the Forest to ask if I could have a bath. The house was owned by a Mrs Coralie East whose husband was a Colonel in the Middle East. Coralie was wonderful: she let me have a bath, she invited Molly to stay, and amazingly enough I got permission to sleep out. Coralie and her husband Geoffrey remained friends for the rest of our lives. It's odd how a friendship can start.

★ ★ ★ ★ ★

"THEN THE DAY DAWNED BRIGHT AND CLEAR AND THE FIRST WAVE HAD GONE.

★ ★ ★ ★ ★

"Our job was the defence of advanced landing grounds and our first V.P. (vulnerable point) was just east of Caen. We were due over D + 3 [the third day after the landings in Normandy].

"That evening Bill Jaques, my troop commander, and I decided to have our last meal at the local pub with Coralie and her friend Bubbles. We had just started to eat when my brother arrived, his opening was 'I looked for you on the beaches, but as I couldn't find you there I knew I'd find you here'.

"Bill had gone straight into the navy from school. He went into mine sweepers in Dover, twelve hours before the actual landing. His sweepers had gone into the Normandy coast partially to sweep and partially, I understand, to jam the German radar. All the ships had been considered expendable but by the grace of God they had all got back.

"Later on his ship was blown up in the Scheldt and he was thrown into the air. His main complaint was that the ship did not sink quickly enough, and instead of coming down in the water he came down on the hard deck which rather messed up one of his knees and he has had a gammy knee ever since.

"Half way through dinner the troop despatch rider arrived to say that Orders had come through to move. I forgot to tell Bill that Coralie had invited us for the meal. He told me later that he only had a shilling on him and he was so worried that he would be expected to pay for the dinner that he was sick in the lavatory. I expect it was partially also a reaction after what he had been through.

"We arrived back to camp to be told that our troops had met 'stiff opposition' east of Caen and as it was unlikely that our first V.P. would have been taken by our appointed time we were ordered to go into action in the Hastings area against V.1 [the new flying bomb] which had just started to devastate London. It was then that I had to get a gun across that gap in the Hastings Pier — the gap I had watched being made three years before during the retreat from Dunkirk.

"The breakout from Caen came and went and still we remained at Hastings potting at 'Doodle Bugs' as the V.1s had now been christened. We thought we had been forgotten and were doomed to stay at Hastings till the end of the war. Then a signal came down to move.

"At the London docks we loaded the guns into American Liberty Ships, a battery of 18 guns to a ship, and set sail for Normandy. About a mile off the coast near the little port of

Arromanches the guns and tractors were off-loaded into landing craft. I was ferried to the beach to control the landing of our battery and the despatching of the guns to the marshalling area. It was all quite peaceful. The first landing craft arrived, down went the ramp and off drove three tractors neatly hitched to three guns. I was directing the drivers to the area when something inside me said 'keep one tractor back'. I did. The second landing craft arrived, down went the ramp but nothing happened. This second craft had all guns and no tractors. However with the tractor I had kept back I was able to tow the guns one by one up the beach to firm ground, and when the third craft arrived with the missing tractors I was able to send them all off peacefully to join the others. Throughout the war odd little things happened like that and I began to believe in Joan of Arc's little voices.

"We were attached to the 2nd Canadian Division and advanced peacefully behind them as far as the Antwerp – Turnhout canal. There we deployed in an anti-aircraft role while a recce' group went on to Rosendaal, our next objective. Unfortunately Rosendaal was still in German hands so the recce' group scuttled back and we were hastily re-deployed in an anti-tank role.

"However the night passed peacefully enough and the next morning we were ordered to park our guns and deploy as infantry just keeping contact with the Germans as they withdrew.

"That afternoon returning to my H.Q., having seen my advanced troops dig in along the edge of a wood, I met a Major from the pukka line regiment that was on our right. He glanced at my Middlesex cap badge and said 'Well, thank heavens we have some real soldiers, all we seem to have is the ruddy artillery playing at soldiers'. I dared not tell him that we were 'The ruddy artillery playing at soldiers'. He then said 'I've got fixed machine guns covering this path and if you have to withdraw those men and want covering fire send up a white flare. Again I dared not tell him that I didn't possess a Verey Light pistol and should not have been too sure of how to use it if I had one.

"It was dark by the time I got back to my driver, who greeted me with 'Got you a good bed for the night, sir'. He led me to a small building which seemed all that was still standing of what had been a large hospital. I felt my way inside and found that he had put my bed out on what appeared to be some sort of shelf and had laid my kit out on a couple of wooden boxes which were alongside.

"I slept well but made a hasty exit when daylight came: the building was the hospital mortuary, the 'Shelf' on which I had been sleeping was the slab on which they washed down the bodies and the 'couple of boxes' were two coffins. My driver was waiting for me and he grinned broadly as I shot out. I never really found out if he did it on purpose or if he really thought that I should be more comfortable in the mortuary than on the stony ground outside.

"Next morning we were told to rendezvous some miles west of our overnight positions. The guns were left in the parking area but we were given our tractors to travel in.

"It was part of a gunner's perks that he could, because he travelled by tractor, take with him far more equipment than, for instance, the Infantry who have to carry all theirs on their backs, and in consequence, individually they were not very mobile. I had drawn the men back and was getting them into the tractors when my little voice warned me again and I said 'You have ten minutes to pack all the kit that is really necessary in your haversack. Stuff you don't really need stow neatly in the tractors'. It proved a Godsend because after that day we did not see our tractors for about two weeks.

"On arrival at the rendezvous the battery commander took me to the edge of a wood, pointed to a village about a mile away and said 'See if the village is occupied; if it isn't, occupy it'. He didn't say what I was to do if it was occupied.

"The only thing I knew about the Infantry was what I had seen in films, so I aligned the troop up in copy book order, detachments on alternate sides of the path, each detachment correctly spaced under its Sergeant, the Bombardiers with me to act as runners between me and the detachments if it was necessary, then off we went across three ploughed fields and into the village which fortunately was not occupied. So I sent back a message to that effect and deployed the men along the banks of a small river that ran the other side of the village. Looking back now we must have made awfully good targets coming across those ploughed fields.

"The only living things in the village were about 10 cows in a barn in a rather unhappy state, so I found one of my men who had been a farmer to milk and feed them. During the 10 odd days we were there no one returned to the village so we handed the cows over to the incoming troops when we left.

"We had moved some miles forward and I was peacefully asleep in a barn on a bale of hay when the Battery Commander burst in, he had been trying to raise us for hours. It would seem that the wire had been cut and 'would somebody bloody well do something about it'. I took out a sergeant and two men and we set out to trace the break. For some reason I stopped by a barn. The night was pitch black. I was waving my revolver about and trying to look like a soldier when I heard a slight noise. I stepped back into the bushes behind me, a stupid thing to do, there was a slight scuffle and two figures glided swiftly and silently past me and disappeared into the darkness, and I was left sitting on my bottom still waving my revolver. When I got back I found I had a slight gash in one arm that might have been made by anything from a knife to a sharp twig. I was never sure what really happened. I felt so foolish at not even taking a pot shot at them that I never mentioned the matter to anyone.

"Some days later we were ordered to pick up our guns, proceed to Nijmegen and deploy in defence of the bridge. The Nijmegen bridge was the number one V.P. of the front and we felt it an honour that we had been given, but I feel its retention by us and the efforts of the Germans to destroy it was purely symbolic because it was never used again.

"We spent the winter of 1944/45 fairly peacefully at Nijmegen. The Germans made a number of half-hearted attempts to destroy the bridge: by frogmen who were captured without doing any great damage, by floating mines down the river which were destroyed by gunfire, by sending down torpedoes which were caught in the torpedo net the Navy had put across the river, by unmanned motor boats packed with explosives, these again destroyed by gun fire; finally they settled down to rather sporadic shelling.

"They also tried infiltration, and on one occasion a small head-on attack which was doomed to failure from the start. It was during this attack that I first experienced how small happenings can be built up when required to make them newsworthy. We were listening to a news bulletin of a rather gory bit of action that was going on somewhere in our sector and were just commiserating with the poor devils who appeared to be getting it when the name of a village was mentioned and we realised they were talking about us. Nothing else was happening along the front so our little attack had been a Godsend to the news room.

"At Nijmegen I was taken to Regimental H.Q. as Intelligence Officer, a name I never really lived down with Molly. My main job was to contact other units in the area including Army H.Q. and to bring back news as to what was happening locally and in other parts of the front which was mainly nil, as it was the time when we were along the Meuse and the Rhine preparing for the crossing.

"Our H.Q. was in a little village called Lent in the area between the Nijmegen and Arnhem bridges. We were in a convent — just a priest and one nun were left. The nun was a round jolly person who played snowballs with the men and allowed me to have a bath in the nuns' bathroom saying rather pointedly 'It's the first time a man has had a bath in here'.

"At Christmas the priest asked the C.O. if we could form a choir for Midnight Mass, and being the only Catholic Officer I was given the job of organising same including a man to play the organ. At midnight when the men were singing 'Silent Night' the Germans fired a barrage straight into the air and sent up flares, so did the troops on our side and found it difficult to stop myself crying.

"After the Mass we were invited to supper. We fed off the Convent's gold plate which had been dug up when the Germans withdrew, but all they could offer us to eat were potatoes. It was the only time I wished I had had the sense to fiddle some rations.

"There was a certain amount of excitement during the Ardennes offensive, wondering if we were going to be cut off in what became known as the Nijmegen Salient. Rumour upon rumour of parachute drops until nobody would trust anyone they did not know personally; but the American stand at Bastogne quickly brought an end to that.

"Just two other points. The convent had a church tower which we used as an observation post. We found later that an Iron Cross had been promised to any German gunner who

could destroy the tower. The second was the lady whom we christened Mary of Arnhem, a lady who broadcast daily from Arnhem, whose signature tune was 'Home Sweet Home' and whose main theme was 'What are you fighting for Tommy, while you are here, at home an American is sleeping with your wife, go home Tommy and save your wife'. She also went into rather lurid details as to what the American was actually doing with your wife and at one time her programme was almost as popular as Tommy Handley's I.T.M.A.

"The crossing came at Wesel south west of us. For 48 hours prior to the crossing every gun in Nijmegen and its surroundings (and it ran into thousands) pounded the area till nothing was left standing. As darkness fell on the first day a sergeant looking round at the brilliantly lit sky turned to me and said 'Just like bloody bonfire night, ain't it'.

"The area to the north of us having been cleared we passed peacefully across the Arnhem Bridge. We knew that there were German troops cut off in the Rotterdam area but not how many.

"When a regiment moves a small advance party establishes a rendezvous point or R.V. Each unit will report to this R.V. and from there is dispatched to its deployment area by the officer in charge. For this move I was in charge of the rendezvous party and as my small group crossed the Rhine and turned north east into Holland the country seemed deserted. When I had established the R.V. a few Dutch youths did appear. They were not over friendly, they looked disillusioned, haggard and worn. They were obviously uncertain as to whether we were here to stay or was it going to be another Arnhem fiasco.

"Dusk fell and all the units had arrived except the R.E.M.E. section. Midnight came and went and still no R.E.M.E. 2.00 o'clock came and went, 3.00 o'clock came and went, my driver and I still waiting by the road side between two large mounds of the type that the Germans had erected along all roads to give some protection against bombing.

"Quite suddenly out of the darkness and from the direction of Rotterdam came lines and lines of men. They seemed to march in complete silence — not even a footfall. They had no mechanical vehicles only a few horse drawn carts, and even the horses' hooves seemed to make no sound.

"They marched to attention, upright and with a certain pride, they took no notice of us, they seemed like ghosts. It took over an hour for them to pass us and although it was a pitch black night they seemed to be surrounded by a red glow and I could see them clearly. They were marching through the night to avoid confrontation with the Dutch, and they were marching to surrender.

"They had twice torn the world to pieces, they had caused millions of deaths, some of their countrymen had behaved in a way that has never been equalled by the most depraved form of life, but in some odd way one felt sorry for them.

"The next morning the R.E.M.E. section arrived. It had been held up by a bridge that would not take the weight of the equipment. With it came a signal that hostilities has ceased.

"So the war was over, it was a strange feeling and I don't think anybody who has not experienced it could really understand it. For nearly six years everyone had had just one objective, to get the war over, barriers of all kinds had been broken down. We never had any doubts about winning *the war, it was just* when, *and now it was over. There was enormous relief of course but in some odd way it was tinged with regret. One had been part of an enormous and in many ways wonderful family machine. Now one was to become an individual again and in some ways one felt lonely and lost. However that came later. The first reaction was a party, any excuse was good enough for a party but this was the excuse of all time and this was the party of all time. I have never felt so ill in all my life.*

"The day after the party I was ordered into Rotterdam to check and list all German installations there. There was not much, a couple of ammunition dumps, a small dump of land mines and a few sea mines and torpedoes. The Army H.Q. and the Gestapo H.Q. were just as they had been left: full ashtrays, dirty glasses, congealed food on cracked plates. My Troop Sergeant Major had never really had a satisfactory typewriter and always coveted one, so I 'liberated' one from the Gestapo H.Q. I've still got it incidentally.

"There were few people in Rotterdam, no rejoicing, just haggard, careworn, half starved faces. A few did gather round my jeep and told me stories of a winter of starvation when about the only food available was potato peelings from the German barracks and even these were obtainable only on the black market. I had a few cigarettes which I dished out to the small group, and as they dispersed clutching their cigarettes a tall comparatively well dressed man came up to the jeep, held out his hand and said 'Please you give me cigarette'. I had to tell him I'd just given all my cigarettes away. He looked at me silently for a moment and then said 'Bloody fine liberator you are' and turned and walked away.

"R.H.Q. was established in Dordrecht and the regiment dispersed in the surrounding area. We had our own small victory parade, our guns were 'put into moth balls' and returned to England, and we settled to a round of rowdy parties which we expected to last until we ourselves were returned to England.

"The Dutch were wonderful and I had not known that Holland had so many beautiful girls. I was paired off with a wonderful, tall, blue eyed blonde; but she was married (her husband had been in a labour camp and was then in the Hague, something to do with the newly established government), also I was married. No one would believe that all we did was kiss goodnight. She was true to her husband and I was, and had been all throughout the war, true to Molly.

"During the occupation my girlfriend had often apparently carried messages for the underground. She told me that if the girls rode a ladies bicycle and got off when stopped by Germans the bicycle would as often as not be commandeered. But if they rode a man's bicycle and stopped with one leg either side of the crossbar the Germans would seldom if ever indulge in an undignified struggle to get the bicycle away.

"There was the usual parade through the streets of shaven headed girls with placards around their necks saying 'I slept with the hun' or words to that effect. There was also a certain amount of 'potting' at German prisoners in their compound at night. Neither things we liked very much and got up against certain sections of the Dutch when we tried to stop them.

"We were using the German prisoners to clear the mines along the edge of the river, a rather tricky business if the plans had been lost or, as they sometimes were, deliberately altered with disastrous results.

"Our men were clearing German ammunition dumps. They were bringing in a lorry of incendiary bombs when it happened. I am not sure if one was booby trapped or it just slipped out of its case but the whole dump went up and five men with it.

"Trying to find their remains at the bottom of the crater was nasty, but the worst thing was having to write to their wives and mothers and tell them that their loved ones had been killed when everyone was still rejoicing at the war's end.

"Unfortunately all good things come to an end. We were to be moved into Germany. The Adjutant went ahead to prepare accommodation and I brought the Head Quarters staff, vehicles and equipment with me. The Adjutant greeted me in Pletonburg with 'Congratulations, John [Travis's name was John Travis, and he was known as John in the army], your promotion has come through, and there is a Don. R [Dispatch Rider] from Div. H.Q. waiting for you. I don't know what he wants'. I hastily stuck another pip on my shoulder tabs and went to see the Don. R who came smartly to attention and said 'The General's compliments and your wife's living with him'. I always thought it could have been differently put.

"However, it appeared that the company was dancing in 51 Div. Area, that Molly was staying in or near Div. H.Q. and I was invited down for the weekend. I hastily got permission to go, collected a motorcycle and off I went, I behind the Don R. Never try to keep up with a dispatch rider. I think he spent most of his time by the road waiting for me to catch up, but it was a wonderful weekend.

"We still had two more moves to make, the first back to Gogh on the Dutch – German border where our job was to prevent the Dutch getting into Germany and the Germans getting out, and in our spare time to try to resuscitate the civilian telephone system which seemed to be completely wiped out.

"It was from Gogh that I picked up Molly in Hamburg and took her back to Brussels for her final journey home.

"Our last move was back to England. I was in command of the advance party. My job was to find accommodation for about a thousand men where they could peacefully await demobilisation. People back in England were not particularly helpful. I remember one young officer trying to insist that each man must collect and sign for his own blankets, as the men were arriving at some unGodly hour. I thought that a bit much so I signed for them myself and distributed them throughout the sleeping huts. I am still waiting for the army to send me a bill for two thousand blankets.

"Numbers dwindled each day as men were demobilised. It was in many ways a sad period. The regiment ceased to be a unit, it just became a number of rather disgruntled individuals rather worried as to what awaited them in civilian life. At last my turn came.

"My driver drove me to the Demobilisation centre. He had driven me and looked after me from Normandy to Rotterdam. He rushed round and opened the jeep door for me, saluting more smartly than he had ever done before. I went up the few stairs to the entrance, turned and returned his salute. We both held it longer than was normal, then he got into his jeep and drove off. I only saw him once more after that. Some years later we were playing in Norwich with the Continental Ballet and we were (as we always were when running a company) completely broke. A very prosperous businessman came to the stage door, it was my driver. He took us in a very large car to lunch at the best hotel in the City (it was almost the first decent meal we had had for weeks); he drove us back to the theatre, rushed round and opened the door for us, as I turned to say my thank yous and goodbyes, he saluted as smartly as he had done at the Demob. centre, so I returned the salute and as he got into the car and drove away I felt tears rolling down my cheeks.

"But back to the Demobilisation centre. I collected the garments the Army considered necessary for civilian life and went out through the exit. No jeep, no driver, no salutes. I had a rather ill fitting suit and a cheque for £95, my gratuity money, and I was on my own. The only thing I was trained to do was dance and I had not done that for about four years. I found myself humming 'Where do we go from here'."

Dance on a Shoestring

Embassy Ballet

The Ballet Guild gave its last performance for ENSA on March 16th 1946, and Maurice Jackson, the ENSA organiser who had arranged the tours during and after the war, continued to show his support. First he recommended that Molly be asked to arrange the dances in "Marrige à La Mode" by John Dryden directed by John Clement which ran at the St James's Theatre London in 1946, and for which Molly received 25 guineas. He set up a new company and to begin to find venues, and he and Molly cast around for a name. Travis was still in the army, and Molly wrote to him asking him to "lay your rank on" so as to obtain a sewing machine box, crossbows, a make up chest, and badly needed materials for costumes. ENSA appeared to have lost the scores of "Giselle", and so Molly had to have the whole ballet re-scored. However, she found someone to paint the new scenery, and everything was going well with the plans for the new company, the management of which was to be called "Terpsichore Ltd". It had six Directors, including Colonel Aldworth, Ben Walker-Smith, Mr Boam (father of the dancer Monique Boam), and Mrs Bantock. Those dancers who had remained urgently needed to work but it was difficult to find suitable venues, and so it was decided to start in what Maurice Jackson called "dust-holes", so as to keep the company together. Molly told the dancers about developments, and "broke the news to them" that they would only receive £4 per week starting in May, and then secretly hoped that they would indeed do so. She gave Jak Carter (who was not only a dancer, but also a composer), £5 for orchestrating "Swan Lake" Act II, as he did not know how he was going to get through the break. Costumes were being tidied up, and old costume baskets repaired, and one of the dancers came to stay with Molly as she had nowhere else to go.

Molly was very worried about the projected company, and told Travis:

> "I know I'll bust, or blow up, or explode if something gorgeous doesn't happen soon. I'm scared as Hell about this change over. I'd like to run miles and miles away tonight and not come back until rehearsals had started with a good tour ahead."

By mid-March Molly was really frightened: dates were very hard to get, and yet she was spending money on new costumes and music, and she did not know whether to tell the dancers that in the end there might be no company at all. And then, on March 18th

> "Something happened today that may save the company's bacon, and incidentally ours, very nicely".

Molly received a phone call from Mary Honer. Mary had been a dancer with the Sadlers Wells Ballet, and she was asked by Anthony Hawtrey, the manager of the Embassy Theatre in Swiss Cottage, if she would like to form a company to be based at the Theatre, and to perform there on Monday nights. Hawtrey worked in the building from an office which had once belonged to the actor-manager Charles Hawtrey. Behind the desk it had a cupboard at the back of which was a low door leading into another part of the theatre. The actor-manager had had many creditors, and whenever one of them approached, his secretary in the outer office would press a hidden bell to warn him and he would escape through the cupboard. It was still there and Travis often wondered whether the present director ever used it to escape from him.

Mary realised the difficulties involved in forming a new company and she was in any case more interested in dancing than in directing, and so she asked Molly if she would like to undertake the job and Molly happily accepted. It was agreed that Mary would dance in the first few performances only. The theatre had a growing reputation, and Molly considered it to be a first class shop window. "It seems too much to hope for; we could live in Springfield Road and not be continually worried and overworked — in fact, *live* for a change. . . . If we can make a go of it, our future should be much easier". The theatre suggested a company consisting of at least fourteen girls and three men, and an orchestra of ten, to which Molly readily agreed as long as she could have her own musical director.

The Embassy Ballet began performing in 1946, and Terpsichore Limited held its first general meeting on June 14th 1947. This managing company was necessary as a means of obtaining relief from entertainment tax for the company, but it later developed and its functions became more diverse. The company, consisting of about twenty dancers, performed at the Embassy Theatre for several weeks, and then went on tour led by Molly, with Johanna Barratt (formerly with the Ballet Rambert), Angela Bayley (originally with the International Ballet, had danced with Molly in Germany), Margot Chandler (Anglo-Polish Ballet), Pamela Sabine (aso from Rambert), Travis, Jak Carter, Monique Boam (formerly with Antony Tudor's London Ballet), and Clifford Williams as soloists. Programmes, which were changed at every performance, were designed, as the *Dorset Daily Echo* of September 21st 1946 stated, 'to satisfy all tastes' and were very varied; they included "Les Sylphides", the second act of "Swan Lake", and Act II of "Giselle" in which Molly later danced the name part; Jak Carter's specially created "Episode (Fantaisie)" to music by Chopin, which was praised by Anthony Tudor;

Keith Lester's "The Dark Mirror" was also performed, and was highly acclaimed. Every programme always included a "Grand Divertissement" consisting of many short dances, some of which were choreographed by members of the company. Not surprisingly this often caused problems with quick changes of costume, and the programme at the Palace Court Theatre Bournemouth for the week commencing August 26th 1946, began with a 'Note' stating:

> "At certain performances slight amendments of the cast are necessary, eg, when an artist appearing in one number would require an elaborate change to appear in the next".

The rest of the repertoire was choreographed by Molly.

They travelled with their own conductor, Alan Bixter, who was well known at the time in the world of music. He had studied at the Basle Conservatoire under Weingartner, and had at one time the unusual distinction of being the youngest conductor of opera in Europe. Before joining the Embassy Ballet, he had conducted the Carl Rosa Opera Company.

Jackson's assistant at ENSA had been Tom Giles (known as Bonzo), and Bonzo had also become so interested in ballet that he now began working full time for Embassy Ballet, obtaining the bookings, negotiating the contracts, going on ahead to venues, and liaising with the local education authorities.

The group toured medium scale theatres throughout England, occasionally also going into large theatres, and the conditions of contract varied from theatre to theatre. The dates were usually negotiated by an agent who took anything from 2% to 5% of the income, and this also changed in each venue: sometimes they paid the theatre £100 – £300 for rental, at others they received from 45 – 70% of the takings, out of which they paid for the get-in and get-out (for the scenery to be unloaded into the theatre and reloaded onto the trucks again). Details of publicity also varied: usually the company was expected to provide posters, but on other occasions, they shared the cost of these with the theatre. Often, as Travis stood on stage in moments between dancing, he would try to count the number in the audience and to calculate whether he would be able to afford to pay the company at the end of the week. They usually appeared eight times per week, although occasionally they were expected to perform twice nightly. At first there were problems with Customs and Excise about exemption from entertainment duty, but by 1949 this was assured.

The railways gave the use of a scenic van free for every twenty five seats which were bought, and the company always reserved this number, even if in fact they required fewer. The scenic van was put in the sidings at the town they were playing, and on a Monday morning two or three lorries would be sent from the theatre to collect its contents, returning them to the van at the end of the Saturday's performances.

While many of the reviewers were obviously knowledgeable about ballet, they all particularly praised the entertainment value of the company's work, showing that as always Molly and Travis were reaching those with whom they wanted to communicate. For example, when the company appeared at the Theatre Royal Bath, the *Bath and Wilts Chronicle and Herald* gave them a glowing review, listing their "originality in the choice of themes, artistry in portrayal, tireless energy, and well varied scenic effects".[1] In Weymouth, the company received a "wonderful ovation",[2] and throughout the season played to packed houses. A.T.P. in the *Southern Times* described Molly as a "graceful creature, tall and slim and light as a zephyr, complete mistress of her lovely art". He concluded

> "This is a great company and is deserving of great support. From Molly Lake and the musical director, Alan Bixter, down to the youngest coryphee, there is not a weak link in its chain of virtuosity."[3]

The company's first visit to Torquay elicited a very favourable review from W.D.M. who had seen several of their dancers when they had appeared with other companies. He told his readers that "local balletomanes will find plenty of cause for gratification this week at the Pavilion", and went on to praise the company's "undoubted talent for burlesque", mentioning several members by name. Another local paper succinctly summed up the impact of the company compared with that of others which had appeared at the same theatre: He was struck by how everyone "has an air of enjoying their dancing" and suggested

> "This is perhaps the nearest to 'everybody's' ballet the Pavilion has seen. Nearly all the presentations have a pastelle quality — very much more pleasant than the usual austere classic air."

He felt that the whole company had a very high standard and that the principal dancers had "quite remarkable expression". An enthusiastic review of the company's peformances in Swindon concluded "they contain features at each house which can be enjoyed by the average theatre-goer who makes no claim to understand the technique of ballet".

This theme, that the company's performance could be enjoyed by everyone, was taken up again and again by the reviewers of the provincial theatres which the company visited. For example a critic from the *Brighton and Hove Herald* felt that

> "The dancing is fresh and full of character, not only in the less familiar sequences where much of the choreography is by the director of the company, Molly Lake, but also in those ballets where tradition and long acquaintance might conceivably detract from the individuality of the performance, as in 'Les Sylphides'."[4]

While praising the company's "technical virtuosity", they referred to those elements of performance to which audiences could relate and enjoy: "dramatic portrayal", "interpretation", "elan", "complete artistry", etc. In the *Hereford Citizen and Bulletin*, R. W. implored anyone who had never seen ballet to go and see the company: "Go now, for you initiation is in the right hands".[5] He felt that Angela Bayley was "the most appealing and controlled Swan Queen that we have seen in Hereford"; Travis's elevation was "particularly worthy of comment... In Giselle, as Count Albrecht, he has caught the spirit of tragedy and gives a dramatic portrayal worthy of the role". He was impressed by the dancers' "clear pure line that remains in one's visual memory", and he praised the performance of the male dancers ("Male roles have not been famed for their appeal in the previous Ballets seen here in Hereford"), the choreography, and the whole company "which rightly takes its place with its contemporaries in the London scene". In the *Southampton Daily Echo*, under the heading "Pavlova would have been proud of Molly Lake", "Patoc" repeated the same message: "there is something to suit all balletomanes — and much that will appeal to those who are strangers to this lovely art".[6]

Of course it is possible to appeal to wide audiences and at the same time to have very low artistic and technical standards; however, the fact that so many of the reviewers favourably compared these aspects of the Embassy Ballet's work with those of other companies which had visited their towns, implies that in the case of this company, standards were not low, and that in addition to the attributes of the other companies, this one did indeed have wide appeal to both balletomanes and those new to ballet. The reviewers sometimes bewailed the fact that the theatres were not always full for performances by the Embassy Ballet, and of course they were not unanimously favourable, but theatre managers were happy to host the company and often told Molly and Travis that, as they had had Ballet Rambert for example the previous year they would try the Embassy Ballet this time.

Travis suspected that Marie Rambert was not pleased about the competition for dates for her company. The Embassy Ballet generally had good houses, in spite of the fact that they usually were only able to get the dates at unpopular times of the year, and theatre managers often expressed their satisfaction at the standards and repertoire of the company in comparison with others. Their repertoires were very different: while Rambert's was, in Travis's opinion, original and often highly sophisticated, that of the Embassy Ballet, and later the Continental Ballet, was geared specifically to entertain provincial audiences new to ballet, and one cannot but remember the controversy which had raged over the quality of the repertoire of Pavlova who had also aimed at a general wide unsophisticated audience.

The Arts Council of Great Britain which had grown out of CEMA, was giving grants to some companies; Molly and Travis applied, and Marie Rambert was sent to assess Embassy Ballet. She did not recommend a grant, and the fact that the company's application to the Arts Council was rejected raises several important issues when assessing the value of an artistic venture. Molly and Travis's main concern was always that of entertaining the audiences, rather than what they called an ''intellectual approach'' and maybe this was not what the ballet world of that time considered appropriate. John Pick propounds the idea that ''CEMA and its followers were moving into a position of social control on 'The Arts' while they narrowed and revalued the term''. He goes on to suggest that eventually the only activities subsidised by the Council were those which the Council itself considered to be worthwhile or ''excellent''.[7]

The practice of representatives of companies which receive financial support sitting on committees and assessing other companies' work is still prevalent today, not only in the Arts Council, but in Regional Arts Associations, and the danger of this would appear to be not that of vested interests possibly inadvertently influencing decisions, but perhaps more importantly the fact that only those artistic ventures which are in line with the thinking of those already in existence might receive official recognition, thus leading to a form of artistic monopoly.

Molly and Travis had worked with the BBC producer Philip Bates before the war, and he now used the Embassy Ballet as a tool to help him train cameramen. Every day for several weeks the company danced as if giving performances, while cameramen filmed them. Some of their work was also transmitted: Molly's ''Nymphenburg Garden'', with ''Victorian Bouquet'', ''Roumanian Gypsy Dance'', and the Pas de Deux from ''Casse Noisette'' Act III, accompanied by the Light Symphony Orchestra of twenty four musicians, conducted by Alan Bixter, were televised on the 19th July 1946, and ''The Last Curtain'' was broadcast three times in fourteen months: on 16th and 21st February 1946, and 21st April 1947. For the last transmission, in which Molly and Travis danced leading roles, as did Jak Carter, Angela Bayley, Margot Chandler and Johanna Barratt, the company received a total of £90 for the rehearsals and broadcast.

Molly continued to give class and take rehearsals. She was always extremely demanding but never strict. She found she could teach anyone and even be "really beastly" to them, as long as she made it clear she was on their side: "Otherwise you can't teach them". She set an example by always doing her own class alone every day, and she had no patience in later years with those who said they could not do this, particularly after cassette tapes were invented. She was particularly aware of the high standards she herself had to keep up, as her dancers always watched her whenever she performed, and this could have led to problems had she not been so respected and on such good terms with them. She thought highly of them also, and felt that they were so much better than dancers in later years because "they actually danced. They felt what they were doing, and they had a magic which has been lost completely". They were also capable of dancing on concrete floors with no music and no backcloth, "and now they don't; they can't".

In spite of the occasional television work and the satisfied managers, the financial worries were very great, and one day Molly and Travis received a phone call which could have resulted in an answer to their problems; it was from a Mr and Mrs Inglesby inviting them to come to talk to them. They had a daughter Mona, and they wanted her to dance with the Embassy Ballet. Mr Inglesby would have been happy to invest in the company, and it looked as if this was just what the Embassy Ballet needed. At that time Helene Wolska was dancing with them and, as Molly had other work to attend to, she arranged for Helene to be in charge of a rehearsal in which Mona would set some choreography. It was a disaster: Helene and Mona fought, and afterwards Helen came to Molly and said she would have nothing to do with Mona, and so Molly was obliged to ring Mr and Mrs Inglesby and to decline their offer. Mona's parents then formed the "International Ballet" in which she usually took the leading roles.

A few years later, Travis saw Errol Addison dancing in revue and suggested he return to ballet and try to work for Mona Inglesby. Errol took Travis's advice and went to dance with her company. He told Travis that all the dancers showed great respect for Mona, and would line the stage and bow as she passed. Molly remembered her as being a very strong dancer with sturdy legs.

When the Embassy Theatre ceased to be available in September 1947 the company was obliged to tour continuously, and as it no longer had ties with the Embassy Theatre, Molly and Travis renamed it the Continental Ballet.

Continental Ballet

Terpsichore Ltd now managed the Continental Ballet, and officially appointed Molly and Travis as its Artistic Directors. The company consisted of about twenty eight dancers which Molly and Travis themselves led, and although unsubsidised it just managed to pay its way. Life was always very precarious, and Molly and Travis often paid themselves less than the youngest member of the corps. In 1952, together with every member of the company, they signed a form stating that they had voluntarily agreed to accept salary cuts, and that they would make no claims upon the company until such time as it showed a "suitable credit balance". The reductions amounted to about one third of each dancer's contracted salary during some weeks of the tour, and Monique Boam refused to take any salary at all for several weeks.

During the financial year which ended in February 1948, the company played for thirty one weeks, and showed a deficit of £1,247.19.11, £900 of which was met by loans and gifts from the Directors of Terpsichore Ltd. The loss was felt to be due to inexperience in negotiating contracts in the beginning, and by the end of the year matters had greatly improved.

Terpsichore Ltd acquired the lease of 44a Loudoun Road in St John's Wood for use as a studio and store during the first year, but there were no funds for new productions, and two new works were added to the repertoire without scenery, and with costumes made from materials already in Molly's possession. The lack of money for new works was to remain a problem for the company throughout its existence.

By February 1949 the Continental Ballet was able to show a credit balance of £1032.16.9d (although this was in part thanks to an unrepaid loan of £100 from one of the dancers, the manager of the premises at Loudoun Road working for nothing, the secretary charging very little for her services, and the donation of a sewing machine by one of the Directors). Minimum salaries were raised from £4 to £5 per week, with corresponding rises for all grades. Mr Maurice Jackson, who had been arranging some of the bookings, now undertook to negotiate all dates in future. A regular stage manager was now employed, three new productions were added, and improvements in scenery and costumes made. More venues were played with orchestral accompaniment than previously, and the Annual Report No 3 of 1949 recorded "a general improvement in the quality and presentation of the show, which is reflected in the box office returns". Affairs were going so well that in December 1948 Terpsichore Ltd gave £10 to Continental Ballet for Christmas celebrations!

The Directors of Terpsichore Limited hoped that they could raise extra funds for the Continental Ballet by presenting foreign companies and thereby gaining exemption from tax. During the second year of the company's existence, they brought to London the Ram Gopal Indian Ballet, the Grand Ballet de Monte Carlo, the Carmen Amaya Spanish Gypsy Dancers, and the Ballets de Paris de Roland Petit, and in some cases arranged tours of the provinces. However, only the Ballets de Paris de Roland Petit made a profit, the losses on the tour of Ram Gopal's ballet being met by Dr Julian Braunsweg, and that of the other companies being covered by a donation from a Mr Bertram Montague.

The Continental Ballet toured the provinces with a repertoire of fifteen ballets, which included "Les Sylphides", Molly's "Salute to Petipa", Keith Lester's one-act version of "Sylvia", and many humorous works also choreographed by Molly. They appeared often in venues unsuitable for dance: some were too small, others had uneven floors, or inadequate lighting, and many did not have room for musicians numbering more than two pianists. Even when there was room finances usually did not stretch to a large orchestra, and it was decided that two well played pianos were preferable to a small inadequately rehearsed orchestra. Sometimes, though, the theatre managers requested that the company be accompanied by an orchestra as for example when the manager of the Theatre Royal Huddersfield explained that since the Continental Ballet's last visit, the Ballet Rambert had performed at the theatre with a full orchestra.

It was an avowed part of the company's policy to bring ballet to new audiences, and this often resulted in financial losses. However the directors of Terpsichore Ltd agreed that "the risk involved was fully justified if the continued presentation of ballet to fresh audiences and the regular working and training of the dancers could be maintained in this way". In its efforts to reach those not already acquainted with ballet, the company performed wherever they were invited. In August 1952 they gave a lakeside performance of "Swan Lake" Act II for an audience of 5000 at Leamington Spa. Later the same week they appeared in Jephson Gardens, dancing on the grass and lit only by spotlights. Sometimes they could not find accommodation, and spent hours on end looking for rooms. In a letter Molly wrote to a Mr Pawney in 1951 in answer to criticisms that the response of the audience was not sufficiently enthusiastic because the decor and size of orchestra did not do justice to the wonderful dancing, she defended the company: she explained that the Continental Ballet did not have Arts Council support as the Vic-Wells and Ballet Rambert had, and no private family fortune like Mona Inglesby. She outlined the cost of a large orchestra which was way beyond their means, and disagreed that the backcloth for "Les Sylphides" was too simple: it was on the contrary more in tune with Fokine's intentions than many of the more elaborate and more expensive ones in use by other companies; she explained that they could not afford to dazzle the spectator with spectacle, but what they offered was life and enthusiasm, and she concluded "without money it is difficult to buy popularity". However they *were* popular, and the reviews and many letters from admiring members of the audience exist to prove it.

"Giselle" was performed frequently, and always evoked particular praise. When the company visited Salisbury in August 1947, Travis received a particular mention for his rendering of Albrecht's "dance-to-near-death... in a temperature that must have utterly exhausted the least active member of the corps".

The company often took ballet to towns and theatres which had never seen ballet before, and it was described by the *Tunbridge Wells Advertiser* as having done more than any other similar company to popularise ballet in the provinces.[1] They were the first full size ballet company to appear at that stronghold of variety, the Palace Theatre Walthamstow, and in September 1948, the Aston Hippodrome Birmingham conducted an experiment: it invited the Continental Ballet to entertain its audiences. They had never seen ballet before, and they were not shy of voicing their reactions; as the music of "The Last Curtain" floated out over the auditorium a rich Brum voice exclaimed "We've had it!", and at the conclusion of the second ballet, "The Four Elements", another voice complained "Nobody's said a word yet". They enjoyed more an Andalusian dance and the "Can-can", and even the second act of "Swan Lake" was received in respectful silence. The *Evening Dispatch* felt there was a lack of discipline among the corps at times.[2] Overall though, the paper considered the experiment a success.

The audience at the de la Warr Pavilion Bexhill one month later was more sophisticated and appreciated the company's wide repertoire: it comprised "'La Revenante'... in which Molly Lake danced as if inspired in a ballet of her own creation... and Travis Kemp was the very embodiment of virility as the bridegroom", Keith Lester's "Les Quatre Elements", "Sleigh Ride", "a frolicsome piece", the inevitable Divertissement, and "the dainty and delectable 'Les Sylphides'."[3]

The only "slight complaint" of H.H.H. of the *Cambridge Daily News* was that "once again, a week of ballet was opened with 'Les Sylphides'.... It does seem strange that it is invariably chosen by companies for their opening night". However, H.H.H. felt that the company succeeded in making extremely enjoyable the performance of the familiar work, which "whilst paying due regard to the traditional grace, had plenty of springy life about it".[4] The critic enjoyed Jak Carter's humorous "Impromptu for Twelve" which poked fun at ballet, and also Molly's "Salute to Petipa" in which the dancing of Molly, Travis, Angela Bayley, Monique Boam and Stanley Newby was particularly noted. On this occasion the company was accompanied by an orchestra under John Andrewes.

It is not surprising that the excellent dancing of Molly, Travis and their soloists was frequently admired, but after the first month or so, the corps de ballet was also highly praised on a surprisingly large number of occasions, for example: "the perfection of training for which the corps de ballet of this company is noted",[5] their "high level of artistic expression".[6]

The *Stockport Express* described the Continental Ballet as presenting a programme "which includes something to suit the tastes of both newcomers to the art and balletomanes",[7] while *The Advertiser* wondered whether the rich varied humorous programme might not have disappointed some who expected to see pure ballet when they came to the Stockport Hippodrome: "'Sleigh Ride' was gay and delightful to watch, but it was not ballet".[8] In contrast, when they appeared on the tiny stage of the Albert Hall, Colchester accompanied by two pianos, the reviewer of the *Essex County Telegraph* reported how in "Flora and Fauns" "every movement, as well as expression, of the dancers seemed to join in the joke", and he particularly praised the simple settings and imaginative costumes which "added to the unsophisticated quality of this Continental Ballet".[9] He recommended that the company be seen by all who had the chance. This suggestion was echoed in almost every town the company visited, sometimes coupled with the regret that the performances were not better attended.

On March 24th they gave a varied programme on television. It consisted of the Pas de Deux from "Casse Noisette", "Giselle" Act II, and the Bluebird Pas de Deux from "Sleeping Beauty" which was coached by Stanislas Idzikovski. On June 9th 1948 "La Revenante" was televised under the English translation of its title "She Who Came Back". It was performed exactly as in stage productions, the only difference being that Molly as the "Revenante", the ghost, always appeared to be transparent. Very often after that, the English title was added in brackets on the programme, below the original name. "Les Quatre Elements" was broadcast on 28th July 1949, and "Fall From Grace" on 18th October 1950.

Molly often spoke on the subject of ballet, and was quoted by the *Cambridge Daily News* as saying that ballet was getting dull, that

> "mere virtuosity is taking the place of real feeling, and that a definite break had taken place with the classical tradition".[10]

The paper went on to record her belief that there was too much stereotyping of physical requirements, and that many girls with possibilities were losing their chance merely because they did not measure up to the required physical standards. (Molly had proved that chubby girls could dance well by engaging as a soloist five-foot-two Angela Bayley, now nineteen years old and weighing nearly nine stone, and Angela repeatedly earned enthusiastic reviews for her "excellent technique and flawless timing"). The piece finished by quoting Molly's opinion of ballet as a career: there was no glamour in it and it was very hard work: "Sometimes one wishes one had become a Chinese washerman, or anything else under the sun. It's a vocation, not a profession."

While they were appearing in Colchester, Molly was struck by the beauty of St Peter's churchyard which was next door to the theatre, and she took the company into the graveyard, where in they were photographed in their "Giselle" costumes for the local newspaper. On another occasion, she took them onto the common at Tunbridge Wells "to blow the cobwebs away", and once, in May 1951, she took them to Abbotsbury Swannery to study the movements of swans. When they performed at Doncaster Arts Centre in 1950, the girls were taken to the British Railways Plant Works, and visited an engine driver in his cab dressed in their "Les Sylphides" costumes.

The company was popular not only when it first performed at a venue, but also pleased its audiences on return visits, and when it went back to Huddersfield in November 1949 after an absence of two years, the enthusiastic audience was composed of both young and old. Among the most popular items were always Molly's humorous works, and one of these was "Fall From Grace" first presented at the Pavilion Brighton in September 1950, and televised on October 18th of the same year. Travis amused and impressed by his comic rendering of the main part, the Grandfather who disgraced his family by marrying a fairy while on a family picnic.

One of the characters in the ballet was a dog (played by the dancer Roy Evans), the inspiration for whom came from Molly's dog Cornelius. He watched every performance from the wing and was a permanent member of the company; in January 1952 a photograph of him with the dancers in costume appeared in the local paper when he was presented with a St Francis medal by the Secretary of the local branch of "Our Dumb Friends' League".[11]

Sometimes the company invited visiting artists to work with them, and in October 1950 Walter Gore and Paula Hinton joined the team and Walter mounted his "Bartlemas Dances". While Paula was dancing with him one evening a hook from his costume caught on her skirt and as she moved away

The company in Molly's "Olympic Antics"

The company in pantomine

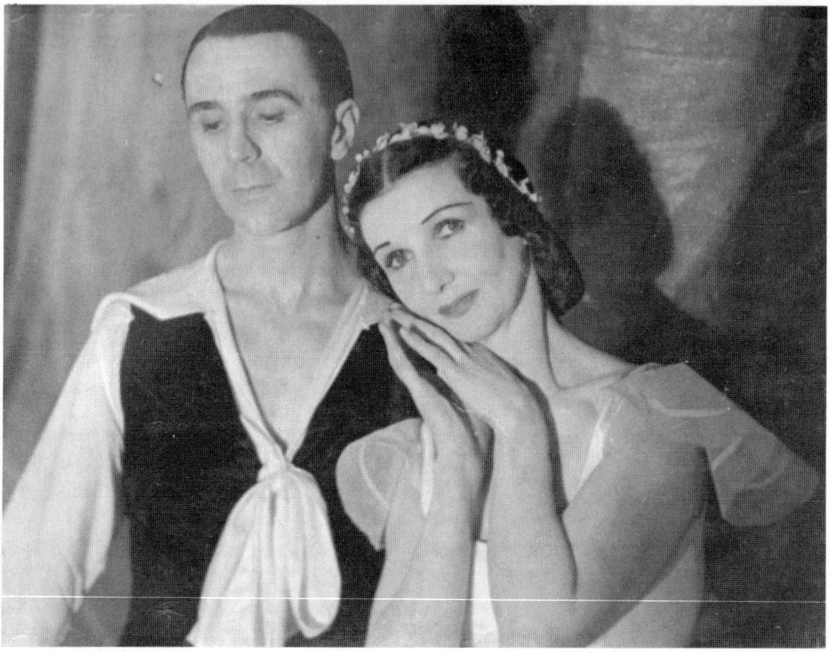

Molly and Travis in Fokine's "Les Sylphides"

Molly and the company in Molly's "La Revenante"

The company in Jak Carter's "Impromptu for Twelve"

The company in Molly's "Fadette"

The company in Molly's "Jeu de la Danse"

Travis as the Prince in "Swan Lake"

Travis, making a film

from him it tore off completely, and she impressed the local critic by managing to complete the energetic dance holding it on with one hand.

During the company's visit to the New Royal Theatre Bournemouth in 1950, an incident occurred which caused the theatre management to lose several hundred pounds as a result of an out-of-date law: the theatre did not hold a regular justice's licence to sell liquor on the premises and was therefore obliged to submit a script of every entertainment to be licensed by the Lord Chamberlain. Of course the Continental Ballet were unable to provide a script, and the local watch committee therefore forced the theatre's three bars to remain closed. They did so, while displaying such notices as: (beside bottles of gin) "It is here, but local regulations will not let you have it" and (next to bottles of whisky) "We are sorry. There is plenty in stock, but we must not sell it."

An example of the different criteria employed by those judging ballet as entertainment for new audiences, and those for whom these considerations were less important, was evinced when Continental Ballet appeared at the King's Theatre Hammersmith in May 1951. *The Times* praised the choreography of their comic works, but said of the company that "burlesque and character dancing in fact lie within these dancer's powers as the testing classical manner does not".[12] Peter Williams in the *Daily Mail* appeared to understand the difference in presentation necessary for the two types of audience although he did not appear to feel that the Continental Ballet had got it quite right. He praised Molly's choreography of "Jeu de la Danse", but felt that "the company, which spends most of its time touring the United Kingdom, has not shed quite enough of its itinerant nature for London presentation".[13]

It was while they were appearing at the King's Theatre that Ninette de Valois asked them if they would like to go out to Turkey to set up a school there. However, the company was enjoying a certain amount of success and Molly and Travis turned down the offer and thought no more about it.

In January 1952, Terpsichore Ltd presented the company in "an entirely new form of Christmas entertainment", when it put on a three-act "Ballet Pantomime" entitled "Cinderella" to music by Tchaikovsky, for one week at the Regal Theatre Southend. Apart from the "dream scene" which was choreographed by Keith Lester, the work was created entirely by Molly who also danced the role of the Fairy Godmother; Travis was Buttons, Margaret Kowak Cinderella, Angela Bayley (later replaced by Rosina Gay) and Rachel Cameron the Ugly Sisters, and Harold Foster the Baron. They had a full corps de ballet and were accompanied by an augmented orchestra under the direction of John Andrewes. In February they took the production to Norwich where A.G.W. in the *Eastern Evening News* found Molly's dancing "dainty but orthodox" and that the

> "quaint miming of the comedy characters makes the greatest appeal. Travis Kemp possesses a mischievous drollness as Buttons, which fails to conceal his polished dancing, and Rosina Ray and Rachel Cameron display the bickering buffeting of two alley-cats as the Ugly Sisters, scoring especially when they emulate the dancing debutantes."[14]

The company's policy of taking ballet to audiences who had never seen it before was educational in its broadest sense, but when in 1947 a Headmaster asked them to give a talk in his school, this aspect of their work began to grow, and gradually became an integral part of all their touring.

For The Young

In 1975 when Roy Shaw came from the world of education to become the Secretary General of the Arts Council of Great Britain, he redefined the aims of its Charter to encompass education, and thenceforth every recipient of revenue funding was expected to undertake educational work.

Some dance companies had been doing a small amount for a few years, but most had not done so. Now they engaged Education Officers who were instructed to introduce young audiences to dance, but they were given minimal budgets with which to do so. The Education Officers, often dancers or former dancers, did not themselves perform, but relied on dancers from their respective companies. This often caused problems as these were often needed for company rehearsals and could not be spared, or they had to conserve their energy for performances and did not want to do educational work.

Some companies involved other departments, music, costumes, scenery, and marketing staff in their projects and often met with resistance from those who did not want children on their premises and could not spare the time to go out to the schools.

It was found to be almost impossible for dancers to be totally involved in their company's programmes and to do educational work as well. Equally the Education Officers were too busy with administration, fund raising and lecturing to be able to consider performing themselves. The post of Education Officer was in any case considered to be a complete job on its own, often for a non-dancer.

For Molly and Travis the educational work was part of their normal activities; from 1947 onwards they organised and administered it, they gave lectures and talks during the day several times a week, and then danced the lead roles in their company's performances in the evenings. Their dancers also appeared in lecture demonstrations for schoolchildren during the day and then gave their regular evening performances. Forty years before the Arts Council of Great Britain and the Department of Education and Science published their report "Dance in Education" and suggested that "a new breed of dancer is needed, one prepared to undertake the rigours of touring and working under different and often difficult conditions",[1] they showed that that breed of dancer had already arrived.

Education had always been an element of Molly and Travis's work; as early as 1938, when they were running Ballet Intime, they gave occasional lecture-demonstrations to young audiences, to whom Travis would explain:

"*Ballet is a way of speaking with your body. If you are in the playground and your friend is over on the other side, with a whole lot of people shrieking, kicking and scratching and fighting in between, and you shout to him 'Hi, I want you', and he shouts back 'what did you say?', and finally you mime 'You come here'. Well, basically, that's what ballet does.*" Travis suggested at one of his earliest educational talks, to 180 girls at Weymouth Central School in September 1946 that ballet's popularity was increasing because "*it takes us away from the struggles and trials of recent years into a dream world — a world of spirits and sprites. . . it gives us colour and music. . . it takes us into a world we read about in books and would like to live in*". He also explained the stories of some of the ballets which the girls would be seeing that afternoon at the schools matinee.

Molly became involved in educational work while she was with the Arts Theatre Ballet, the first occasion being a week spent in Barking schools in 1940, when they gave two performances each day at 10 am and 2.45 pm. Molly caught a workman's train at 7.20 in the morning, and did not arrive home until after 7.00 pm, having given a class after the two performances. The school had a fine stage, the audience composed of elementary school children was appreciative and well-behaved, and Molly hoped that they had done their bit towards creating a future ballet public. The programme was very varied consisting of many short items, including "something classical, something amusing, something of character work, national work, and something terrifically live, with no long waits or fanciful costumes, slap slap one after the other". Molly and her colleagues obviously knew what research thirty years later found: that in order to introduce children to dance it is necessary to have a very varied programme of short dances.

In February 1941 the Arts Theatre Ballet presented a series of lecture demonstrations, each programme lasting about an hour. The 1 o'clock performance concentrated on the Russian school of ballet, the 2.15 on the French, and the 3.30 on the Italian. All began with a demonstration and exercises given by Molly; a rehearsal of a new ballet with choreography by Keith Lester was shown, and the programme finished with a performance of a pas de deux.

Molly and Travis learnt from their educational experience and continued to develop this aspect of their work, and the importance of this activity and of the way in which they were doing it, was recognised by Ninette de Valois who had a deep commitment to education and suggested that they specialise in it. She asked Molly to write a paper on ballet in education (which in the event was never published), and in the foreword which she wrote for it entitled "Entertainment as Education", referring to the educational work undertaken by several companies during the war, she attributed the success of ballet which had "in the space of twenty five years become an important cornerstone of English Theatre", to the fact that during the war there had been "a tremendous drive to bring the younger generation in to closer touch with the arts of the theatre", and she felt that it was therefore only "common sense" to enlarge on this experience. She admired the practical way in which Molly and Travis were bringing knowledge of ballet into the classroom, and she described how students were being taught to appreciate "the finer points" before seeing a performance in a theatre.

Molly and Travis's lectures, the content of which were very thoroughly thought out, covered nine subjects:

"1. *A GENERAL OUTLINE OF BALLET*
How a simple knowledge will increase the appreciation not only of ballet, but of its sister arts.

2. *THE HISTORY OF BALLET*
The evolution of the technique, choreography and costumes. Famous dancers and famous people associated with them. The effect of world history on ballet.

3. *THE TRAINING OF A DANCER*
The physical demands made by ballet, and how these demands are met. The physical and mental discipline required of the dancer.

4. *FRENCH*
The main language of ballet. How a knowledge of that language can be increased through the eye by associating movements with words.

5. *CHOREOGRAPHY*
The language of the dance. How a ballet is built. The close collaboration necessary between the choreographer, dancer, musician and painter.

6. *DANCING, A MEANS OF EXPRESSION*
The dancer should use the steps of the dance to tell a story or create a mood. As the words of a play can be meaningless or otherwise according to the emphasis used by the actor, so a ballet can become meaningless should the dancer worry only about the steps and not the atmosphere those steps should create.

7. *THE ASSOCIATION OF COLLATERAL APPRECIATION OF TWO OR MORE ARTS*

   How a knowledge and liking for the dance can create and assist the desire to know and appreciate other arts.

8. *THE DANCERS*

   The classical dancer. The demi-character dancer. The character dancer. The mental and physical requirements of each. How each can be appreciated. The necessity for the various styles in order to create a well balanced programme.

9. *THE INTERNATIONAL ASPECT OF BALLET*

   Ballet, having no speech has no national boundaries. The effect of national dances on ballet and the effect on ballet of the national temperaments, in countries in which it has been fostered."

During the company's visit to Southport, they gave several schools' matinees for which the children were charged 2/- each. They included:

"1. A short general talk on ballet.
2. A description of the ballets to be presented, with danced excerpts enabling the lecturer to point out the methods by which the choreographer got his or her effects.
3. The presentation of three ballets as follows:
   a) A classical or Romantic Ballet such as Swan Lake, Les Sylphides or Giselle.
   b) A modern ballet on classical lines emphasising the difference between the present day productions and those of the last century.
   c) A comedy ballet showing that ballet does have a lighter side."

The importance of point number seven has only recently been appreciated by those concerned with education, with the setting up in 1983 of the School Curriculum Development Committee (SCDC), to monitor the relationship between the various arts, and between them and the school curriculum.

Molly developed very clear views on the educational value of entertainment if suitably presented, and in view of the fact that this very issue is still being hotly debated among those involved in dance in education, it is worth quoting Molly's opinion:

> "The value of entertainment as education is now widely known. A subject presented as a task becomes irksome, but create entertainment out of that subject and it ceases to be an imposition, it becomes a pleasure and is alive in the mind of the student. Conversely then it is of interest to find what educational value is contained in existing entertainments.

> Ballet has been described as an entertainment for the connoisseur; to fully appreciate it, it was considered necessary to have a knowledge of the various subjects related to the Dance, as well as of the Dance itself. It is possible therefore to draw *from* ballet (should it be presented in the right manner) the knowledge which originally had to be gained *elsewhere* in order to fully appreciate it.''

In March 1984, in ''The Glory of the Garden'', the Arts Council referred to the necessity of breaking down ''attitudinal barriers to the arts, sometimes created by such factors as social class'',[2] and several education officers of dance companies have also reported a certain prejudice. It would seem that this was not the experience of Molly and Travis.

From 1947 onwards Molly and Travis gave a matinee for schoolchildren in almost every town they visited, preceded by a talk whenever this was requested. On one occasion, on the Continental Ballet's first visit to Grantham — it was in fact the first visit of any ballet company to the city — there were over 2000 applicants for 719 seats, and the manager of the theatre in conjunction with the company manager, invited the unsuccessful applicants to attend performances during the week at the reduced price of 1/-. Every member of the audience was a girl, as boys had applied too late. In the absence of Dance Advisers the talks and lecture demonstrations were sometimes arranged by the ''Organiser for Physical Education'' of the local education authority, and some were more helpful than others: some only helped publicise the lectures and matinees in the schools, while others took a very active role.

In November 1950 the manager of the Theatre Royal Huddersfield collaborated with the local education authority and Molly in an educational venture which covered several days. Two matinees were given for 2000 primary and secondary schoolchildren who had first attended lectures given by Molly and Travis at the Huddersfield Technical College. This was a conscious decision on the part of the organisers who did not want the theatre to be used for a purely educational purpose. The lectures, entitled ''The History of Ballet'' and ''The Trend of Ballet since Diaghilev'', were given by Travis, and one called ''The Music of Ballet'' was delivered by the company's musical director, Trevor Widdicombe. In the evening Travis gave a talk on ''The Science of Ballet'' which was followed by a demonstration by Molly, with Angela Bayley, Marguerite Stefan, Monique Boam, Rachel Cameron, Marya Gerante, Richard Brown and Roy Walker. During one of the matinees ''Fall from Grace'' was presented, while at the second the company performed ''Les Sylphides'', first in short sequences, with a commentary explaining the steps and the idea behind the ballet, and the second time uninterrupted. Molly wanted to dispel the idea that ballet was not for boys:

> "I shall try to give the children an idea of what a ballet dancer's life is like. What looks to the audience like effortless movement comes only after strenuous training, the glamour is achieved only by a lot of unglamorous hard work.... It requires one hundred per cent physical fitness, stamina, and skill."

During the lecture, one of the men in the company demonstrated what was described in the local paper as a "'rather difficult' triple spin in the air"[3] and later, as if to prove the strength of ballet dancers, while they were performing the work Travis received what the local paper reported under the heading "Fairy Packs a Punch", a "fourpenny one": he lost a front tooth when he was accidentally hit in the mouth by one of the dancers during "Fall from Grace".

Art students from a local technical college were invited to watch and sketch rehearsals and classes, thus giving them the unusual opportunity of working with moving models.

The reactions of the audience were carefully monitored and evaluated, and it was found that the introductory talks were very helpful in aiding understanding and appreciation of the ballets, they were "lucid, uncomplicated, and of just the right length"; however, a few of the children who attended the performance of "Les Sylphides" found them to be a little too long. The majority of the schools stressed that ballets with a story had a stronger appeal, whereas "abstract" ballets such as "Les Sylphides" and "Children of Space" were "somewhat severely criticised". Many children observed that they would have preferred an orchestral accompaniment to the two pianos which they heard, and it was felt that the economics of running a ballet company should also be explained.

The "Times Educational Supplement" described the "Experiment in Ballet" and concluded that a "valuable contribution has been made to the history of ballet",[4] and it is difficult to understand why these findings were not taken seriously by the ballet and education world and used as a basis for further educational work. Other companies working in the 1960s and 1970s reached similar conclusions, and yet these also have been ignored, and conferences, forums, and numerous projects have been initiated to try to find out the best way of introducing young people to the appreciation of dance. The Huddersfield experiment was considered to be so successful and popular that the following year the company was asked to increase the number of matinees to three.

In September 1949 Travis gave a talk at the Usher Art Gallery in Lincoln, where Molly was asked to open an exhibition of prints and paintings.

Sometimes Travis or Molly gave a class in the local ballet school but their educational work was so highly regarded that even those trained in other methods requested their lectures. In May 1952 they were asked to talk about ballet and the company at The Training College, Bognor Regis, where the students had had basic dance training "according to Mr Laban's theories", and schools sometimes asked Travis's advice on which books on ballet they should acquire for the school library. The lectures were usually given free, and in appreciation, after a talk in which Travis mentioned that dancers "usually eat all they can lay their hands on", some girls cooked a cake for them. In June 1950 Molly was asked to give a series of lectures on ballet at a residential course of Music and Ballet organised by the County Council of the West Riding of Yorkshire for about fifty adults. She received the sum of four guineas for each address.

Contacts with colleges of art led to the suggestion in October 1948 that students from the School of Arts and Crafts in Southend should prepare designs for a new production of Swan Lake, and that if liked these would actually be used by the company. Travis travelled down to Southend to talk about the ballet, but no designs were ever used.

Their education work took them not only to schools and colleges; in the 1980s ballet companies who perform in hospitals and prisons are considered to be pioneers, and this is probably because it is not realised that the Continental Ballet did this forty years earlier. Their presentation for the "Church of England Children's Society" in May 1947 was voted by the children "the loveliest afternoon they had ever spent"; in April 1948 Travis and Angela Bayley danced sections from "Casse Noisette" for the patients at Southend General Hospital, and in November 1950 other members of the company gave up their afternoon off to dance for the children at Bradley Wood Sanatorium. They gave a performance for physically handicapped children in West Kirby in June 1949, and a special performance for wounded ex-servicemen at Gifford House, Worthing.

On November 22nd 1950 the company gave a performance in Broadmoor Criminal Lunatic Asylum, where some of the inmates provided the musical accompaniment. The programme was enthusiastically received by an audience of over three hundred men and women, all convicted for crimes of violence, most of whom had never seen ballet before. After the performance, which was preceded by a talk by Travis, it transpired that one of the musicians had worked with Molly when she entertained the troops in England in Germany just after the war, and in 1946 she and Travis obtained permission to have tea with the man, who was in Broadmoor for murder and was then found to be insane.

Molly and Travis were gradually becoming more and more immersed in education. In December 1952 Molly took time off from the company to visit South Africa and Rhodesia, where she examined nearly three thousand children for the Cecchetti Society and the Imperial Society of Teachers of Dancing, and also produced two ballets. Hardworking as ever she rejoined the company in Exeter after only twenty-four hours at home.

In 1954 Ninette de Valois again asked Travis and Molly to go to Turkey, and this time they accepted. They closed the company and travelled nearly 2000 miles to begin a totally new life which was to bring them even closer to education, and which was to last twenty years.

The Building of a Ballet

The padre of the parish in which the Old Vic was situated had been for many years Father Hutchinson. He became very interested in the Vic-Wells Ballet, and spent much of his free time in the theatre watching the dancing.

In 1947 he was sent to Turkey as padre of the British Embassy in Istanbul. He saw that there was a State Theatre, and National Opera, but no ballet company and when one day he found himself talking at a cocktail party to the Minister of Education who was responsible for theatre, he suggested that one be established and proposed Ninette de Valois be asked to set it up. The Minister agreed and de Valois was duly invited.

She went to Turkey and established a school in Yesilcoy, a small village just outside Istanbul, with twenty five seven-year-old girls and boys. It was at first difficult to find students, as the theatre was not considered a suitable profession for respectable Turkish children and some were therefore recruited, as they had been for the world's first ballet school in Paris in 1672, from a local orphanage, and in 1948 de Valois sent out Joy Newton and Audrey Knight as the first teachers. Four years later the school was moved to Ankara where it became part of the state conservatoire, and the children were expected to move with it. However most did not do so, as it was three hundred miles away and parents did not want to be separated from their children, and in spite of the fact that this was to be a state school with all expenses paid for by the state, during the first years there were very few new pupils in the school. In 1950, when Joy Newton left after a year in Ankara, de Valois asked Molly and Travis to go and teach in her place, but as the Continental Ballet was doing so well at the time, they refused, and Beatrice Appleyard was sent out instead.

In 1954 the Director of the Conservatoire was changed, and Beatrice Appleyard and Audrey Knight left the school, but Beatrice remained in Turkey and married the outgoing Director; later, at Molly's request, she returned to teach.

Travis had by now become a member of the executive committee of the Royal Academy of Dancing, and at a meeting he was again asked by Dame Ninette to go to Turkey. This time he accepted, as the Continental Ballet, like most other touring companies at that time, was no longer thriving. Travis suggests several possible explanations for this: firstly, television was becoming increasingly popular and was reducing theatre audiences; secondly, when they began touring, the bulk of their audiences comprised families — father, mother and children — who made weekly visits to their local theatre, but gradually nude shows were introduced into many theatres, and parents stopped bringing their children; eventually men stopped bringing their wives, and theatre audiences fell off even more. *For many weeks we followed a show called "Nudes of all Nations". I often contemplated what the differences must have been.*

When Molly and Travis arrived in Turkey in 1954 accompanied by their assistant Dulcie Pyne, they were surprised to find a school of only about fifteen small children, none of whom had been there for more than three or four years. There were, in addition, three girls and two boys in the state opera. The previous four years had produced nothing lasting because few students had applied for enrolment, and even some of these had drifted away.

Molly and Travis decided on a different method of recruitment. They:

"had to start at once to show the Turkish public what ballet actually was when produced in the theatre. No one, least of all the few students in the conservatoire had any idea what ballet could be. For most people ballet dancing meant belly dancing, so we decided our policy must be performances, performances as soon as possible and as often as possible, not only in Ankara but throughout Turkey. It was no use waiting for conditions to be 'just right'. If we did this, conditions would never be 'just right'. So at the end of our first year, using the four dancers from the opera, and dancing ourselves, we put on a performance at the state opera house. The policy paid off; at the end of our first year we had had twelve applicants to join the ballet school all of whom we took, but at the end of the second year there were approximately a hundred and fifty, and we could start to pick and choose. Also, the Minister of Education, and the Director General of Fine Arts, and the Director of the Conservatoire became exceedingly interested and helpful. Money was provided for scenery, costumes, musical equipment, etc, and within limits we received almost anything we wanted. Towns throughout Turkey were encouraged to organise performances for us and the embassies of other countries, especially the American, became involved and helpful."

That first performance was a tremendous success and after it Molly and Travis happily packed and prepared to go home to London for their summer holiday. (They usually drove there and back, and Molly kept a detailed log of journey times, state of the roads, weather, and even petrol prices). However, on this occasion they suddenly became aware that there were posters all over the city announcing repeat performances, and so their holiday had to be postponed.

"During the second year, we produced a number of performances both in the conservatoire theatre and at the state opera, using the students from the conservatoire. It was hoped that the four opera dancers would work amicably with those from the conservatoire, but they

expected to be stars with the conservatoire students as their corps de ballet; we on the other hand always considered that the best dancer for a role should dance that role, and as the dancers from the conservatoire were rapidly outstripping those at the opera, the latter withdrew from the performances. They then applied to teach at the conservatoire, but it was considered that their knowledge was insufficient at that stage so they withdrew to the opera, and so commenced a feud between the opera and the conservatoire which was to last many years.''

News of the ballet performances given by the conservatoire dancers had begun to spread, and early in 1956 Molly and Travis were asked to take their young students to perform in Izmir; they agreed to go during the holidays so as not to interrupt their regular training, and Molly wrote an account of the trials and tribulations which beset them:

A Trip to Izmir

''It was all very sudden. Nobody was pleased at the prospect, the first tender seeds of enthusiasm were just appearing, but were not proof against the dire fact that a week's holiday would be lost, that the weather was appalling and that nobody knew what would happen to us when we got to Izmir. Where were we going to dance? What were we going to dance? It was all delightfully vague.

''A programme sufficiently long for an evening's entertainment was hastily collected, the necessary costumes packed and pointe shoes overhauled — no dear, you can't dance with black elastic on your shoes — if you lost your frilly pants at the last performance why didn't you say so? Half the Sylphides wreaths are missing, but there are some nice red roses instead — I'm sorry you have a sore throat, no you can't go home — yes I'm afraid you will have to dance, even if you toe is 'very ill'.

''Finally everybody and everything was rounded up and dispatched on a morning of ice, snow and sleet to the station for the slow Izmir train, a matter I think of about twenty-four hours. Travis and I were dancing at the Opera at that time in an operetta named ''Paganini'', and as there was a performance that night we were to travel by 'plane the next day.

''The weather the next day was even worse than the day before, no 'planes flying. A major panic finally got us on to the Izmir motor train express. We relaxed. Now for a little peace before the battle of Izmir.

''After about ten hours of what turned out to be false security we became aware of a current of excitement and apprehension circulating in the train, much talking, much pattering up and down of corridors, much leaning out of windows and finally a slowing down of speed to almost stopping point. Travis and I refused to be disturbed, we were comparatively warm, and nobody had been able to "get at" us since we got on the train. The longer we drifted on the better we should be pleased.

"We crawled through the darkness and finally almost stopped. We must look out, we supposed. We did and were shaken to see the train in a vast lake of flood water with a sizeable bow wave in front of the engine. Would we be asked to swim, if so where to? We were now about sixty miles from Izmir — "It was quite impossible to get there, but they would try and get us to Manissa about ten miles further on."

"An endless time later (about midnight) we got to Manissa expecting to spend the night comparatively comfortably in a siding. "Oh no, nothing like that. Nobody could stay in the train." We were all bundled out into a night of hard little biting stars and icy cold. No waiting-room? No there never had been one at Manissa. How did we get to Izmir? Maybe we could charter a bus or maybe we couldn't it was all in the hands of Allah and absolutely nothing to do with the Turkish railways.

"There was one train already stuck in Manissa station and there was no room in it for any more passengers. Enviously we went down to look, and to our amazement, there in a comparatively comfortable fug, well padded up with bursting parcels of food, were the dancers who had departed from Ankara thirty-six hours before, floodbound too. We were glad to see them comparatively cheerful, but two nights in the train without sleepers and a continuous consumption of very solid food boded ill for the ballet-seeking public of Izmir. Our hearts sank if possible, even lower.

"With chattering teeth and icy feet we left them to their sleep and went in search of our fellow sufferers on the platform. Indignation was high, conversation furious.

"A bus must be found to take us to Izmir." "Well if you want a bus go and look for one. Maybe some driver will be foolish enough to take you the forty odd miles over the icy mountain roads to Izmir."

"Finally having found a bus we set off and had not climbed far before we decided that the railway official had been right. Not only was the bus driver mad, but so were his passengers to trust themselves on this road at night.

"I was squashed into a window seat, Travis next to me, on his lap not only our own suitcases but those of several other passengers too; his chin hardly came over the top of them. He went to sleep and was so spared any realisation of the terrors of the road.

"Hooray we are round another corner! Bit of a skid there!"

"The driver sang, forcing the crazy old bus with all his might. Treetops waved dizzily from below. Occasional lights glimmered so far down that they appeared to be under water.

"As we tore and skidded along the passengers argued furiously, protesting that the driver had overcharged them and telling him so in no uncertain terms. Occasionally and without slackening speed he turned round to hurl a telling bit of repartee at them, but mostly he just sang.

"Gradually the noise subsided and the passengers with that knack which the Turks possess of being able to sleep anywhere, at any time and under any conditions passed out peacefully: that they did not wake up in Paradise must have been due to a particularly watchful Allah, it certainly had nothing to do with the bus driver. After six and a half years in Turkey I can never believe that any journey on the roads will end anywhere but in a ditch, if you are lucky, or in the mortuary if you are not. In this case we managed to avoid both, heaven knows how, and crawled into bed at our Izmir hotel at 5 am for the undeserved luxury of two hours sleep.

"At the appointed zero hour we got up, amazingly enough quite cheerfully, and set out with high hopes and nicely polished haloes "to bring ballet to Izmir".

"Izmir was so beautiful, set between the mountains and the sea — those awful mountains of last night — a spacious waterfront, pleasant houses set in their own gardens, and trees, trees everywhere, what a change after the barren Anatolian plateau. Our goal was the Conservatoire of Music which we could see at the extreme end of a rocky point jutting far out into the sea.

"The wind was apalling, it almost took one off one's feet and having failed to do that, did its best to bite one in half.

"After about half an hour's struggle, blue and battered, we arrived at the Conservatoire — Here we are — How nice — everyone was charming. We admired the view over the sea, which was lovely, and were shown over the entire building including a pocket-handkerchief sized stage which Travis and I pretended not to notice. Time passed, we were to open that night; Travis and I got more and more restive, finally our charming host said "Now, I think if you are ready we will go and look for somewhere for you to dance" — Had we heard aright? Perhaps we had gone over the edge in the night after all. But no, we were about to do just what our host said — go and find somewhere to dance — in that wind too — it couldn't be true! Two hours later, back at our point of departure, the Conservatoire, we knew that it was only too true.

"We had been blown all over Izmir. We had inspected cinemas, crawling under screens then pointing out that it was impossible to dance on the half dozen feet available — visited locked and sealed buildings which, we were told, would be wonderful if only we could get into them. We even located one possible place, only to find that it was being pulled down or re-decorated, I do not remember which, so could not possibly be used.

"The Conservatoire stage or nothing, the small dreary little platform passed in front of our eyes, the dusty, icy hall; perhaps it would have been better had we tumbled off the mountain road or even been drowned at Manissa. The answer to a final question sealed our misery. "Had there been any publicity?" "Oh no we did not know where you were dancing don't worry about that, we will put off the first performance until tomorrow night and InşAllah all will be well."

"Too weary and defeated to argue we crawled off, or rather were blown off, to locate the dancers; had they arrived or were they still sitting in Manissa station?

"They had arrived and were installed cold and cross in a small hotel as far away from the Conservatoire as it could well be.

"We were received without enthusiasm.

"No performance tonight!
Oh!
You had better come across to the Conservatoire for class and rehearsal.
Oh!
They were cold!
So were we!
They were tired!
So were we!
They did not like Izmir!"

"We could not answer that one and left them before they could think of anything else.

"That afternoon we all, or as many of us as there was room for, assembled on the stage of the Conservatoire — all hating each other like poison.

" "Come on, let's do a good barre you will feel better after it" a statement completely lacking in any conviction on my part. Blue hands clutched the edge of the dusty platform — cramped and creaking muscles and protesting overloaded stomachs were forced into reluctant action.

"The barre was not a success, the space was completely insufficient, the dust and cold were awful. Everyone kicked everyone else, mostly on purpose, and either there was an immediate row between kicker and kickee or both burst into tears. After twenty minutes of sniffles and protests I gave it up and tried rehearsal instead.

"The first section of our programme was to consist of a demonstration. Now one of the greatest assets of the Turkish dancers is their big free movement, their ability to cover ground. I saw them eyeing the mean little stage, their ears well back, and feared the worst, not without reason, they demonstrated their ability to cover the space in one jump and to land without difficulty in the audience when the occasion arose, and having warmed themselves up in the process, spirits rose to boiling point. Having got them going the question was how to stop them?

"Pirouettes! How many? Four, five, six! Canturk is down but Ferit and Husnu are still on their feet.

"Come girls! Quicker, faster, lighter, wings on your feet and fly. For heaven's sake stay on the stage though! It's a four foot unguarded drop into the audience and no footlights to warn you.

"For twenty minutes the very young Turkish Ballet showed the seeds of those qualities which if they are preserved will one day make them outstanding in the ballet world — attack, vitality, spontaneous dance quality and musicality of movement.

"Next on the programme for rehearsal was "Les Sylphides", a rash choice? I am not sure that it was. The Turkish dancers, even embryo as they were then, had a certain feeling for its lovely musical quality, they approached it gently and with a reverence that made one forgive them their immaturity and lack of control. It was at any rate an improvement on the competence, confidence and complete lack of understanding with which the general run of present day dancers and producers approach this most elusive and difficult of all classical ballets. Little obvious technical strength appears and there are no stunts what-so ever to fire the frenzied applause of the gallery, so this lovely balletic poem has become as much of a bore to the dancers as it has to the audience. 'Ou n'en quelle pays?" is its melting misty quality, its long poised pause like an arrested sigh, its floating skimming movements. Where is the flock of white birds of which Michel Fokine used to speak? Perhaps we shall see them come floating down, summer moonbeams to make endless lovely patterns on the green lawns of our imagination.

"This rehearsal of "Les Sylphides" at Izmir on that particular cold and uninspiring occasion reduced the green lawns of my imagination to a ploughed field of misgiving — heavy, dishevelled and panting young horses — not white birds — it was hard to forgive oneself — another burnt offering of "Les Sylphides". Michel Fokine's "thing of beauty" was certainly not "living for ever" that day, and my choice seemed not only rash, but disastrous.

"Last came the divertissements the more boisterous of which were executed with terrific gusto. Smoke and flames almost came out of their nostrils — my spirits rose a little. Last of the divertissements was the pas de trois from the first act of ''Swan Lake''.

''What a crazy thing to put on! After seeing it countless times I should have realised that not even the most experienced of ''war horses'' can ever make anything of this dance. The most they can hope for, after expending a great deal of effort, is to get to the end in good order. One always waits for a grand climax, something really exciting always seems due to happen, but never does. In this case lots of exciting things happened but not the right sort of things, and no one got to the end in any sort of order at all.

''Both girls lost courage early on complaining that their cavalier made no effort to lift them, he retorted by saying they were too heavy to lift anyhow, they then stated that their ''toes were very ill'' and limped heavily whenever they remembered to. When it came to the boy's solo he decided that the size of the stage made it impossible to show off his quite spectacular jump and to prove it jumped off the stage in the middle of the dance and did not reappear.

''Firm and immovable gloom had set in — no good going back on it — no good talking, the dancers had too many unanswerable arguments on their side, the only thing to do was to go wearily and drearily home hoping that a good meal would materialise from somewhere — this last proved to be undue optimism.

''Next morning, a hopeless dawn, cold and windy as ever. Travis and I went early to the Conservatoire, some sort of lighting had to be contrived, some sort of entrances engineered through the torn and rusty black curtains. The wings were almost non-existent and any dancer exiting with even a modicum of speed was likely to end teeth on into a brick wall.

''The dressing rooms were in a derelict boiler house across the garden, the garden being in full view of the street. Two dirty little cubby holes, no tables, chairs, mirrors, hanging space, or water and of course no heating.

''Poor children — after all they were only children — How would they continue to cope with such impossible conditions? They had already had three days of great strain and discomfort. It was all so new they could not be expected to understand the tradition that ''the show must go on'', and what other incentive had they? We did not even know if there would be an audience. Travis and I wondered how there could be, as no publicity what so ever had been done.

''A little later the dancers arrived wind blown and blue with cold, but amazingly cheerful, and they refused to be daunted by anything, not even the dressing rooms. Class and rehearsal were got through with a great show of enthusiasm — they would show ballet to Izmir, and if Izmir did not like it, it would be no fault of theirs. Even the ''Pas de Trois'' finished, if not in good order, at least without any major disaster.

"So not withstanding the minute stage, the appalling chaos in the unheated dressing rooms and the icy trek in costume across the garden the dancers danced their best. All three performances were packed — publicity must have been done by bush telegraph — Izmir liked its first introduction to ballet. The hard-tried dancers could say truthfully "We are a success" a success against these odds too. We all patted each other on the back and told each other how wonderful we were, everything was fine until it came to clearing up after the last performance. This was a minor labour of Hercules.

"The dancers had shot their bolt, given all they had and a bit more too, and were sitting around in dejected heaps amid piles of discarded costumes in the dark, dirty and perishingly cold dressing rooms. Two had developed high temperatures and were coughing and shivering miserably. Skinned and bleeding toes were thrust accusingly up for my inspection. All complained that if they did not get a meal and some warmth quickly they would die. But packing had to be done, costumes must be collected and counted and missing bits and pieces found.

"Tempers became very frayed. "I did put my Sylphide dress in the hamper, there it is" "No you did not that one is mine, you are sitting on yours" "Yes, there are three petticoats missing, does it matter?" "Only five pairs of frilly pants out of sixteen?" "Oh they will turn up, most of them still have them on" "For Heaven's sake don't lie down on these costumes" "You must take more of that make-up off, you have wiped your eye black all over your face."

"Having finally got the costumes packed and collected the dejected girls we began to depart. Suddenly we realised that Canturk was missing. After searching everywhere in vain, one of us happened to look out of the window at the rocks below, and there, swimming in the icy sea was Canturk. I was so relieved to see him that all I said was "You must never do that again, especially not in your 'Swan Lake' tights."

By the end of 1956 there were 62 pupils aged between nine and nineteen in the school, of whom most were boarders and all of whom were state sponsored. They were taken into the school at the ages of between nine and twelve, and were required to pass examinations which could lead to their being dismissed at the end of any year, advanced or even jumped one year. The course was designed to take seven years to which two more years were later added for exceptional students, although this was not rigidly adhered to as Molly and Travis preferred to proceed at the pace of their pupils. In June 1957 the first graduations took place and the successful candidates were drafted into the Opera.

In December 1956, *Dance and Dancers* published an article by Travis entitled "Starting from Scratch". In it he explained the thinking behind giving performances with young children — that as only a few would graduate each year, it would not be possible to give performances with fully trained dancers for several years, and by that time those who had completed their studies in previous years would have drifted away. It therefore became increasingly necessary to hold the interest of both the graduated and the non-graduated students, and in addition there was the task of building up audiences, and of breaking down the prejudice which existed in Turkey against the stage as a career, particularly for girls.

In those first two years Travis noted that the Turks had a "very fine national dance tradition, particularly as far as the male dancer was concerned, had retentive memories, were quick to learn, had a natural facility for pirouettes, a feeling for movement, and in the case of the girls, strong feet for point work". However, he also listed the problems which necessitated very careful handling — for example, the lack of self-discipline — but they responded well to firm, friendly imposed training discipline in class and rehearsal "but only if great vitality and enthusiasm are shown on the part of the teacher".[1]

The students loved Molly and Travis, but did not feel so much in awe of them they could not play an April Fool's joke: every class began with pliés in second and the students were expected to be ready to begin the moment Molly or Travis walked in. One year, on April 1st, they entered the studio and found it empty except for rows of shoes standing in perfect second positions next to the barre. The humour of the situation was of course appreciated but did not prevent Travis writing "They still have to absorb the devastating truth that only through blood, sweat and tears can a ballet dancer be made". He put this down to three main causes:

> "They have had no opportunity of seeing ballet other than in an occasional film: they have only recently come into contact with so arduous and vocational approach as that demanded by the classical dance; the emancipation of women is so very recent."[2]

It was necessary therefore not only to create physically the dancers and choreographers, but these had to be moulded mentally to achieve an understanding of "the tradition of service required by this most exacting art".

Molly found the students very easy to teach as they had bodies which were perfect for dance:

> "Not only strong, they were rhythmical to a degree, and they were also expressive and enormously dramatic. I think that the Turkish boys were quite the best male dancers that I've seen for years, and years, and years."[3]

Molly and Travis staged ‘‘Les Sylphides’’, the second act of ‘‘Swan Lake’’, revivals of two of Molly’s ballets ‘‘Fadette’’ and ‘‘Music Hall’’ and Keith Lester’s ‘‘Faust’’, as well as producing two new works ‘‘Soirée de Vienne’’ and ‘‘The Musicians of Bremen’’. In later years they were to commission scores from Turkish composers and to base ballets on Turkish folklore using authentic Turkish folkdance. In December 1956 de Valois wrote to Travis suggesting sending over someone to mount Tudor’s ‘‘Soirée Musicale’’, Cranko’s ‘‘Beauty and the Beast’’ and Howard’s ‘‘Death and the Maiden’’. Molly and Travis felt that if they were to build a local audience, they had to present works which would be of more relevance than imported works from the Royal Ballet and the Ballet Rambert. De Valois agreed with them that eventually the Turks had to express themselves in their own dance and music, and that, as she wrote in a letter which was published in the magazine printed in 1988 to commemorate the fortieth anniversary of the company:

‘‘They have, of course, the heritage of their wonderful national dances, for here is found the national style of every state ballet company’’; however, she also wanted British choreographers to be represented.

After producing the second act of ‘‘Swan Lake’’ Molly and Travis came to the conclusion that the European classics were inappropriate at that stage of the schools’ development, whereas de Valois’ philosophy had not changed since she had formed her own companies: that a classical state company must have as its basis the ‘‘universal’’ classical repertoire.

Molly described the company and the philosophy behind her and Travis’s decisions on repertoire and training in an article which was published in *Dance and Dancers*.[4] She explained how, because the children did not lend themselves easily to discipline and yet were open to the music they showed ‘‘a much more spontaneous reaction to musical movement than is usual today’’. She was sure that their eagerness should be ‘‘jealously preserved if the Turkish ballet is to attain the international reputation which it will, we hope, later deserve’’. Molly talked about their natural ability to execute technical feats, and their lack of concentration leading to their unwillingness to polish this technique. ‘‘The problem is to obtain this polish without destroying their lovely natural qualities many of which are so lamentably lacking in today’s dancers’’. She went on to say that these dancers were not, at the time, yet suited to

> ‘‘the more rigid of the old classical ballets which can so easily bring out all their bad points and extinguish their good ones. It would seem that ‘‘Giselle’’ is the only one which would possibly give them a chance of showing their mettle. Let us hope that the very young Turkish ballet will gradually acquire a repertory suited to their own peculiar and very varied

talents, that they will continue to develop along their particular and delightful lines and will not become a dim replica of the already established companies whose idiom is not their idiom.''[5]

In a piece in *The Week* in February 1957, it was reported with pleasure that the students would give performances every month and all the readers were heartily recommended to go and enjoy them. The article concluded:

''Please excuse this rave review, dear reader, but we are terribly enthusiastic about this promising ballet group. And while we reflect that the average age of the leading dancers is only about sixteen, and foresee what they will be like three years from now if they continue to work hard under the same good direction we can happily prophesy that the Turkish Ballet will become as fine as its opera and drama.''[6]

By December 1958 the school was developing rapidly, Dulcie Pyne had left, and Travis expressed the need for two more teachers in the school to replace her; de Valois offered to send two of her students, Valerie Deakin and Julia Cross to work for Travis and at the Opera. She did not consider them to be completely ready for the task, but arranged many extra classes and rehearsals for them to attend to groom them for the job, and she also insisted that when on holiday in England at the end of the first year they attend more classes and courses to acquaint them with professional dancers and ballet company procedures. Julia Cross only stayed for one season, as she had hoped that she would have more responsibility for rehearsals and choreography, but Valerie Deakin remained for many years, and remained friends with Molly and Travis ever since.

The conservatoire company's success increased from year to year. In April 1957 Nadia Nerina and Alexis Rassine joined the conservatoire students in a performance which included Molly's ''Salute to Petipa'', the second act of ''Swan Lake'' specially put on for them, Dulcie Pyne's ''Macar Dansi'', and again Molly's ''Soirée de Vienne''.

In April 1958, as a result of an invitation from Travis and to everyone's surprise, the legendary Margot Fonteyn with her partner Michael Somes came and danced with the conservatoire student company. They rehearsed at the conservatoire but gave the performance at the Opera House, and Molly described vividly the magic of their arrival and the worry of the children at performing with such wonderful artists.

True Artists

''Margot Fonteyn, her mother and Michael Somes were to arrive at nine o'clock that morning by plane from Istanbul, where they had passed the night. The conservatoire was bubbling with excitement and joyous anticipation.

"Certain lucky students, three girls and three boys, were to accompany the British Council Representative, Travis and myself to the airport. Armed with large bouquets and with spirits on top of the world we arrived there with about ten minutes to spare before the Istanbul 'plane was due.

"A gorgeously sunny, but very windy morning and now in a minute we would see Margot Fonteyn! The gale made it impossible to hold on to a bouquet and keep your skirts down at the same time, modesty prevailed, the cellophane covers were blown off the bouquets, flowers scattered themselves lyrically and fittingly all over the airfield and hair was blown into a bacchanalian state of disorder.

"The plane is in sight, all eyes went up to the sky, to the little silver plane — bigger, bigger, bigger, coming down. She's down! she taxied up to unload.

"Everyone stood stockstill suddenly overcome with shyness and aware of windblown hair and dishevelled bouquets.

"The steps were up, the door was opening, pull yourselves together — now is the big moment.

"Several solid, sombrely clad, sombre faced individuals came unenthusiastically down. Then a pause — this must be them; no! a large woman in red, a very old man, some children, more solid sombre individuals "Tamam" Finish! No more!!! anticlimax.

"We waited one and a half hours for the next plane and hardly dared to watch it come in — perhaps if we looked the other way she would be there when we turned back — she was.

"In almond green with a small almond green hat, looking as enchanted a princess as one could hope — she was followed by her mother and by her partner Michael Somes.

"Famous people are rarely the modest and unegotistical figures which they are popularly represented to be, they seem more often than not to be only too aware of their own importance and to act accordingly. Would that they could model themselves on these two great stars of the ballet world, no people could have been more charming — though, as it transpired after, they had been subjected to a series of events enough to infuriate anyone, let alone two V.I. V.I.Ps.

"Both these world famous dancers were giving their services in order to encourage the development of the embryo Turkish Ballet, and had sacrificed a few days of badly needed leisure in order to come out to Ankara at the invitation of the British Council, yet on arrival at Istanbul airport the night before, no one had met them — insufficient accommodation had been booked for them in the hotel and by some inexcusable oversight no financial provision had been made for them there. The representative of the British Council in Istanbul had to be dragged from his bed in his pyjamas in order to clear up the situation.

''The chapter of accidents did not end there; next morning when they returned to the airport to take the local plane up to Ankara as scheduled they found that reservations had been made for Margot Fonteyn's mother and for Michael Somes, but that there was neither reservation nor vacant seat for Margot Fonteyn herself, they would have to wait for the next plane, hence their late arrival in Ankara.

''Still here they were at last — charm, friendliness, a kiss, the battered remains of the flowers presented — arrangements made for practice and a rehearsal that afternoon and still bravely smiling, the poor tired creatures were taken off to lay a wreath on Ataturk's tomb.

''The rehearsal was on the stage of the conservatoire theatre — the second act of ''Le Lac des Cygnes'' with the half-trained and quite inexperienced Turkish dancers as corps de ballet. That they were then unworthy of their two great principals was obvious, that they were at their most unworthy in ''Lac'' was so unfortunate as to be disastrous.

''More or less the same could be said of the conservatoire orchestra, but the dancers at least would do as they were told whereas the orchestra would quite likely dig its toes in and insist that it knew best regarding tempi etc. Nothing to be done, nowhere to run to.

''The curtain went up, there in front was a packed audience of professors and students! ''Oh'' said Margot Fonteyn ''Oh dear.''

''It was explained that to clear the theatre would be a terrible disappointment to the audience. A heavy sigh! ''Oh well! But could you tell them that this is only a rehearsal and not to expect too much.''

''It was a shattering afternoon for Travis and what it must have been for the guest dancers I shudder to think. We can never thank them enough for their forbearance and understanding.

''The corps de ballet were quite shocking, they forgot everything of grace that they had ever learnt and gallumped all over the place impeding the Swan Queen and her Prince at every turn.

''The orchestra was erratic, tempi often unrecognisable, the conductor bewildered and unco-operative. At the end nobody knew what to say to anybody — we had disgraced ourselves, what was there to say? That Margot Fonteyn of all people should have had such a terrible time! Even now I can hardly bear to think of that shocking afternoon.

''Next morning there was to be an orchestra rehearsal at the Opera House where the performances were to be held. What would happen? Would it be worse? Would it be better? Let's run away!

''It was neither worse nor better, it was much about the same and made one want to hide under the seats. The corps de ballet by this time painfully aware of its own deficiencies hardly dared to move in case they got in the way. The orchestra worried and inaccurate was never helpful, but Margot Fonteyn only said ''Don't worry, don't try to get them right, as long as I know where they are wrong I can manage. If you try to get them right they may go wrong somewhere I don't expect.''

''Manage she did. Quietly and beautifully she went through the rehearsal, her lovely, lyrical interpretation in no way blurred by the horrors around her.

''After ''Lac'' she and Michael Somes rehearsed the pas de deux and variations from''Casse Noisette'', and neither of them were satisfied with their work. ''They had not done 'Casse' for a long time''. ''It felt rusty''. ''It simply could not go on like that''. ''Might they go and work again at the conservatoire that afternoon?''. Then having drawn small circles in white chalk round the worst pitfalls on the stage, a warning to keep away from them, they thanked everyone — heaven knows what for — and went quietly back to the Embassy where they were staying.

''The performance that night was probably a little less bad from the corps de ballet point of view, the frame was in no way worthy of its principals. The Turkish dancers were pushed beyond their powers, we knew that, poor children. But a start had to be made to create a company, they could not remain any longer as the clumsy students they then were.

''Now, when many people acclaim the Turkish Ballet as something to be reckoned with, it would be as well to remember the pioneer performances which enabled them to attain the first rung of the professional ladder.

''Still, however unhappy that evening was for us, I shall always remember Margot Fonteyn's ''Swan Lake'' with a nostalgic gratitude. For me she represents the last link with the great dancers and artists of yesterday, Pavlova, Karsavina, Spessiva.

''Distant and lonely, still more bird than human, long dipping lines, always that suggestion of flight, beautifully gentle arms and head, a nostalgic picture of the lost and loving ''Odette'' — so different from the adolescent incipient fire birds with their busy arched and writhing arms with which a rather limp and blase Siegfried copes languidly. These admirable young athletes have lost the ability to create an illusion, surely ballet's most precious gift and one which Margot Fonteyn possesses to the n'th degree — they are oh so completely earthbound.

"One wonders too what, if anything, a variety of Prince Siegfrieds have learnt from Michael Somes. When these elegant young princes appear with their wiry athletic partners there seems so little contrast — so little romance and emotion. One can never believe that Odette could really fall for a young man more preoccupied with the beauty of his own legs than the beauty of hers, or that he on his part could have any use for her once she became human and made demands on him other than supported arabesques.

"It is perhaps as well that the whole sad tale does not go beyond the arabesque stage and is continuously so well clothed with pirouettes and fouettes that the audience demands nothing more. The third act, the famous thirty-two fouettes, fireworks at the Crystal Palace — the whole ballet seems to wait for this Albert Memorial of period vulgarity.

"A few more memories of Margot Fonteyn. In the conservatoire after her practice, dressing for an ambassadorial lunch — no mirror in the room, so doing her hair and pulling on her hat by the aid of her dim reflection in the glass doors of a bookcase.

"A blazing hot day, hatless in a flowered black frock, trailing up the precipitous and dusty street of old Ankara perched on its hill, sheet precipices falling away from its surrounding walls.

"Exploring the old grain market on the extreme summit with its lovely view of clustered roofs and tortuous streets winding downwards to the bare plains where many coloured shadows chased each other to the ring of mountains beyond.

"Examining the gold and carven treasures of the Hittite museum.

"With Michael Somes packing after the final performance, the meticulous care taken by both of them of their costumes, headdresses, shoes and tights, their courtesy and consideration to each other and to every one else.

"Always gracious, charming, eager and friendly. Would there were more such V.I.Ps."

Travis's memories of Turkey were not all of dancing:

"'Keep calm and stay in your homes'. We were woken by blaring radios from the other flats and people rushing up and down the stairs outside. I looked out of the window and

saw a rather worried looking soldier, his rifle at the ready, walking rather warily up the street. Everyone stuck their heads out of the windows and applauded madly: we were in the middle of revolution! I hastily put on some clothes, told Molly to stay in bed, and went down to the main hall where all the other occupants of the flats seemed to be congregating.

"Good luck to the revolution, but they wanted breakfast and no one had any bread. No one wanted to go out, but they were sure I, as a foreigner would be safe. So off I went with lots of bits of money wrapped up in lots of bits of paper on which was written each person's requirements. As I was coming out of the bakery, about twenty loaves balanced precariously in my arms, a tank came up the road with about half a dozen infantry men on each side, under the command of a young officer. As the tank was passing me I tripped and dropped the loaves. The tank stopped, the infantrymen stopped, the young officer politely piled all the loaves back into my arms, saluted smartly and went on with his revolution.

"The revolution must have been well planned and carried out for after a couple of hours there was literally no disruption to normal life. I believe three or four people were killed and rumour had it that the bodies had been put in the deep freeze department of the city's meat store. Whether this was right or wrong I don't know but no one would eat mince meat for days.

"There were three revolutions while we were there, but eveything returned so rapidly to normal that one barely noticed that they had happened."

De Valois accompanied Fonteyn and Somes to Turkey, and the Turko-British Association and the British Council presented the largest cultural programme they had ever organised. The ballet performances were a "Ballet Festival", and the poet John Betjeman, Sir John Rothenstein, Director of the Tate Gallery, and the actress Rosalinde Fuller, were invited to appear. There were exhibitions, one on the History of the Theatre, and the other on The Art of Photography, a number of lectures were given, and de Valois was thanked and honoured for having made it all possible.

A long review by Metin And in *Ulus* rhapsodised about the honour of being visited by "the fairy and her prince", praised the young dancers' performance in Jak Carter's "Impromptu for Twelve", and was full of hope for their potential success:

> "If we get hold of this art well, there is no doubt that we can advance more in this field than we can in the fields of opera and theatre, and turn it into a national art of which we can be proud."[7]

The following year another cultural event was presented. The Pipes and Drums of the Sutherland Highlanders were invited by the Turkish military authorities to play at the stadium, and they marched down the Ataturk Boulevard in full regalia. A concert of Chamber Music was devoted to the music of Henry Purcell. In spite of having had no previous training or experience, Molly and Travis acted in a performance of Oscar Wilde's "The Importance of Being Earnest", and there was again a ballet programme which Travis directed, with Maryon Lane, Anya Linden, David Blair and Peter Clegg appearing with the conservatoire ballet at a gala in the State Opera House, and in a production of "A Maske of Comus" at the British Embassy the following month.

There were now two companies: the ballet at the opera, the State Ballet, which at last had enough fully graduated dancers to be able to give performances without Molly and Travis and their students, and the conservatoire ballet.

Having built up the school and the companies, Molly and Travis naturally expected to continue to supervise them, and to carry on their work of presenting ballet to Turkish audiences, but de Valois wrote to them stating categorically that it would not be possible for them to take on work "that requires a different form of direction and which would take you away from the academic duties that you both excel at", or to "take on both jobs". Molly and Travis were surprised by these remarks, considering that they had successfully run ballet companies for longer than they had taught children.

After Molly and Travis had been in Turkey for about five years, they were asked to give a private performance with the conservatoire company for the Shah of Persia and his wife. The Shah and his wife sat alone in the theatre which was heavily guarded by tanks, and it was a very exciting event. They were later invited to have tea with the wife of the Iranian Ambassador to Turkey and in conversation it transpired that she had been a soloist with Pavlova many years before. Molly asked her if she knew her first teacher, Hilda Bewicke, to which she received the reply: "Don't be silly Molly; I *am* Hilda Bewicke". Molly felt "very small indeed". She and Travis learnt that the Shah had been so impressed with the performance he had seen that he wanted them to come to Persia to advise on setting up a similar school and company, and in view of the uncertainty about their future roles in Turkey, they decided to look into the matter, and Travis went there for a month to explore the situation.

Ninette de Valois began to send a series of Royal Ballet dancers to Turkey to teach the State Ballet, to choreograph for it, and to work at the opera. Robert Harold, Richard Glasstone, Andree Howard, Claude Newman and John Gilpin all worked there for some time but none stayed very long.

The director of the conservatoire in Turkey continued to be delighted by the way in which both the schools and the company were being run by Molly and Travis and by the fact that their own performances wer encouraging an interest in ballet; he gave them complete freedom as well as enough money to continue to do so in any way they wanted.

In 1958 the Opera Director began to put on operas which required a greater number of dancers than he had, such as "Faust", and so he asked the conservatoire for dancers to perform the main ballet which was choreographed by Molly and Travis, the character dances being executed by the graduates. It was a great success, and thenceforth they were asked also to arrange the movements of the opera singers. In 1963 de Valois asked Richard Brown, who had danced in the Continental Ballet and had later helped at the conservatoire, to choreograph the opera ballets, the responsibility for which Travis and Molly had at first not wanted to take on. By this time they had graduated about thirty dancers, many of whom were dancing there, but the antagonism between the Directors of the Opera and the conservatoire made collaboration between the two organisations very difficult.

Molly and Travis continued to present works which they considered suitable for the temperament of their students, and these developed from what Molly called the "Nursery Rhyme stage" to two ballets by Todd Bolender, "Création du Monde", a jazz ballet which Molly described as being a "study in psychological emotionalism". Todd had come to them as a result of the helpfulness of the American cultural attaché, who had offered to send an American to choreograph for the conservatoire: he gave Molly and Travis a list of names from which they chose Todd.

"Giselle" was the only "classical" piece which they produced and they were very proud of their leading dancers, who were students in their final year. Molly wrote an article for *The Week* June 1961 most of which was devoted to the performances of these dancers, and which finished

> "We believe in, like and admire the Turkish dancer, even if we did spend the first two of our seven years here in trying to find the right approach to develop their obvious talents. The temperament of the Turkish dancer needs considerable understanding, and a probationary period to obtain their full potentialities is necessary for any teacher or producer who has their welfare at heart."[8]

Molly enlarged on her description of the first cast of "Giselle".

> **Meric Sumen, the first Turkish "Giselle"**
>
> "Not quite seventeen, very childish, very beautiful, she looked the part, slim, rather tall with a lovely long neck and throat, a little sleek dark head

and a delicate featured face with large grey very innocent eyes.

"Her first attempt at portraying the role was not particularly successful; she approached it tentatively and self-consciously. One wondered if such a faint sketch would ever be visible at all. However egged on by her admiring fellow students she turned Giselle into a rather "tarty" village belle, and when it came to the mad scene let it rip as an operatic tragedy queen; this last effort followed on the advice of a visiting choreographer who told her to practise every gesture in front of a mirror, with the inevitable disastrous result. Would she ever find Giselle?

"Then suddenly one day while trying to explain to her that very difficult first entrance, a child coming from the cool and sober protection of her mother's cottage into the sunshine of her first love — she understood. She portrayed her own youth, beauty and innocence. Mischievous but never coy, tender but never amorous, gently loving to her mother and her comrades she used her beautiful lightness and her budding technical ability to convey her happiness and love of life.

"Later her complete bewilderment, her refusal to accept Albrecht's perfidy leading to heartbroken realisation and breakdown. The shattered child wandering terrified and alone in the dim shadow world of her vaguely remembered happiness. The almost exultant gesture of the last sword thrust to free herself from her shadows. Too late poor child, she realises that her own impending death is the most terrifying shadow of all. To be so cold in all the sunshine — so many people near and no one to help her — seeking for comfort, too young to accept death, the shadows closing in, the cold gripping her — poor loving frightened child.

"One could perhaps call this very young dancer "Giselle" and not Meric.

Sait Sokmen, the first Turkish "Albrecht"

"To see Sait in the role of "Albrecht" is the only way to realise its stature. One can say that his technique and acting were excellent, that he had nobility and that his partnering was equally excellent. But all these superlatives become meaningless unless the depth of his understanding of the character of the rather shallow and self complacent early Albrecht and his transformation to the broken penitent of the second act can be conveyed.

"It is easy to be touched by the obvious tragedy of poor little Giselle, but until I saw Sait as Albrecht I have never felt the least sympathy for him. Mostly I have felt a vague irritation that such an obvious young spiv should come poking round the village with such complacent snobbishness. It was impossible to forgive Albrecht his shabby destruction of Giselle, but after seeing Sait, from his fury of uncontrolled despair at the end of the first act to his agonised endeavour to catch and keep his beloved shadow in the second act, I realised that in destroying Giselle he had also fittingly and tragically destroyed himself.

"The utter resignation to grief and despair, despair for all eternity, that he managed to convey at the last curtain fall. Poor Albrecht. But perhaps as one of the stage hands at the Arts Theatre once said to me while leaning sentimentally on the cross "If he couldn't 'ave 'er in life 'e 'ad 'er in death". I only hope he was right. Certainly no other Albrecht has made me believe that he felt anything much beyond the necessity of wearing decorous and of course becoming mourning, and bringing a nice bunch of flowers while keeping a weather eye on the effect produced by his coupé jetés etc.

"It still remains to find an aspect of Bathilde that does not make one want to cut all her scenes as short as possible. What can we do with the poor girl? Perhaps place her in the secure pages of *Woman and Home* where later she will doubtless meet a member of the Corps Diplomatique and create a cosy corner of Kensington in foreign parts — which after all is a "Far, Far Better Thing" than chasing unstable Albrechts through damp German forests.

At the same time, Travis also wrote a poem about this ballet which they both loved so much. It was inspired by the memory of the complaint of a lady in Bradford: "I've paid good money to see 'Swan Lake', but you've changed the bloody programme, and I've had to sit through something called 'Lac de Cygnes'.

To be spoken in a north country accent, and with apologies to Albert and the Lion

Now, this is a story of sorrow,
A very sad story to tell,
Of a gallant young Duke christened Albrecht
And a young peasant girl called Giselle.

Giselle was the "Belle" of the village
Loved by all for her beauty and grace
And especially by one called Hil-Ari-On
Who wore a red beard on his face.

Duke Albrecht had heard of her beauty
And thought him that he'd try his luck
So he got himself up as a peasant
Just returned from a day carting muck.

He hid his fine clothes in a cottage
Next door to Giselle's mother's inn

But his dastardly plan was found out by the man
Who wore a red beard on his chin.

Now always a Duke or a Baron
Denoting his rank, wealth and pride
Wears a sword with a gold plated handle
From a strap on his belt at his side.

Now Albrecht was proud of his weapon
He'd worn it midst battle and din
It was left with his clothes in the cottage
Next door to Giselle's mother's inn.

He met her that day in the village
They exchanged lovers' vows on a bench
For her it was marriage or nothing
She weren't that kind of a wench.

A flower that she plucked said he loved her
They parted as all lovers should
She went to help Ma with the washing
He went for a walk in the wood.

The hunt came along shortly after
All the folk from the house on the hill
With the Prince who was Duke Albrecht's neighbour
And a stag they had managed to kill.

The Prince was escorting one Bathilde
A lady of beauty and wit
Engaged to be married to Albrecht
And she wore the Duke's ring on her mitt.

The hunt had been hot and exhausting
The party were weary and pale
So they knocked at Giselle's mother's cottage
And asked for some cakes and some ale.

They were served on a bench in the open
By the delicate hands of Giselle
And to show her respect for the gentry
By the hands of her mother as well.

Giselle liked Bathilde's hunting costume
Bathilde liked Giselle's pretty face
Giselle gave Bathilde a deep curtsey
Bathilde gave Giselle a necklace.

Yener Durukan, Sait Sokmen, Tanju Tuzer, with Molly, Travis and Koko

Molly and Jane

On tour with the Conservatoire Ballet

Students of the State Conservatoire

Students of the State Conservatoire

Students of the State Conservatoire

Students of the State Conservatoire

Graduates of the State Conservatoire

Students of the State Conservatoire

Molly taking rehearsal in Ankara

Giselle danced with joy round the garden
But her mother thought dancing a sin
So she went to the door of her cottage
And invited them all to come in.

The Prince took his horn from his shoulder
Called his servant and said to him "Mate
Here's my horn if I'm wanted just blow it"
And he hung the thing up on the gate.

The gentry went into the cottage
The huntsmen went off for a talk
The peasants went back to wine pressing
Duke Albrecht came back from his walk.

Giselle left the cottage to meet him
Their love for each other were plain
She gave him a kiss on the forehead
And made to dash off down the lane.

Hilarion crept round the corner
And saw the two lovers at play
He got all worked up in a temper
And thrust himself in Giselle's way.

He told the poor girl that she'd had it
And swore a foul oath by the Lord
Told her Albrecht was not what she thought him
And proved it by showing his sword.

But Giselle would have none of his nonsense
She lashed him with anger and scorn
So he rushed to the gate of her cottage
And blew a long blast on the horn.

The huntsmen came up right and smartly
The peasants came on at a run
The door of Giselle's cottage opened
And the gentry came out one by one.

The Prince saw the Duke and said "Crikey
What doeth thou Duke in this place
With the beautiful belle of the village
And that man with that hair on his face."

Giselle was now properly flummoxed
"The Duke Sire? that surely can't be

That young man is my Ma's next door neighbour
And he's going to be married to me.''

Lady Bathilde then thrust herself forward
And said ''What you say is not true
Him and me had a private arrangement
A long time before he met you.''

Giselle thought the Duke had betrayed her
She were really quite rattled poor lass
After throwing the beads back at Bathilde
She collapsed in a heap on the grass.

Her mother came out at that moment
And said ''What's this frightful affair''
She went and knelt down by her daughter
And let down her dark shiney hair.

She raised up her girl and embraced her
But Giselle pushed her mother away
She couldn't expire for five minutes
There was still that much music to play.

She rushed round the crowd so demented
Amidst all their horror and cries
It was marvellous the way that she did it
Cause her hair covered both of her eyes.

Then she stopped in the midst of her rushing
And her Ma gave a sort of a squeal
As her body tensed up and went rigid
'Cause she'd touched Albrecht's sword with her heel.

She picked up the sword with emotion
Then giving a sort of a start
Did a relévè, coupe and jétè
And shoved the damn thing in her heart.

She was buried at night in the forest
Cos she'd taken her life with her hand
And her ghost join some others called Willis
A truly remarkable band.

They were led by a Willi called Myrtha
Who torn by frustration and spite
Had a dastardly plan to destroy every man
Who strayed in the forest at night.

The first man to come to the graveside
Was the bloke with red hair on his chin
He was chased through the forest by Willis
To the edge of a lake and shoved in.

Then Albrecht arrived with some lillies
Which he laid at the foot of the tomb
He was kneeling in vain supplication
When Giselle's ghost appeared in the gloom.

They danced through the glades of the forest
The Duke and the ghost of Giselle
Till they came across Myrtha and T'Willis
And Myrtha were angry as hell.

"If you find a man in the forest
Report straight to me that's my law
Its fair shares for all in this band love
That young man must die before four."

But Giselle was not going to be beaten
And give in without showing fight
She protected the Duke from the Willis
And danced with him through that long night.

The sun rose up over the hilltop
While Albrecht still danced with Giselle
The clock in the village struck loudly
And Albrecht was saved by the bell.

Giselle and the rest of the Willis
When the clock in the village struck four
Slowly returned to their coffins
Leaving Albrecht flat out on the floor.

All Dukes take a note of this story
And to save further sorrow and gloom
If you go a'courting a peasant
Leave your sword back at home in your room.

The director of the Theatre now decided to expand his activities and to present musicals. The Director of the Opera refused to co-operate, and so Molly and Travis were approached and they agreed to help, using the dancers of the conservatoire. Todd Bolender directed "My Fair Lady" and choreographed several of the dances. Molly and Travis also created some pieces for the production which was very popular.

Although Molly and Travis only danced themselves during the early years, and then only on special occasions such as galas, they continued to do their daily class as they did not believe that it was possible to teach unless they were in training; ''You lose the rhythm of it, you lose the feel'',

While in Turkey, Molly and Travis made several visits to South Africa. In 1962 Molly taught and mounted some works for the Johannesburg City Ballet (later known as the Ballet Transvaal and finally the P.A.C.T. Ballet): the peasant pas de deux from ''Giselle'', her own ''Walpurgis Night'' and Jak Carter's ''Impromptu for Twelve''. In 1963 she and Travis staged the complete ''Giselle'' with guest artist Yvette Chauvire. Molly was extremely popular with the dancers, who were quoted in the *Johannesburg Star* as describing her as an ''excellent teacher'', ''a wonderful person'', ''so inspiring'' and a ''wonderful choreographer''. Trevor Dodd, one of the four male dancers in the company said about her:

> ''She keeps a company together. And she has got our respect. Some teachers shout for hours, and don't get what she gets in minutes.''[9]

Molly and Travis were asked by Hermien Dommisse, who headed the management committee, to stay with the Ballet Transvaal, but they decided to remain in Turkey in spite of the internal politics and rivalries which had beset almost all their dealings from the moment they arrived.

But by 1974 world politics began to intrude and these were not so easy to deal with: one night a bomb was thrown against the wall of their house. It appeared that terrorists had wanted to distract the police so that they could blow up an important building elsewhere.

''The night before, Molly had burnt the gas stove out, and when I heard the bang I shouted 'Molly, Molly, what are you doing this time?' It blew all the windows out on the coldest night of the year. There was glass everywhere.

''We felt that twenty years was enough. When we first went to Turkey, we were not allowed to accept invitations from the Russian embassy without permission from the Ministry of Education, or to put a Russian dance into our programme. The Russians were constantly offering to provide teachers to be paid by them and not by the Turks, but at first their offer was refused. However, by the time we left, the climate had changed, and our leaving gave the Russians a chance to get in and they have been there ever since.''

Molly and Travis left their beautiful house on the beach and returned to London to start yet another new life.

By the time they left Turkey they had started and had built up three state ballet schools each with over a hundred pupils, one in Ankara, one in Istanbul and one in Izmir, and two state ballet companies each of approximately seventy dancers, one in Ankara and one in Istanbul, as well as nurturing growing audiences for the repertoire which they had so carefully developed.

In spite of the problems, the twenty years which they spent in Turkey were among the happiest and proudest of Molly's life. She never ceased to talk about her wonderful students in Turkey, and never tired of looking at and showing the film which had been made of their class and performance, and to tell her current students and friends how marvellous they were. Many of the students, especially the men, became principal dancers in ballet companies throughout the world. For example, Tanju Tuzer with the Harkness Ballet, Azkan Aslan with the Stuttgart Ballet and later with the Festival Ballet, and Yener Durukan with the ballet in Hanover.

When the news of Molly's death reached Turkey in 1986, the company put on a special performance of "Giselle", with a glowing tribute to her in the programme, and describing with gratitude and affection how it was she who had first mounted the work in Turkey. And when the school celebrated its fortieth birthday in June 1988 Travis, together with Joy Newton, and Barbara Fewster the Associate Director of the Royal Ballet School representing Dame Ninette de Valois, was invited to the festivities at the expense of the Turkish government, and was afforded every honour due to one who had contributed so much to the creation of the companies and schools.

Journey's End

The Place

The dance world in London to which Molly and Travis returned in 1974 was very different from the one they had left twenty years earlier: firstly, ballet training had changed; secondly, Robin Howard had introduced Contemporary Dance into the country in 1967, and now ran a performing company and a growing school which, while building on Martha Graham's technique, was teaching a form of contemporary dance which was developing in a way suitable to the English temperament and bodies. He felt that most ballet dancers at that time were incapable of doing modern dance but that this was primarily because of their attitude resulting from the way in which they had been trained, rather than being a physical impossibility. He greatly admired classical ballet "when it is what I think it should be",[1] and believed strongly that a ballet discipline was necessary in the school of London Contemporary Dance; he began looking for someone who could instil this in a way different from most of what he had seen in this country, and engaged Cleo Nordy. When she left the school he asked the advice of Ninette de Valois whose opinion he greatly respected, and she immediately suggested Molly and Travis.

She was not the only one to recommend them; when they had been running the Continental Ballet, they had asked Eileen Grundy, the administrator of the Arts Educational Trust for dancers for the company, and she had sent several along to audition. Molly and Travis selected four, one of whom was Clare Duncan, who they later learnt was Eileen's daughter. Clare stayed with the company for several years, going on to study contemporary dance at the school which Robin Howard had set up. She danced with its company, the London Contemporary Dance Theatre, and then became Principal of the school, which was now based at The Place. When she heard that Molly and Travis were leaving Turkey, she immediately suggested that Molly be invited to teach at The Place. Soon after this she herself was asked by Ben Stevenson to teach at the Houston Ballet School, and she recommended that Travis replace her as Principal. And so Molly and Travis both started work at the same time at what was then called the London School of Contemporary Dance.

They arrived at the school with the firm belief that, if well taught, ballet training was sufficient to enable dancers to dance in any style whatsoever, and that no other method was necessary, and many lively discussions ensued between them and Robin Howard. However, they all had enormous respect for each other, and agreed that there are only two kinds of dance — good and bad — and there were many points when their opinions coincided, and many occasions when Molly and Travis saw the good in contemporary dance more than the contemporary dancers saw in classical ballet. Their understanding of dance, their different way of looking at it, meant that their assessment of a work was often invaluable, and they could often explain why a given piece was not successful. Travis remembers Robin Howard as being:

"a very great person not only as far as dance was concerned but as a citizen of the world. Anyone who overcomes a deformity as Robin overcame the loss of his legs during the last few weeks of the war, tends to become a strong person in all ways.

"We found Robin not only a man of great strength of character but a delightful person of great kindness. Unfortunately the great kindness sometimes led to his being imposed upon.

"In spite of having two false legs, he would sometimes stand at the back of a class and try to feel the rhythm of a movement through his body, often more successfully than some of the students, and sometimes more successfully than some of the teachers.

"Robin also had a wicked sense of humour and it was often some minutes before one realised one was being 'got at'. His favourite reply to anyone who asked him what he considered to be the main difference between classical and contemporary dance was 'Classical goes down to go up, while contemporary goes up to go down', which I suppose in many ways is true.

"Robin had given his life's energies and his personal fortune to creating contemporary dance in England, and his relationship with the Contemporary Dance Trust in the last year of his life was tragic and to my mind contributed to his early death."

Molly and Travis both believed that nowadays much ballet training in England omits the development of the use of the torso and of different dynamics, and that this gap is now filled by contemporary teaching. Travis feels that another change in ballet dancers' accomplishment is caused by the fact that many years ago, dancers would come to class half an hour before the start of the lesson in order to limber and warm up and to strengthen certain parts of their bodies. This is no longer done, and the contemporary technique now incorporates into the class structure a development of many of the exercises which ballet dancers used to execute before starting work.

Molly and Travis very much enjoyed teaching the students, and loved their enthusiasm and the fact that they worked hard and were not only accomplished contemporary dancers but also good at classical ballet. Molly taught Robert North who was "lovely to teach and such a nice person", and Tom Jobe "the most wonderful looking person I ever saw, and always tying his legs round himself". The students loved Molly and Travis and at times missed contemporary classes in order to attend theirs; many company members also came to their lessons whenever their work schedule allowed. The school had a vibrant atmosphere: everyone was enthusiastic and there was an exciting feeling of building something new, of belonging to a venture that was living and unfolding. However, there was an area of disagreement, as Travis remembers:

"For the most part contemporary dancers work equally as hard if not harder than the average ballet dancer, but unfortunately contemporary dance is inclined to attract an element for whom dance means emoting in corners, walking round in various directions at varying speeds, breathing hard and choreographing to the sound of flushing lavatories. Regretfully there was a small element of this in the school which gnawed away at the vast majority of goodness like a maggot in an apple. I tried to eradicate it but unfortunately this approach to dance is considered by many to be highly intellectual, and it was easier said than done. So although I had enjoyed my time at the 'Place', and for the most part had found it vital, hardworking and overflowing with original ideas, it was not completely with sorrow that I reached the age when I had to retire.

"There used to be a song 'Old Soldiers Never Die, they Only Fade Away'. It's rather the same with dancers: I thought we could retire gracefully but of course we couldn't.

"I had envisaged a small school of fifteen to twenty hand-picked students from amongst whom Molly could create some really worthwhile dancers, if necessary teaching them for nothing.

"We started the venture with Natasha and Bishek Lisak who at that time had a studio in Golders Green. Dame Ninette de Valois, Dame Alicia Markova and Sir Anton Dolin all agreed to become our Patrons, Dame Ninette opening the school at a party held at Ivy House, calling it the 'London School of Classical Dance', not realising at the time that it had the same initials as the London School of Contemporary Dance, and caused Robin to change the name to 'London Contemporary Dance School'. During this period Molly was invited by Clare several times to go and teach in Houston, which she loved doing, as she found the dancers were physically very strong and hard working.

"Three years later we parted from Natasha and Bishek and opened our own school in a studio near our house in St John's Wood, calling it the 'Lake School of Dance', our Patrons very graciously moving with us."

The new brochure of the Lake School of Dance stated:

"The school believes that professional dancers for the theatre can be better produced by teachers who have had a long association with the theatre — teachers who are a direct link with the great dancers and teachers of the early part of the century.

"The classical technique correctly taught is a foundation for all forms of dance, and a body correctly created through the classical technique should be capable of adapting to any form of dance."

In spite of this the broad curriculum included not only ballet (taught by Molly and Travis), but also contemporary dance and choreography (Naomi Benari), national (Robert Harold), pas de deux (Travis), repertoire (Molly), historical dance (Belinda Quirey), and music (Maria Garzoh). For a short time the school also ran a junior department for children, and the dance in education company Dance For Everyone was linked to the school, thus affording opportunities for the students, several of whom were later accepted into classical companies, to work for children in their schools.

Molly was as demanding as ever, and she demonstrated every exercise, never sitting down once throughout her classes, which were a joy. In Molly's opinion, placing was one of the most important aspects of technique. While she was teaching at the London Contemporary Dance School, Molly had been invited to Australia as a guest teacher with the Australian Ballet, and writing about her in the *Sydney Morning Herald* of December 20th 1978, Jill Sykes remarked how she noticed Molly constantly moving the dancers' torsos to a precise point in relation to their feet. Molly explained the reason for this was that "the placing of a dancer is as logical as engineering", and she told Miss Sykes that Pavlova, whom she admired so much, never missed a performance due to injury because she was so beautifully aligned over her feet. Molly was full of praise for the Australian dancers, who she felt to be as good as the Stuttgart Ballet, which at that time she considered to be "one of the best in the world".[2] The emphasis on placing continued to be the focal point of Molly's teaching until her death and all her students, however talented or otherwise they may have been, were always perfectly placed.

As part of a very strong technique, Molly taught and expected a dance quality which is rarely seen nowadays. This was not a sugary icing on top of the technique, but an integral part of each movement — it was not possible to execute them in any other way. This was how Molly had been trained by Cecchetti, and she was very anxious that his teachings should be preserved; she looked very frail and there was an unspoken determination among the students who adored her to do as she asked. They made a special effort to learn and remember what she taught them, because they knew that her health was deteriorating and that she would not be with them for long; they wanted to be able to continue to teach in the same way after she had gone, because they knew that that was what she wanted above all. But Molly now began to teach less and less.

"Molly throughout her life could rarely be persuaded to see a doctor, but as she became weaker I insisted. Tuberculosis was diagnosed. Tuberculosis in its early stages can now be easily cured, but Molly had left it too long and at this stage there was little that could be done. Reluctantly I closed the school."

After dance, Molly's greatest love was for animals, and in Turkey she and Travis at one time had as many as thirty cats and ten dogs, for she picked up every stray. Now in London they had only four cats and two dogs, some of whom they had brought back with them from Turkey. Every Christmas and birthday, Travis used to send a card to Molly from each of the animals, with poems and drawings about their antics, and above all expressing over and over again his, disguised as their, undiminished love for her.

"Molly sank into a state of semi-consciousness and I spent all my time at her bedside. One morning the voice which had helped me during the war suddenly said: 'Sit and hold her hand'. I did. There was a pulse beating at the side of her neck. The voice seemed to say 'When that pulse stops Molly will be dead'. Almost at once the pulse did stop and the journey was over."

Thoughts On Dance

Molly's admiration of Cecchetti had inspired her all her life, and the lessons she had learnt from him were passed on to Travis who has incorporated them into the wealth of knowledge he has accumulated throughout his life of dancing with the greatest of this century.

Molly wrote of Cecchetti:

> "The very warmth of his personality makes the word 'method' in its dry as dust implications to my mind unsuitable. His was a way to dance, not a 'method', an essentially professional teacher of professionals and potential professionals; he helped to sustain the glorious company of Diaghilev at the height of its dance capacity and to guide his young and improved students towards the magic entrance to the theatre. To think of him only as the creator of a 'Syllabus', a 'method', is to underrate him and to lose the view of his importance as an inspired purely professional teacher. With the best will in the world it is impossible to transmit the genius of a particular teacher to paper, the result is apt to become as flat as the paper. It was a mighty and praiseworthy effort to attempt the task of transferring Cecchetti to paper. That it has been successful is, I think, greatly in doubt. The skeleton is there to a certain extent, but the spirit and understanding is missing. The syllabus has become an end in itself and is used as a yardstick by which to measure the pass or fail of a candidate: 'She knows the syllabus, she must pass'. This is I think death to the memory of a great teacher. I find it very hard to hear Cecchetti belittled and ridiculed by many people who have never bothered to find out the fundamental logic and beauty of his teaching. Nor are they altogether to blame; take away or rather distort the line particularly the arms, lose the co-ordination, breadth of movement and elevation he so loved, and what is left — stiff and apparently out of date exercises, a series of syllabi, more and more syllabi, each getting further and further away from their alleged originator. I do not think it possible to tie down Cecchetti to the arbitrary detail that is so often insisted upon in the examinations. There is a lack of continuity which is very far removed from the great teacher of great dancers — the exciting explosive and very often careless teacher of detail, inspired teacher of fundamental truths that he was."[1]

In spite of common belief, Cecchetti did not have a "set" class for every day of the week; each skill did indeed have its special day allotted to it, but his classes were never the same as there was enough in each day's syllabus to last at least eight hours, and Cecchetti always selected from his wealth of material which Molly likened to an encyclopaedia. It was only in his last years, when his memory was failing, that he allocated exercises to different days of the week to be certain that every aspect of technique would be covered and would not be forgotten. When Cyril Beaumont formed the Cecchetti Society in 1922 to ensure that the work of the great teacher would be perpetuated, Molly was asked to join the committee, together with Marie Rambert, Ninette de Valois, Margaret Craske, Derra de Moroda, and Jane Forestier. Molly was truly one of the few dancers in England who really understood the work of the great Maestro and was able to teach it. At the Golden Jubilee Dinner of the Cecchetti Society in 1972, Molly's address, which was read by Travis, was on "Cecchetti the Teacher", and in it she amusingly described the experience of being one of his pupils (see Appendix A).

When Molly returned from Turkey, she had been invited to see the "Cecchetti" syllabus as taught in some of the larger ballet schools. Molly did not make a value judgement, but said that good as it might be, it was not Cecchetti. She wrote:

> "The approach to ballet today and Cecchetti's own approach are two very different things. Let me make it quite clear, that this is not in praise or condemnation of either point of view, not an endeavour to illustrate how and why they differ, but just to emphasise the fact that they differ very widely.
>
> "It is not, I think, constructive to bypass his quality and alter his syllabi to suit a very different concept of dance and call it modernising Cecchetti; even that which is being 'modernised' has ceased already to hold the quality of his dance.
>
> "Let us remember that it is the dance of Pavlova, Karsavina and the artists and choreographers of the great Diaghilev period which is being changed almost beyond recognition to fit the requirements of a very different style.
>
> "To adapt his approach in the name of 'modernisation' is not constructive nor is it fair to the original. Cecchetti's own very different understanding of dance would be far more useful at the present time when ballet in England has gone a long way to becoming a monopoly of style and presentation."

Molly asserted that while Cecchetti might have developed his way of teaching had he still been alive, it appeared that the fundamentals of dance and the syllabus were not being taught in the way Cecchetti himself would have done. She expressed her views in a talk which she gave at the International Cecchetti conference in 1976 and these were printed under the heading "Cecchetti Remembered" in *Dance and Dancers* in November 1976 (see Appendix B); at the Easter Seminar of the Society in 1977, Molly was invited to give a class in which she gave "emphasis to the quality of movement" of Cecchetti's training. She also expressed her ideas on quality in an article entitled ''Teaching for Quality'', which was published in *Dancers and Dancers* in 1962 and reprinted after her death (see Appendix C).

In December 1919 Molly had received Cecchetti's diploma, which he gave to pupils who had successfully completed a course of study with him; it stated that she had ''regulièrement suivi ses cours de Danse Classique Théâtrale'', and she was given authorisation to pass on his teachings. Travis stresses that the training was in *theatre* dance, and is convinced that the best teachers can be drawn from ex-dancers who have a successful career behind them: they have not only their knowledge of technique to offer, but also their experience of performing in the theatre, of communicating with an audience, of pacing themselves, and of understanding how to get the maximum effort from a muscle or a joint with a minimum of strain, thus enabling them to give eight performances per week in spite of tiredness and without injury. None of these skills can be taught by someone who has never experienced them.

Travis would also like to see successful former dancers join the examining bodies, and a professional dancers' diploma added to the present examination system, which would indicate that the recipient would stand a reasonable chance of being employed by a professional company. The assessment would take the form of an audition or performance, and would judge the quality of movement and the ability to use technique to create every form of emotion. The examining board would include representatives from the major companies, who would thus be constantly aware of what was being produced and would, on the other hand, keep the examining bodies informed of what they wanted. Travis believes very strongly that as the ultimate in professional dance training is the theatre, the assessment would have to relate to the companies' needs, and he is hopeful that such a diploma may soon be introduced.

Travis has carried this concern for the relationship between dance training and the theatre to the training of young children. He had been for some time on the Council of the ''Sunshine Dance Competitions'', which organised competitions as theatrical performances to help raise funds for the blind, but when, in the early 1980s, it began to lose money it ceased to operate, and in his efforts to promote the concept that dance is performance rather than examinations, Travis conceived of the idea of forming the ''All England Dance Association'', which would arrange children's dance competitions all over the country culminating in a bi-annual gala performance in London. He wrote to fifty people and put together a committee. Travis himself was the Chairman until 1987 when he handed over to Richard Clarke, Alicia Markova graciously agreed to become the first President, Malcolm Hickling became the Secretary, and John Gandolphi the Treasurer. The organisation flourished, and is now a major force in the world of festivals, thanks largely to the untiring efforts of Malcolm Hickling. At a committee meeting in November 1989, further changes and developments were decided. As Travis explained:

"We wanted to bring back the magic of the dance, and we knew that while some children have a dance quality within them at an early age, it has to be nurtured and encouraged; we hope that the competitions will give them the opportunity to develop it, to bring it out, and thereby to bring back the magic of the dance. It is therefore necessary that the competitions appear in no way to be examinations. Technique is *necessary, but only as a means to an end, and not as an end in itself.*

"The festivals should be run as much as possible as professional theatre performances. We talked about reaching out into the black void of the auditorium, grasping the audience, and making it react to whichever emotion is being transmitted. But in many festivals, that black void becomes a half-lit hall, in which mothers and children are milling about, talking quite loudly, and making it impossible for the dancers to feel any form of theatricality.

"We decided that the festivals have to be run in such a way as to relate entirely to the theatre, the adjudicants must relate to the theatre, and their criticisms and remarks must relate to the theatre. If we can do this, it will be one corner where the magic of the dance is being revived."

Travis believes that the difference between dance training for the theatre and that given for other purposes is not always fully appreciated, and that the dance training of those who wish to become professional dancers is sometimes too analytical.

"Dance lessons are given for a variety of reasons: to help deportment, to give self confidence, to help the handicapped, to help athletes to obtain a supple movement, to keep slim, to help 'Mums with tums', and so forth. BUT THEY HAVE NO RELATIONSHIP TO TRAINING A DANCER FOR THEATRE. Some people say that one comes out of the other and mix them together much to the detriment of both sides. They are completely different from the word 'go'. One says 'God has given you a body, do what you can with it for your own enjoyment'. The other says 'God has given you a body, discipline and train it so that it will do what ever you want it to do for the enjoyment of an audience in a theatre'.

"Movement cannot be satisfactorily translated into words. We can give a step a name but the name will be meaningless until the step has been demonstrated. Even so, in the classical dance one step may have a number of names. For instance, petit tours, enchainé, deboulé all mean the same thing. If one knows the names of a sufficient number of steps one can write out a syllabus but again the syllabus is meaningless without demonstration.

''Some steps are there to help build the body instrument, others to help that instrument transmit, but unless these steps are correctly done they often do more harm than good and can even damage the body irrevocably. There can be good syllabi and bad syllabi, but the syllabus is not of major importance, it is the way that syllabus is taught, and the ability of the teacher to transmit the fundamentals of movement that lie behind it.

''It has been said of the English that they give a thing a name, pigeon-hole it and think they understand it. It is only a step to analysing a thing and thinking we can do it. A teacher who does not fully understand through personal experience the fundamentals of movement tends to fall back on analysis: 'The eyes should be here, the nose should be there, the third finger of the left hand does this, the first finger of the right hand does that'. With such an academic approach any natural co-ordinated dance quality that a student may have is killed. Conversely, it is possible for a teacher to put every part of a pupil's body in the right position, but unless that pupil has a natural feeling for co-ordinated, rhythmical movement, commencing in the centre of the body and radiating to infinity there will be no dance.

''We used to go to a 'teacher', now we attend a 'school', and the teacher becomes subservient to the school. This is reflected in the present application forms for accreditation, which want to know the number of studios and of students, the course of study, and the number of years the school has existed, etc. etc., but the names of the teachers are never requested. Few of those great masters such as Cecchetti would have been accredited today as the premises in which they taught would not today be considered satisfactory. Many of the old teachers were idealists who would teach a gifted pupil for nothing if he or she considered that they had the necessary potential, but would rarely have encouraged an untalented one to continue to study.

''The great teachers of the past would bring into the studio a lifetime of experience in the theatre, while now a school often advertises 'fully qualified staff', and sometimes 'fully qualified' means that the teachers in question have obtained qualifications to teach dance having never put a foot on a professional stage, and while these may be excellent 'teachers', their scope is limited as it is rarely possible to transmit satisfactorily that which one has not to some degree experienced.

''The body is the 'instrument' on which the dancer 'plays', and the teacher has the dual job of creating that instrument at the same time as he or she is helping the dancer to acquire the technique to play on it, and that instrument for dancing must be developed by dance. If the body has been satisfactorily developed it should respond freely to any form of dance, and if the dancer has been given a satisfactory technique he or she should be able to execute any form of dance. But a good body and a good technique are not sufficient; there is a third element, which enables the dancer to use the body and technique to make the audience forget the body and the technique and be conscious only of the emotion being transmitted. It is this element which creates the magic of the dance.''

Travis is convinced that for some time choreography has not been used as a vehicle for communication, but has been more a means of showing off acrobatic ability or "exploring new ways of moving", although he would question the use of the word "new". For example, are falls and dancing off balance really new? When Fokine demanded in "Les Sylphides" that his dancers drift and float and fall, was he not asking them to play with their weight? Because ballet had become so rigid, it was necessary to create new techniques, and jazz and contemporary dance have filled these gaps also. Musicals and musical films which are revived today require dancers with jazz or contemporary technique, and yet when they were first produced, many of the dancers who had had only ballet training (which included a little character or national dance), were able adequately to execute what was demanded of them. He remembers how each ballet demanded a different quality of movement which every dancer was able to produce, whereas in England he now often sees a "balletic" style superimposed on every ballet.

He feels that some post-modern dance has become the focal point of those interested in the avant garde and that, in their obsession with the new and the different, some post-modern dancers have lost their way, and have forgotten how dance can create atmosphere and mood, and above all can communicate emotion and excitement without which it ceases to interest a wide public.

Dancers either have to use their art and technique to evoke emotions, "*to make the audience laugh, cry, stand up, sit down, shake them, make them do what you want — if you can, you are an artist, if you cannot, you should give up*", or they have to be such virtuosi that the movements themselves create the excitement. But for that, their technique, in spite of the progress which so many claim to see today, is not good enough. Thirty or forty years ago, eight or ten pirouettes from a male dancer was a usual occurrence, and when they did a double turn in the air finishing on one knee, they finished the tour, established the kneeling position while in the air, and then landed — "*so much more exciting to watch*".

However, he is very optimistic about the future; he is constantly being approached by established professional dancers who feel that something is missing in the way they dance, and who want to learn from him how to use their often considerable technique in order to gain an emotional quality, and to communicate with their audiences. They are often surprised that Travis's teaching also helps them achieve greater technical feats with a reduction in effort. Travis on his part is constantly gratified by the increased warmth and power of their performance as they dance in ballets in which he has coached them.

And so Molly's wish is being fulfilled: young dancers are again learning to dance as her beloved Cecchetti would have wanted, and Dance as she knew it will not die.

APPENDIX A

Cecchetti Society

"Dear Maestro Cecchetti. Small, round and rosy, benevolent, eager, irritable, sometimes indignant (as he was on the occasion when my father tried, quite unsuccessfully, to disentangle his income tax) and, when our general inept idiocies became too much for him — QUITE FURIOUS.

"What love he gave us. . . . And what energy he expended, trying with every atom of his dynamic force and enthusiasm to make us realise the necessity of understanding the basic principles of his teaching. I think we can never under-estimate the value of these basic principles to ballet then, now and always. The straight, poised body, the weight carried by those strong muscles in the stomach and lower part of the back, the top part of the body without tension, lightly lifted off the hips until one could almost sense an airborne quality. 'Into the floor as far as you go over it.' 'Take the weight slap over the feet, no matter how wide and high or how light and swift you go.' Everything is logically placed in order to give the body the utmost chance to master the demands of his method and at the same time create an impression of ease and beauty. Strength and relaxation must go together to achieve dance quality.

"One of his favourite remarks was: 'You must first make a good violin before you can play a beautiful air on it'. (A remark to me: 'Vous êtes jolie belle fille mais un morceau de bois'. That placed me well below Stradivarius level.) His French, incidentally, was colourful but extremely peculiar.

"One recalls his insistence that every line and every movement must be followed through to its ultimate conclusion. The arms, legs, head and body co-ordinating and continuing through to the next movement without a break. This of course necessitates complete control of demi-plié. No twist, no distortion of the hips was allowed. Wide, balanced arms and no tension or strain in the shoulders. 'Cover the ground my children' 'Wings on your feet' 'Stand in the air' 'The ground is your best friend, stroke it, sink gently into it, never hit it.' It we could only master a modicum of this, then we had some glimpse of that rare avis, 'dance quality'.

"Nothing, so to speak, was to be put on from the outside. Classic simplicity — no coyness, no mannerisms, just an inner understanding without meaningless decoration. All the great Diaghilev dancers of the day came to Maestro. Spessivtseva, Dubrovska, Schollar, Nemchinova, Tchernicheva and many others. And what dancers they were. And all in class with the shaggy young students and being corrected as we were corrected. They worked as hard as we worked and that was very hard indeed. And they all worked with the enthusiasm with which he inspired us. Think of the opportunities we had to learn as we watched them. Alas, where are the snows of yesteryear?

"What fun the Maestro was too. Running round the room in a fury caricaturing our horrible attitudes: 'Attitude de petits chiens'. Hurling his stick with unerring aim at one's legs for sloppy work. (Learning to jump over it greatly improved one's elevation.) Hearing those sarcastic words 'ma belle' that meant that you were in for it in a big way. One day ending a pirouette en dedans with great enthusiasm in a wildly thrown back efface position, I heard the fatal words: 'Ma belle, ça c'est pas une grace, c'est une disgrace.' Sometimes when he could no longer bear our uninspiring efforts to do a renversé, he would rush into the centre of the room and execute a renversé such as one dreamed of — so swift and exciting a movement it was. In those days I thought that his plump tummy must help him balance. Now I know he was merely applying his principles of placing.

"He told us that in his youth he shaved in attitude on the half point to attain more strength and control. Now perhaps when shaving is rare and a good attitude rarer still, the value of this may be somewhat obscure. When I first joined him I was given a week to learn the entire work covering his major syllabi. After a week one took one's chance in front of the class when called and one was expected to know, at any rate, the body of his daily programme. This meant hours of homework, racking one's brains to remember and write out each enchainment as it came up. Later he would send new students to me to learn their daily programme before he would take them into his classes.

"For the few of us left who were lucky enough to come into contact with his personal genius, we can show our gratitude to him by endeavouring to pass on something of the treasures we learned, and keep his teaching as near the inspired source as possible. Salute to our dearly beloved Cecchetti."

APPENDIX B

Cecchetti Remembered by Molly Lake

One of the most popular talks at the International Cecchetti Conference, organised by the Gulbenkian Foundation, was that given by Molly Lake and heartily endorsed by Derra de Moroda, Dame Peggy van Praagh and Mary Skeaping. She warns about the dangers of syllabus work swamping the true quality of his dance.

Cecchetti, ballet master to the Diaghilev company and to Pavlova, teacher of most of the great dancers in his day, was a creature of the theatre quite individual in his approach to dance. So, the further we go from him in time, the fainter, more adulterated, more diffused and distracted becomes the quality of the original and what was in his case inspiration becomes a series of written lists conveying nothing of his quality.

To see Cecchetti's little round figure jumping from his chair in a flurry of indignation and executing a renversé or a pirouette with a brilliance and excitement unknown today, was an unforgettable experience. What are we doing with the genius of Cecchetti?

Granted none of us has his genius, but could we not have endeavoured to keep some of those qualities he loved best instead of analysing, pruning, and pigeon-holing the bare bones until the vital essence is gone for ever?

Why are we going so far away from his dance — not method — not syllabi but movement?

Syllabi can be confined to paper but movement is a language in itself and cannot be translated into the written word, and movement is *dance*. Cecchetti *is* a classic teacher — I use classic in the sense that it implies the best — and I use *is* not *was* because these classic teachers have no enclosed period. Many of them vanished long ago, but what they had to hand on to future generations in their basic knowledge of rhythm and movement can never vanish as long as *dance* remains. His syllabi have been modernised — a pity, I think, to chop up beautiful and valuable exercises, but not entirely destructive provided the basic rhythm and dance quality of the emerging dancer can be kept in view. It is not a question of technical facts, it is a question of subjecting those facts to the rhythm and movement of dance. Technique should be a servant to dance; it has no value in itself.

Why is this invaluable gift of dance being lost? First, I think, because many of the teachers of today have concentrated on the written word and found their strength in analysis and the examiners have followed their lead. Second, because the word "technique" is so often misused and misinterpreted: it certainly implies the strength and ability to execute a wide range of difficulties, but it should also imply the style, dance quality, and understanding with which they are done.

Once the basic rhythm of dance has been analysed out of the body, we are virtually killing that which we aim to produce.

Stance

Let us try to see how destructive is the tense stance of today to Cecchetti's dance. His strong lift was from those muscles across the stomach and in the *lower* part of the back (not in the upper part as taught now) thereby taking the weight off his hips, legs and feet. Above the waist a lightly lifted, poised, almost airborne quality enabled the dancer to take his or her weight right over the feet no matter in what direction or with what speed the dancer moved.

This is a different picture from the arched back, thrust forward ribcage and over all tension seen now. How can a rigid and impacted body fly or float, dart or leap or create any magic of movement? Where is the brilliance and vitality of Cecchetti's day?

Line

What has happened to Cecchetti's arabesque, where is his beautifully balanced line? The front arm lifted at eye level, the head raised looking along the hand, the hips and shoulders facing the same way, the raised leg continuing the line of the front arm, the back arm raised about two inches directly above the raised leg. Now we often see a twisted and raised hip with an almost ugly, over high extension of the lifted leg, the front arm at a bare shoulder level, the other arm at a right angle to the side and a head without lift. Perhaps today's tense and impacted stance make it anatomically impossible to execute Cecchetti's line.

Why are his arm positions lost? The fifth en bas shortened, held and stiffly away from the body so cramped that the arms resemble the claws of a crab. The fifth devant equally cramped and ugly. The fifth en haut not only shortened and cramped but held too far back. Where is Cecchetti's wreath for the head and face, the raised hands held where the eyes could see them without straining the head and neck?

Why can we no longer give the illusion of projecting line beyond ourselves as we could in the days of Cecchetti's light stance?

Where is that easy and flowing coordination of arms, legs, head and body allowing the dancer to fall naturally into those movements and rhythms that make up dance quality?

Cecchetti loved elevation and ballon. "Use the floor, the floor is your best friend. Never hit it. Sink into it as far as you would go over it and stand in the air." It would be lovely to see that again.

See, too, that flow, continuity and coverage of ground, that almost animal quality joining one movement to the next instead of the hard little jumps seeming without follow through.

How can we cover ground or jump without understanding the use of the floor, or achieve continuity or fluidity with every muscle tense? Strength and tension are replacing poise, lightness and lift.

"Terre à terre" work, those light skimming movements where the supple play of the feet takes the place of height and depth, played a large part in Cecchetti's dance. He asked for speed, lightness and a great coverage of ground, accented rhythm and a great accuracy. Accuracy, I am sure, is there now, but over tension and the inability to keep the weight always over the feet, combined with heavy pointe shoes, make speed and supple footwork almost impossible.

Nostalgically I can still see Cecchetti's first studio in London, in that dark, very dirty, semi-comic centre of revolution, Chandos Hall, where the strains of his whistling became entangled with the strains of the "Internationale" or the "Red Flag" or what ever it was called.

Later, and still more nostalgically, I can see him coming into the Shaftesbury Avenue studio, often grumbling to himself, his overcoat down to his ankles, his stick in one hand, a bag of food and a small bottle of milk for his cat Mamie in the other.

Having fed the cat he sat himself down in his small wooden armchair waiting for the daily kiss which he expected and received from each one of his students. What warmth and friendliness was there. The new students, "the little rats", all mixed up with the famous names.

In the centre, his class was placed in a semi-circle moving round one place every day so in due course one found oneself standing in front of some famous star.

I can see him pointing to Spessivtseva, that frail and lovely creature, and saying triumphantly in his very bad French "Voilà la danse".

I can see Lopokova hiding in the dressing room rather than face one of his particularly demanding pirouettes. . . .

Sad to say that with him went that eagerness, vitality, sense of theatre that was so much a part of his dance.

I know that it was impossible to enclose Cecchetti's dynamic personality in the written word, but could we not have kept more closely to those basic principles of dance which he laid down so clearly?

In our concentration on analysis and detail are we losing sight of the fact that the real Cecchetti, the timeless teacher of dance, is in danger of being lost for ever?

Let us think about this modernised Cecchetti, or, more important, the way it is being applied, and ask ourselves how much longer we can go on calling it *his*.

Let us go back to Cecchetti as it was; after all, who are we to improve on it?

A dancer trained as Cecchetti taught — with his beautifully balanced, well thought out exercises, the accent on his light easy stance and poise, his long line, his co-ordination and continuity of movement and coverage of ground, his rhythm and use of the floor, is as timeless as *he* is and can fulfil the needs of any period.

APPENDIX C

Teaching for Quality

Many people think that dance teaching, especially in Britain, is not achieving what it could and should do. In coming months we intend to present several points of view on this subject and, through this, to initiate a necessary public debate. Here, to start the series, is a voice from the past, that of Molly Lake, who died a few months ago. In September 1962 she contributed an article to *Dance and Dancers* about qualities that were in danger of being lost. Her thoughts then are still relevant today, so we reprint what she wrote for a new generation of readers, audiences and dancers.

As we become more and more addicted to the reproduction of the old classical ballets so we seem to go further and further away from the placing and quality needed for their execution.

The stance which appears now to be insisted upon in the training of a dancer is one with the rib cage expanded, ''Lead with your chests, children'', the back arched and the shoulders forced back, ''Crack a nut between your shoulder blades, dears'', the arms tense, contracted and forced back even further than the line of the shoulders. Surely all the facility and beauty of the classical, or any other dance, is defeated by this position — try it yourself and see how it is virtually impossible to move easily in any direction.

How is it possible to execute a ballet like ''Les Sylphides'' with the melting, floating quality and the lightness and poise which Fokine declared was its essence with the body in such a position?

That the dancers of the Bolshoi Ballet should favour this stance and be able to survive, in my opinion only goes to prove what marvellous athletes they are, but the same cannot be said of the English dancers, who have neither the same strength nor vitality.

Think back, those of us who can remember, to the dancers of the Diaghilev period and to Anna Pavlova. What an illusion of flight they could create, what speed, poise and elegance were theirs! I spent three years with Anna Pavlova, watching her dance every night. I was always dazzled by the swiftness and brilliance of her movements and her quite incredible balance, not realising that it was the perfect placing of her weight that allowed her to dance as she did. Later, in Paris, I was privileged for six months to watch Olga Spessiva at her practice in the old Olympia Music Hall — was there ever such a perfect placing as hers? She explained to me that all the strength for the dance should be taken from the lower part of the spine to the waist and from the base of the stomach to the waist, lifting the weight right off the hips and legs. That the upper part of the body should be only lightly lifted and be supple enough to follow the quickest movement of the feet so that the weight could always be centred and there was no limit to speed and lightness of movement.

Almost any young dancer of today would tell you: ''We have far more technique than they had''. Have they? It all depends what one calls technique. They have very strongly trained legs and feet with a very high extension usually with a very much displaced hip, and they are able to cope with the ''concrete'' point shoes they appear to insist upon, the busy tap of which does not seem to disturb them at all, though it is reminiscent of Karsavina's dance in ''Parade'', which was executed to the tapping of a typewriter. What other claims to technique have they? Elevation is still rare (at least in British ballet), and even when there is elevation it seems to have more the quality of an athletic feat than the soaring flight of the dancer. Speed and brilliance are rarer still, small batterie requiring either of these qualities is almost non-existent. Pirouettes? Yes, plenty of them, mostly strong and straight, but lacking something of the speed and sparkle which gave a pirouette its raison d'être, and here again we come to placing. With all the strain and strength in the upper part of the body as it is now, it is impossible to use the head with sufficient flexibility to give the ultra-sharp ''flick'' on each turn which makes a pirouette worth looking at. There is, as I said before, an enormously high extension of leg, but even then the hips are usually displaced — hence the lower part of the body and the thighs are often thickened. The displacing of the hips makes it impossible to lift the base of the spine, where the strength of the ballet dancer should really be. By forcing the shoulders and arms back and examining the rib cage the upper part of the body is irretrievably thickened, and though the present-day dancer is usually thin she is rarely tapered and fine — her placing makes it impossible. Dance is movement; surely it is common sense to place the weight in such a position as to facilitate that movement.

A straight back, a light lift over the feet and off the hips, and a flexible and unstrained upper torso, is surely the basis on which to build your race of super dancers. Must we have all this tension? What is it for, where does it get us? Ask a dancer to do some very simple movement, and enough strength is brought into play to qualify them as all-in wrestlers.

What about present-day arms, too? Again, tense your shoulders and your well-thrown-forward rib cage and see what flow or follow through of arm movement remains; how is it possible to project your line beyond yourself when that line all too often ends somewhere by the ribs? The upper part of the body being a sort of uneasy superstructure bearing no relation to the lower. Touch the arms and hands and one meets with the quality of well-stretched wire, which is not the most rewarding of mediums to ''express'' with.

There is also, I think, far too much emphasis laid on barre work and far too little on a balanced lesson which will teach the dancer how to apply what we hope he or she has learnt at the barre in the way of placing, etc. It is very nice to see a developpé à la seconde taken at ear level, and if it can be done lightly and straight as Spessiva did it, it can look very beautiful, but done on an ugly spread hip it has little merit, especially when the shoulders and arms are strained almost beyond endurance.

I often hear it suggested that ''Ballet is so dull now, there is no excitement''. It is hard not to be dull, hard to move freely and expressively, hard not to lack rhythmical co-ordination, excitement and emotional reaction to music if the body has become a cage of unbalanced and tense bones and muscle which defy their owner to express anything other than sheer physical and mental strength in order to move at all (MOVE is the operative word) in such a position. Why, oh why?

NOTES AND SOURCES

The British Library
The Theatre Museum Library and Archive
Jane Pritchard, Rambert Dance

I. **As It Was In The Beginning** (1899 – 1909)

II. **The Consequences Of A Strike** (1914 – 1926)

III. **Molly Spreads Her Wings** (1909 – 1922)

1. *Dance and Dancers*, August 1954

Molly's notebooks

IV. **What Shall We Do With Travis?** (1926 – 1934)

1. *Morning Post*, September 25th, 1931
2. *The Times*, February 1st, 1934

V. **Pavlova Years** (1922 – 1926)

Molly's notebooks and diaries
Letters from Cecchetti to Molly 1920 – 1923

1. "I Remember Pavlova" in *Dance and Dancers*, December 1950
2. *Dancing Times*, September 1923
3. Listed as O. Oliveroff in programme of November 7th, 1922
4. Arnold Haskell, "Anna Pavlova", London, The London Museum, 1956

VI. **In The Wilderness** (1926 – 1934)

1. *The Referee*, June 1928
2. Mary Clarke, "The Sadlers Wells Ballet", London, A. & C. Black, 1955
3. Georges Chapelot, in forward by Jean Laurent, to "Boris Kniasseff, 25 Années de Danse 1918 – 1943"
4. Conversation, 1985
5. Molly's Notebooks
6. February 8th, "Manon" with ballet
   March 28th, "Samson and Delilah" with "Scherezade"
   March 29th, "Traviata"
   April 2nd, "Salome", with "Scherezade"
   April 4th, "Carmen", with ballet
   April 5th, "Salome", with "Scherezade"
   April 10th, 14th, 16th, a Kniasseff ballet
   April 11th, "Tosca", with "Prince Igor"
7. Molly's Notebooks
8. *Musical Times* 1929
9. *Brighton and Hove Herald*, May 24th, 1930
10. *Daily Express*, July 28th 1930
11. Peggy van Praagh, "A Life for Dance" Macmillan, 1986
12. Molly's Notebooks
13. Conversation 1985
14. Molly's Notebooks

VII. **A Moment In Time** (Dandré) (1934 – 1935)

1. Molly's Notebooks
2. *Cape Argus*, May 29th 1934
3. *Cape Times*, May 29th 1934
4. *Cape Times*, July 15th 1934
5. *The Old Vic and Sadlers Wells Magazine*, No. 19, Vol. 2, September – October 1934
6. Conversation 1985
7. *The Star*, December 24th 1935
8. *Times of Ceylon*, February 15th 1935
9. *Bourse Egyptienne*, Cairo, April 4th 1935

VIII. **Fish And Actors** (Markova-Dolin) (1935 – 1937)

Conversation with Alicia Markova 1989

1. Molly's Notebooks
2. Molly's Notebooks
3. Conversation 1985
4. Conversation 1985
5. *Glasgow Herald*, April 24th 1937
6. *Nottingham Journal*, November 26th 1935
7. *Liverpool Daily Post*, November 21st 1935
8. *The Times*, December 24th 1935
9. *The Times*, December 24th 1935
10. *Glasgow Daily Record & Mail*, April 23rd 1936
11. *Newcastle Chronicle*, November 19th 1936

12. *Yorkshire Post*, November 12th 1936
13. *Edinburgh Evening Despatch*, May 6th 1936
14. *Nottingham Journal*, April 13th 1937
15. *Glasgow Herald*, April 29th 1936
16. *South Wales Echo and Express*, October 5th 1937
17. *Manchester Evening News*, May 23rd 1936
18. *Leeds Mercury*, April 13 1937
19. *Birmingham Post*, March 24th 1936
20. *Bristol Evening World*, December 11th 1936
21. *Evening News*, March 16th 1937
22. *Manchester Guardian*, March 23rd 1937
23. *Nottingham Journal*, April 13th 1937
24. *Nottingham Guardian*, April 13th 1937
25. *Bristol Evening World*, November 20th 1936

IX. **Interlude** (Ballet Intime) (1938 – 1939)

1. *Observer*, March 13th 1938
2. *What's On*, March 18th 1938
3. *Bexhill Observer*, June 11th 1938
4. *Guernsey Evening Press*, August 30th 1938
5. *Clacton Graphic and East Coast Illustrated News*, October 8th 1938
6. *The Granta*, January 25th 1939

Molly's Diaries

X. **Ballet and Bombs** (Arts Theatre Ballet) (1940 – 1941)

Molly's Diary

1. Arts Theatre Club programme, May 8th 1940
2. *Bystander*? 1940
3. Programme week beginning February 12th 1940
4. Programme week begining February 12th 1940
5. *Harrogate Herald*, July 24th 1940

XI. **You Are About To Become A Soldier** (1940 – 1942)

XII. **Nissen Huts and Aeroplane Hangars** (Ballet Guild) (1941 – 1945)

1. *Picture Post*, August 20th 1942
2. *Bath and Wilts Chronicle*, April 16th 1941
3. *Dance Magazine*, July 1988
4. *Dancing Times*, August 1941
5. *Weston Gazette*, April 1941/2?
6. *Yorkshire Post*, April 29th 1941
7. *Harrogate Herald*, April 30th 1941
8. *Evening News*, July 1st 1942
9. *The Queen*, February 24th 1943
10. John Pick, "Managing the Arts? The British Experience", London, Rhinegold, 1986, p. 37.

Molly's letters to Travis

XIII. **Camp Followers** (1945 – 1946)

Molly's Diary

1. *Polar Bear News*, November 16th 1945

Molly's letters to Travis

XIV. **I Looked For You On The Beaches** (1942 – 1945)

XV. **Dance On A Shoestring**
Embassy Ballet (1946 – September 1947)

1. *Bath and Wilts Chronical and Herald*, September 19th 1946
2. *Dorset Daily Echo*, September 26th 1946
3. *Southern Times*, September 27th 1946
4. *Brighton and Hove Herald*, September 7th 1946
5. *Hereford Citizen and Bulletin*, April 18th 1947
6. *Southampton Daily Echo*, May 6th 1947
7. John Pick, "Managing the Arts? The British Experience", London, Rhinegold, 1986, p. 41.

Molly's letters to Travis

Continental Ballet (1947 – 1954)

1. *Tunbridge Wells Advertiser*, 22nd September 1947/8?
2. *Birmingham Evening Dispatch*, September 7th 1948
3. *Bexhill-on-Sea Observer*, October 23rd 1948
4. *Cambridge Daily News*, October 4th 1950
5. *Recorder*, June 30th 1949
6. *Varsity*, November 6th 1948
7. *Stockton Express*, June 2nd 1949
8. *The Advertiser*, June 3rd 1949
9. *Essex County Telegraph*, August 25th 1950
10. *Cambridge Daily News*, October 4th 1950
11. *Southend-on-Sea and County Pictorial*, January 25th 1952
12. *The Times*, May 1st 1951
13. *Daily Mail*, May 1st 1951
14. *Eastern Evening News*, February 19th 1952

XVI. **For The Young**

1. "Dance in Education", Arts Council of Great Britain and Department of Education and Science, London, 1982
2. "The Glory of the Garden", Arts Council of Great Britain, 1984
3. *Huddersfield Daily Examiner*, November 15th 1950
4. "Experiment in Ballet", *Times Education Supplement*, 1948?50?

XVII. **The Building Of A Ballet** (Turkey) (1954 – 1974)

Conversation with Dame Ninette de Valois, 1989

1. Travis Kemp, "Starting from Scratch", in *Dance and Dancers*, December 1956
2. *Dance and Dancers*, December 1956
3. *Dance and Dancers*, December 1956
4. *Dance and Dancers*, November 1960
5. *Dance and Dancers*, November 1960
6. *The Week* (First English News weekly), published by Vedat Aut, February 6th 1957
7. *Ulus*, May 19th 1958
8. *The Week*, June 1961
9. *Johannesburg Star*, February 7th 1962

XVIII. **Journey's End** (1974 – 1986)

1. Conversation with Robin Howard, November 1988
2. *Sydney Morning Herald*, December 20th 1978

XIX. **Thoughts On Dance**

1. Notebooks

Conversation with Dame Ninette de Valois

Bibliography

Bibliography

Clarke, Mary. THE SADLERS WELLS BALLET (London, A. & C. Black, 1955).
Jackson Shiela. BALLET IN ENGLAND, A BOOK OF LITHOGRAPHS (New York and London, 1945).
Haskell, Arnold & Richardson P.J.S.(eds). WHO'S WHO IN BALLET 1932 (Dancing Times).
Kerensky, Oleg. ANNA PAVLOVA (London, Hamish Hamilton, 1973).
Lazzanini, John and Roberta. PAVLOVA (New York, Schirmer Books, 1980).
Pick, John. MANAGING THE ARTS? THE BRITISH EXPERIENCE (London, Rhinegold, 1986).
Rambert, Marie. QUICKSILVER (London, Macmillan, 1972).
Sexton, Christopher. PEGGY VAN PRAAGH, A LIFE OF DANCE (Australia, Macmillan, 1986).
de Valois, Ninette. STEP BY STEP (London, Allen, 1977).

"Starting from Scratch" in DANCE AND DANCERS (Hansom Books) Vol. 7, No. 12, December 1956.
"She Taught Diaghilev's Dancers" by Molly Lake, in DANCE AND DANCERS, August 1954.
"A Moment in Time" by Travis Kemp in DANCE (ISTD) Number 5, January 1988.
"Dance" (ISTD), No. 182, May 1988.
"Cecchetti Remembered" by Molly Lake, in DANCE AND DANCERS, November 1976 (Molly 2).
"The Dancing Times" March 1920; 1922 (p. 1011); May 1928 (no. 212); February 1935; August 1941; September 1941.
The Old Vic and Sadlers Wells Magazine, No. 19, Vol. 2, September – October 1934.
"Cecchetti the Teacher", Address by Molly Lake at Golden Jubilee Dinner of the Cecchetti Society, July 24th 1972.

Newspapers:

Bath and Wilts Chronicle and Herald, April 16th 1941; September 10th 1946.
Bexhill Observer, June 11th 1938.
La Bourse Egyptienne, 20th April 1936.
The Cape Argus, May 17th 1934; May 19th 1934; May 29th 1934.
Cape Times, May 19th 1934; May 29th 1934.
Daily Sketch, June 30th 1941.
Dorset County Chronicle, September 26th 1946.
Dorset Daily Echo, September 21st 1946; September 24th 1946; September 25th 1946.
The Evening News, July 1st 1942.
Evening Press (Guernsey), August 30th 1938.
Evening Standard, September 30th 1940.
The Glasgow Herald, April 29th 1936.
The Granta, January 25th 1929.
Harrogate Herald, August 3rd 1938; April 30th 1941.
Harrogate?, July 1940.

Hereford Citizen and Bulletin, April 18th 1947.
Isle of Thanet Gazette, June 18th 1938.
Kent Messenger, April 11th 1947 (or 1st?).
The Leeds Mercury, April 13th 1936.
The Polar Bear News, Neheim, November 16th 1945; December 7th 1945.
Picture Post, August 28th 1943.
The Queen, July 2nd 1941; February 24th 1943.
Radio Times, April 18th 1947.
The Sketch, May 1st 1940.
Southend Times and Recorder, October 30th 1946; November 6th 1946; November 13th 1946.
South Wales Echo and Express, October 5th 1937.
Southern Daily Echo, May 6th 1947.
Southern Times, September 20th 1946.
Sunday Times (S. Africa), July 15th 1934.
The Star (Johannesburg), February 7th 1962.
The Sydney Morning Herald, December 20th 1978.
The Times, February 1st 1934; March 22nd 1944.
Weston Gazette, April 1941.
Weston Mercury, April 26th 1941.
The Western Mail (Perth), January 17th 1935.
Wolverhampton Express and Star, May 13th 1941; May 5th 1943.
Yorkshire Post, April 29th 1941.

Letters from Cecchetti to Molly 1920 – 1923.

Repertoire

This list of ballets in which Molly and Travis danced and those which Molly choreographed, is based on their archival material and is not necessarily complete. The dates refer to the first time their appearance in a work is referred to in each company.

From 1925 onwards both Molly and Travis were principal dancers. Where their role is not listed, this is because they often danced different roles in the same work on different occasions.

Where the exact date of the premiere is known, this is given below.

Where the choreographer was not mentioned in a programme, this has been left blank.

Where no designer was mentioned, this is because there usually was none.

	Choreographer	*Music*	*Design*
1917			
London *Coliseum Theatre 13.7.1917* BEFORE DAWN (THE SWINBURNE BALLET) Molly — Solo	Astafieva	Norman O'Neill	Sheringham
Kingsway Theatre HOLOFERNES (Play) Molly — Solo			
1920			
Coliseum Theatre *With Karsàvina 15.3.1920* THE TRUTH ABOUT THE RUSSIAN DANCERS Molly		M. Helmund	
1921			
Paris *Pavlova Ballet* "CHEVRE PIED" Molly	Ivan Clustine		

DIVERTISSEMENT			
PRIMAVERA		M. Helmund	
Molly			

1922

Bournemouth
With Tamara Karsavina

BACCHANALE		Glazunov	
Molly			

Far East Tour with Pavlova
1922 – 1923

AUTUMN LEAVES Molly	Pavlova	Chopin	(Korovine)
CHOPINIANA Molly	Fokine	Chopin	
COPPELIA (Act I) Molly		Delibes	(Soudekine)
THE MAGIC FLUTE Molly — Oberon, dressed as a Hermit	Petipa**	Drigo	
THE SLEEPING BEAUTY (Ballet in 1 act) Molly — Lilac Fairy	arr. Clustine	Tchaikovsky	
SNOWFLAKES (Ballet in one act from Nutcracker) Molly — Pas de Trois	arr. Clustine	Tchaikovsky	Urban
DIVERTISSEMENT Molly			
BLUE DANUBE WALTZ		J. Strauss	
BOHEMIAN DANCE		Minkus	
MAZOURKA	Petipa	Glinka	
RUSSIAN DANCE	(Clustine)	Tchaikovsky	

London
Covent Garden 1923

DON QUIXOTE	arr. Novikoff	Minkus	Costumes and Scenery: Korovine
INVITATION TO THE DANCE		Carl-Maria Weber	arr. Zaglich

Pavlova Tour U.S.A.

1924

AMARILLA Molly — a Marchioness	arr. Clustine	Drigo, Glazunov	Barbier
BLUE DANUBE WALTZ Molly		J. Strauss	
DIONYSYUS Molly	arr. Clustine	Tscherepnine	de Lipsky
THE FAIRY DOLL Molly — a Porcelain Doll	arr. Clustine	Bayer, et al	Soudeikine
ORIENTAL IMPRESSIONS Molly — C. Krishna and Rada	F. Uday Shankar	Colomata Banerji	O. Allegri
VISIONS (from THE SLEEPING BEAUTY) Molly — Fairy Lilac	arr. Clustine	Tchaikovsky	Bardas
DIVERTISSEMENT: Molly			
RAPSODIE		Liszt	
OBERTASS		Levandovsky Russonoff*	
GYPSY DANCE		Dargomyjski	
RUSSIAN DANCE		Rubenstein- Tchaikovsky	

1925

Berlin GRIECHISCHER TANZ Molly		Brahms	
Queens Theatre, London 8.12.1925 Sunshine Matinee THE ARTS OF THE THEATRE Molly — Dancing	de Valois	Ravel	K. Dillon

1927

Cambridge Festival Theatre Cambridge 28.11.1927 A FLORENTINE TRAGEDY Molly — Irony	de Valois		

1928

Royal Court Theatre London 26.11.1928 Academy of Choregraphic Art POISSONS D'OR	de Valois	Debussy	A. Phillips R. Patrick

SCENE DE BALLET Molly — Pas de Trois	de Valois	Gluck	K. Dillon
SCENE VENETIENNE Molly — Romantic Lady	de Valois	Respighi	R. Patrick
LES TROIS GRACES Molly	de Valois	Stravinsky	de Valois

Recital at Rudolf Steiner Hall
Molly

ETUDE		Debussy	
MINUET		Debussy	
HINDU DANCE		Carpenter	
MAZURKA FANTASTIQUE		Kopylov	
MEXICAN DANCE		Partichelas	
PERIE		Schubert	
SPANISH DANCE		Joaquin Nin	
WALTZ		Chopin	

1929

Cambridge University Ballet Society 5.5.1929

PRIMAVERA Molly		Dabell	
SMORGASBORG Molly			

Old Vic Theatre 9.5.1929

THE PICNIC (The Faun) Molly — Phoebe	de Valois	Vaughan Williams	Briggs

1930

Russian Ballet in Variety Bill
West Pier Theatre Brighton May 1930

MANNEQUIN Molly			
POLKA Molly	Molly Lake		

Marilyn and Jani Group/The Marilyn Dancers
Molly

In Monte Carlo

1930 – 1931
Molly

HELEN IN EGYPT (Opera)		R. Strauss	
DANCES FROM PRINCE IGOR		Borodin	
MANON (Opera)		Massenet	
MAZURKA		arr. Glinka	

UNE NUIT A VENISE (Opera)		J. Strauss	
SALOME (Opera)		R. Strauss	
SAMSON AND DELILAH (Opera)		Saint-Saens	
SCHEHERAZADE		Rimsky- Korsakov	
LA TRAVIATA (Opera)		Verdi	
Commodore Theatre, London February 1931 With Victor Leopold and Company Travis			
Vic-Wells Ballet *London* **1931**			
CEPHALUS AND PROCRIS Travis — Attendant on Cephalus	de Valois	Gretry	Chappell
FETE POLONAISE Travis — Mazurka	de Valois Judson	Glinka	Smyth Premiere: 23.11.1931
THE JEW IN THE BUSH Travis — the King	de Valois	Gordon Jacob	Bernard Guest Premiere: 16.12.1931
Old Vic Theatre DIDO AND AENEAS (Opera) Travis		Purcell	13.11.1931
RIGOLETTO (Opera)	de Valois	Verdi	Premiere: 21.9.31
LA TRAVIATA Travis — Pas de Trois	de Valois	Verdi	Premiere: 19.11.31
Cambridge Theatre JOB (Camargo Society) Travis — a Son, a Messenger	de Valois	Vaughan Williams	Raverat Premiere: 5.7.1931
Savoy Theatre 29.11.1931 A DAY IN A SOUTHERN PORT (RIO GRANDE) Travis	Ashton	Lambert	Burra
1932			
DON GIOVANNI (Opera)	de Valois	Mozart	2.4.1932
DOUANES Travis — a Gendarme	de Valois	Toye	Briggs 11.10.1932
HOMMAGE AUX BELLES VIENNOISES Travis — Tyrolese	de Valois	Schubert	Smyth

ITALIAN SUITE Travis — Pas de Quatre	de Valois/Dolin	Lalo Cottrau Cimarosa	P. Dolton 4.3.1932
JOB Travis — a Son, a Messenger	de Valois	Vaughan Williams	Raverat
MIGNON (Opera) Travis	de Valois	Thomas	25.2.1932
NURSERY SUITE Travis — a Bear	de Valois	Elgar	Allen 19.3.1932
LES PETITS RIENS Travis — Tircis	de Valois	Mozart	Smyth
REGATTA Travis — Cabin Boy	Ashton	Gavin Gordon	Chappell
Old Vic Theatre 17.10.1932 THE LORD OF BURLEIGH Travis — Edward Gray	Ashton	Mendelssohn	Sherringham
Savoy Theatre, London 13.6.1932 THE ORIGIN OF DESIGN (Camargo Society) Travis — Attendant on Eros	de Valois	Handel arr. Beecham	Chappell
Camargo Society LE LAC DES CYGNES Act II	Ivanov	Tchaikovsky	6.6.1932
GISELLE Travis — a Huntsman	Coralli	Adam	2.7.1932
THE INFANTA'S BIRTHDAY Travis — Bull, Toreador	P. Spencer	E. Luytens	R. Whistler
BBC Television SONGS AND DANCES Travis			
The English Ballet *Royal Theatre, Copenhagen 25 – 28.9.1932* JOB Travis — a Son, a Messenger	de Valois	Vaughan Williams	Raverat
THE LORD OF BURLEIGH Travis — Edward Gray	Ashton	Mendelssohn arr. Evans	Sheringham 17.10.1932
Ballet Club *Mercury Theatre* **1932 – 1933**			
AURORA'S WEDDING Travis	Petipa	Tchaikovsky	
CAPRIOL SUITE Travis	Ashton	Warlock	Chappell

CARNAVAL Travis — Pantalon	Fokine	Schumann	
LE CRICKET Travis — The Umpire	Salaman	Benjamin	Salaman
Paris			
SYMPHONIE CLASSIQUE Molly	Kniasseff	Prokofiev	
With Anna Ludmilla			
TO VIENNA Molly		Drigo Kalman Lehar Messager Sarasate J. Strauss Thayer	
Grüsse uns Alles Molly			
Vic-Wells Ballet			
1933			
THE BIRTHDAY OF OBERON Travis — rural dances	de Valois	Purcell arr. Lambert	7.2.1933
COPPELIA (Acts I + II) Travis — a Village Dancer	Ivanov rev. Sergeeff	Delibes	21.3.1933 Edwin Calligan
LA CREATION DU MONDE Travis — a God	de Valois	Milhaud	Edward Wolfe 12.12.1933
THE ENCHANTED GROVE Travis — a Gentleman	Rupert Doone	Ravel, Debussy	Duncan Grant 3.1.1933
FETE POLONAISE Travis — Pas de Deux	de Valois/ Judson	Glinka	Smyth 10.10.1932
THE LORD OF BURLEIGH Travis — Edwin Morris	Ashton	Mendelssohn arr. Evans	Sheringham
NURSERY SUITE Travis — The Prince	de Valois	Elgar	Allen
ORPHEUS (Opera) Travis	de Valois	Gluck	29.11.1933
LES PETITS RIENS Travis — Corydon	de Valois	Mozart	Smyth
POMONA Travis — Attendant on Vertumnus	Ashton	Lambert	Bell Premiere: 17.1.1933
LES RENDEZVOUS Travis — Pas de Trois	Ashton	Auber	William Chappell Premiere: 5.12.1933

THE SNOW MAIDEN (Opera) Travis — a Tumbler	de Valois	Rimsky- Korsakov	E. Polunin 12.4.1933
TZAR SALTAN (Opera) Travis — a Dancer, a Clown	de Valois	Rimsky- Korsakov	V. Polunin 11.10.1933
Lyric Hammersmith 21.6.1933 THE FANTASTICKS (Play) Travis	de Valois		

1934

CARNAVAL Travis — Pierrot	Fokine rev. Evina	Schumann	Elizabeth & Marsh Williams
CASSE NOISETTE Travis — Danse Chinoise	Ivanov rev. Sergeeff	Tchaikovsky	Briggs
COPPELIA (Acts I + II) Travis — Franz	Ivanov rev. Sergeev	Delibes	Edwin Calligan
THE ENCHANTED GROVE Travis — a Warrior	Rupert Doone	Ravel, Debussy	Duncan Grant 26.3.1934
GISELLE Travis — Peasant pas de Deux	Coralli-Perrot	Adam	Allan
SAMSON AND DELILAH (Opera) Travis	de Valois	Saint-Saens	
SNOW MAIDEN (Opera) Travis — A Tumbler	de Valois	Rimsky- Korsakov	E. Polunin
Ballet Club DANCES FROM LAC DES CYGNES Act II Travis — The Prince	Ivanov	Tchaikovsky	
Royal Albert Hall 12.2.1934 ELIJAH Molly	Euphan Maclaren	Mendelssohn	

Dandré-Levitoff Ballet
1934 – 1935

BALLET VISIONS (Sleeping Beauty) Molly — The Good Fairy	arr. Petroff	Tchaikovsky	Scenery: Bardas
BALLET EGYPTIEN Molly — Principal Role		Luigini/Verdi	
CARNAVAL Molly — Florestine, Estrella Travis — Pierrot	Fokine	Schumann	Boris Anisfeld
CASSE NOISETTE (Pas des Fleurs) Molly	Ivanov	Tchaikovsky	

LA FILLE MAL GARDEE ACT I Molly and Travis — Bohemians	Petipa arr. Petroff	Hertel	Scenery: Allegri May 1934 Scenery & Costumes: Georges Barbier
THE MAGIC FLUTE Molly — Stranger, Oberon, Dressed as Hermit	Arr. Petroff	Drigo	Scenery & Costumes: Georges Barbier
PRINCE IGOR (Polovtsian Dances) Travis — a Warrior	Fokine	Borodin	Scenery: Korovine
PROMENADE (OLD VIENNA) Molly — a girl, Valse Travis — He, a Cavalier	Petroff	J. Strauss	
SWAN LAKE ACT II Molly — a Swan Travis — a Friend of the Prince	Petipa	Tchaikovsky	Scenery: Korovine
LES SYLPHIDES Molly	Fokine	Chopin	Scenery: Anisfeld
VENUSBURG From Tannhauser Molly — a Bacchante Travis — a Young Greek	Petroff	Wagner	Anisfeld
DIVERTISSEMENT			
CLAIR DE LUNE Molly	Molly Lake	Debussy	
SUITE FROM COPPELIA Molly — Mazurka, Chardaz Travis — Chardaz		Delibes	
DANCE OF THE HOURS Molly		Ponchielli	
ETUDE PLASTIQUE Molly — principal role	Molly Lake	Liszt	
GRAND PAS FROM PAQUITA Molly and Travis		Minkus	
ICE MAIDEN Molly and Travis		Grieg	
LIEBESTRAUM		Liszt	
MEXICAN DANCE Molly		Padilla	

PAS DES FLEURS (from CASSE NOISETTE) Molly — corps de ballet		Tchaikovsky	
PAS DE QUATRE Travis		Chopin	
PAS HONGROIS CLASSIQUE (from RAYMONDA) Molly		Glazunov	
POLKA Molly and Travis	Molly Lake	Linter	
WALTZ Molly		Fetras	
WALTZ		Chopin	
TREPAK Travis		V. Launitz	

1935

The New Dance Group

THE MISTLETOE BOUGH Travis — a Guest	Stanley Judson	Schumann	
THE REAL PRINCESS Travis — The Wolf	Molly Lake	Grieg	

(Molly — THE ICE MAIDEN Choreography: Margaret Craske)

DIVERTISSEMENT

ADORATION Travis	Stanley Judson	Schumann	
CLAIR DE LUNE	Molly Lake	Debussy	
POLKA 1840	Molly Lake	Linter	
SUITE OF COUNTRY DANCES WITH A TEUTONIC FLAVOUR	Molly Lake		

Royal Opera House
with Marie Rambert's dancers
Opera ballets

Travis — Schwanda the Bagpiper	Antony Tudor	Weinberger	

Markova – Dolin Ballet

1935 – 1938

AUCASSIN AND NICOLETTE Travis	Toye	J. Holbrooke	Motley
BEETHOVEN SUITE	Molly Lake	Beethoven	

GISELLE Molly — Myrtha		Adam	
LES SYLPHIDES	Fokine	Chopin	
DIVERTISSEMENT CAN CAN Molly	Molly Lake	Waldteufel	
GRANDE VALSE	Lester	Tchaikovsky	
1935			
DAVID Travis — a Son of Jesse	Lester	M. Jacobson	Meninsky 12.11.1935 scenario P. Vanda
SHOW FOLK	Salaman	Offenbach	Salaman
1936			
CASSE NOISETTE (Act III) Spanish Dance	Ivanov rev. Sergeeff	Tchaikovsky	Chappell Doubojinsky
HUNGARIA Molly — a Gypsy	Derra de Moroda	Folktunes arr. Miklos Rozsa	Costumes: Sandor Decor: H. Briggs
THE NIGHTINGALE AND THE ROSE Travis	Dolin (Based on story of Oscar Wilde)	Frazer-Simson	P. Dolton
PAS DE QUATRE Molly — Taglioni	Lester	Pugni	Decor: R. St. John Roper 18.6.36
BACH SUITE	Nijinska	Bach	
DIVERTISSEMENT GRANDE VALSE	Lester	Tchaikovsky	
1937			
THE BELOVED ONE Molly — The Lioness	Nijinska	Schubert Liszt arr. Milhaud	G. Kirsta (scenario Benois)
LES BICHES (HOUSE PARTY) Travis	Nijinska	Poulenc	Laurencin
1938			
BEETHOVEN SUITE	Molly Lake	Beethoven	
OLYMPIC ANTICS Travis — Hercules (Solo sometimes given separately in Divertissement)	Molly Lake Peter Michael	Offenbach	

DIVERTISSEMENT			
LA LECON	Molly	Delibes	
POLKA 1840 Molly and Travis	Molly Lake	Linter	
TITANIA AND THE TAR (Molly — Titania)	Lester	Mendelssohn	
THE VIXEN	Molly Lake	Schumann	

Ballet intime

1938 – 1939

THE THREE GRACES Molly and Travis — Pas de Deux		Pugni	
VALSE FINALE	Molly Lake		
DIVERTISSEMENT			
A L'ESPAGNOLE Molly and Travis — Pas de Deux	Molly Lake	John Hawkins	
ARABELLA DANCES	Molly Lake	Linter	
CAN CAN	Molly Lake	Waldteufel	
CLAIR DE LUNE	Molly Lake	Debussy	
LES ENFANTS TERRIBLES Travis and John Pygram	Molly Lake	Lohr	
HERBERT SKATES Travis	Molly Lake	Waldteufel	
HERCULES From OLYMPIC ANTICS Travis	Molly Lake	Offenbach	
PERPETUUM MOBILE	Molly Lake	J. Strauss	
TWILIGHT WALTZ	Molly Lake Peter Michael	Chopin	
TYROLEAN	Molly Lake	Schubert	
VALSE FANTAISIE	Lester	Glinka	

Westminster Theatre, London 18.7.1939
R.A.D. Production Club

LA DANSE Travis — Man	Helpmann	Ravel	Chappell
L'ESPAGNOLE (By arrangement with Ballet Intime) Molly and Travis — Pas de Deux	Molly Lake	J. Hawkins	

PUSS IN BOOTS Travis — the King	arr. N. Bush & M. Davies	Mozart	Dorothy M. Thoday
GRAND FETE DE BALLET Travis — Dauberval (in Pas de Trois)	de Valois		R. Furze

Great Ormond Street Hospital
Pantomimes
Concert Parties

Travis with Ballet Club
Mercury Theatre and Birmingham Repertory Theatre May – June 1939

AURORA'S WEDDING Travis — Corps	Petipa	Tchaikovsky	
BAR AUX FOLIES-BERGERE	de Valois	Chabrier	Chappell after Manet
FACADE Scotch Rhapsody	Ashton	Walton	Armstrong
LE LAC DES CYGNES (Act II) Travis — Prince	Ivanov/Petipa	Tchaikovsky	
LES MASQUES Travis — The Lover	Ashton	Poulenc	Fedorovitch
PARIS-SOIR Travis — Anarchist	Gore	Poulenc	Swinstead-Smith
VALSE FINALE	Gore	Ravel	Fedorovitch

June – July 1939

LADY INTO FOX Travis — the Huntsman	Howard	Honneger	Nadia Benois
LE JARDIN AUX LILAS Travis — Her Lover	Tudor	Chausson	Stevenson

Travis with Ballet Rambert
Duchess Theatre November – December 1939

BAR AUX FOLIES BERGERES Travis — Gustav	de Valois	Chabrier	Chappell after Manet
CZERNYANA Travis — Sucre et Pastorale	Staff	Czerny	Swinstead-Smith Premiere
FACADE	Ashton	Walton	Armstrong
LADY INTO FOX Travis — Huntsman	Howard	Honegger	N. Benois
LES MASQUES Travis — A Personage	Ashton	Poulenc	Fedorovitch
MERMAID Travis — Prince's Companion	Howard/ Salaman	Ravel	Howard

PARIS-SOIR Travis — Policeman	Gore	Poulenc	Swinstead-Smith
THE TARTANS Travis — Laddie	Staff	Boyce	Chappell
LES PAS DES DEESSES	Lester	Pugni	Guthrie/ Stevenson

Travis in Sheffield

FAUST — A Pageant Production

Arts Theatre Ballet

1940 – 1941

BACH SUITE IN B MINOR	Lester	Bach	
CASSE NOISETTE Act III Travis — Spanish	Ivanov	Tchaikovsky	
ECOSSAISE	E. McLaren		
LES ENFANT TERRIBLES	Molly Lake	Lohr	
LES FEES AUX FLEURS	Lester Molly Lake	Pugni	
FLORA AND FAUNS	Molly Lake	Ponchielli	
PAVANE	Molly Lake		
POLKA 1845 (was Polka, POLKA 1840, BOHEMIAN POLKA) Molly and Travis	Molly Lake	Linter	
SERENADE Travis	H. Turner	H. Wolf	D. Gould
QUEEN OF THE MEADOW	Molly Lake		
DIVERTISSEMENT			
CAN-CAN Molly, with Gould and Vernon	Molly Lake	Waldteufel	
THE FOUNTAIN OF ARETHUSA	Molly Lake		
GALOP FINALE		Delibes	
TITANIA AND THE TAR	Lester		

1940

DE PROFUNDIS Molly	Lester	Chopin arr. Lucas	Joseph Carl
THE FOUNTAIN OF ARETHUSA	Molly Lake		
GISELLE (Act II) Molly — Giselle Travis — Albrecht	Coralli/Perrot	Adam	Joseph Carl

THE GLEN Molly — Demon Queen, Theolinda, a Sylph Travis — Demon King	Lester	Mendelssohn	Eleanor Watts
PERSEUS Molly and Travis	Lester	Stanley Bate	Pamela Bowden Premiere 2.7.1940
SYLVIA Travis	Lester	Delibes	

Ballet Guild

1941 – 1945

BEETHOVEN SUITE	Molly Lake	Beethoven	Decor: Joan Jefferson Farjeon
BLACK ETUDE Molly	Lester by Poppaea Vanda	Moussorgsky	Decor: Van Hengelaar Costumes: B. Dean 15.8.1941
CANCION Travis — A Rider	Celia Franca Based on Lorca	Turina	Edwin Kersley 5.7.1942
FANTASY	Lester	Chopin	B. Dean 15.8.41
FLORA AND FAUNS	Molly Lake	Auric Chaminade Delibes Puishnoff Tchaikovsky	
MIDSUMMER DAYDREAM (Later FALL FROM GRACE)	Molly Lake	Lord Berners	
PAS DE QUATRE	Lester	Pugni	After Chalon 15.8.19
DIVERTISSEMENT			
CLAIR DE LUNE	Molly Lake	Debussy	
LE DOUX PENSEE Molly	Molly Lake	Weber	
POLKA 1840	Molly Lake	Linter	
ROUMANIAN GYPSY DANCE	Molly Lake	Bartok	
SERENADE	Molly Lake	Rachmaninov	
LE SOUPIR	Molly Lake	Liszt	
VALSE TRISTE	David Ellis	Sibelius	

1941			
THE DARK MIRROR Molly	Lester	Weber	Decor: A. Lidderdale Costumes: S. Green, Premiere: 15.4.1941
GISELLE Molly — Queen of the Willis	Coralli/Perrot	Adam	
JEU DE LA ROSE	Molly Lake Devised by Cyril Beaumont		Costumes: S. Green
1942			
MR HENRY'S BALL	Molly Lake	Offenbach arr. Tunnard Theme: Derek Lynham after Albert Smith	Sylvia Green Premiere 17.5.1942
LA PETITE FADETTE	Molly Lake	Fauré arr. Tunnard	Decor: B. Dean, Costumes: S. Green, Book: Lynham
SOIREE MUSICALE	Tudor	Rossini/ Britten	Stevenson
LA VALSE	Molly Lake	Ravel	Decor: Joan Jefferson Farjeon, Costumes: Sylvia Green, Premiere: 22.11.1942
DIVERTISSEMENT			
LECON D'APRES DEGAS	Molly Lake	Delibes	5.7.42
SWAN LAKE (Pas de Deux and Variation) Travis — the Prince	Ivanov		
1943			
CHARTRES	Sheila Nicholson	Respighi	Costumes: S. Green
NYMPHENBURG GARDEN	Molly Lake	Mozart arr. Norman Frankus	Costumes: A. Lidderdale
LES SYLPHIDES	Fokine	Chopin	
VICTORIAN BOUQUET	Molly Lake	Rossini	Costumes: B. Dean

DIVERTISSEMENT		J. Strauss	Costumes: Sylvia Green, Premiere: 21.2.1943
VALSE VIENNOISE Molly			

1944

THE LAST CURTAIN	Molly Lake	Weber arr. Neville Marriner	Costumes: Eva Melova, Decor: William Holmes, Premiere: 30.3.1944
PHANTOM PROCESSION	Molly Lake		
DIVERTISSEMENT			
ETUDE ROMANTIQUE			Premiere 9.12.1944

Chichester Ballet Club
Molly opened this club in January 1944 and later gave demonstrations with Travis

1945

DIVERTISSEMENT			
MIDSUMMER DAYDREAM (Later enlarged into FALL FROM GRACE)	Molly Lake	John Andrews	Costumes: Joan Nunn, Decor: Stanley Newby

1946

St James's Theatre

MARRIAGE A LA MODE (Play)	Molly Lake		

Embassy Ballet

1946 – 1947

BEETHOVEN SUITE	Molly Lake	Beethoven	
GISELLE Act II Molly — Giselle		Adam	Decor: Joseph Carl
THE LAST CURTAIN (Televised 16.2.1946, 21.2.1946, 21.4.1947)	Molly Lake	Weber arr. N. Marriner	Decor: Wm Holmes, Costumes: Melova
NYMPHENBURG GARDEN	Molly Lake	Mozart	Costumes: Lidderdale 5.10.46
LE SOUPIR	Molly Lake	Liszt	Costumes: E. Melova 6.5.1946

SWAN LAKE (Act II)	Ivanov	Tchaikovsky	Joseph Carl
LES SYLPHIDES	Fokine	Chopin	
VICTORIAN BOUQUET	Molly Lake	Rossini	
DIVERTISSEMENT			
CAN CAN	Molly Lake	Waldteufel	
CASSE NOISETTE Pas de Deux, Act III Travis	Ivanov	Tchaikovsky	
CLAIR DE LUNE	Molly Lake	Debussy	
FLORA AND FAUNS	Molly Lake	Ponchielli	
HERCULES Travis	Molly Lake	Offenbach	
LA LECON	Molly Lake	Delibes	
ROUMANIAN GYPSY DANCE	Molly Lake		
SERENADE	Molly Lake	Rachmaninov	
SLAVE TO CIRCE Travis	Molly Lake	Holst	
VALSE OUBLIEE		Liszt	
VALSE VIENNOISE	Molly Lake	Strauss	

1946

EPISODE (FANTAISIE)	Jak Carter	Chopin	Sylvia Green
LA PETITE FADETTE	Molly Lake	Fauré arr. Tunnard	Costumes: Sylvia Green, book: Lynham

Continental Ballet

1947 – 1954

BARTLEMAS DANCES (BARTLEMAS FAIR — Nov 1950) (Televised: 18.10.1950)	Gore	Holst	
FANTAISIE (Was EPISODE)	Jak Carter	Chopin	Costumes: Sylvia Green 28.6.1949
FAUST	Lester	Gounod	Lester
GISELLE ACT II	after Coralli	Adam	Joseph Carl
IMPROMPTU FOR TWELVE Travis	Jak Carter	Rossini	Costumes: Kenneth Symonds

LES OMBRES Molly and Travis	Lester		
LE SOUPIR	Molly Lake	Liszt	
SWAN LAKE (Act II) (Grand Pas de Deux Act III)	Ivanov	Tchaikovsky	Costumes: Sylvia Green
LES SYLPHIDES	Fokine	Chopin	Joseph Carl
VICTORIAN BOUQUET			
DIVERTISSEMENT			
FLORA AND FAUNS	Molly Lake	Ponchielli	
GYPSY DANCE	Molly Lake	Bartok	

1948

NYMPHENBURG GARDEN	Molly Lake	Mozart	Costumes: Alice Lidderdale
LA REVANANTE (From August 1949: SHE WHO COMES BACK) Molly — Title Role Travis — Bridegroom (Televised: 9.7.1948)	Molly Lake	Alkan	Sylvia Green Decor: Mary Turner
SYLVIA (In one Act)	Lester	Delibes	Decor: Phyllis Dexter after drawings by Botticelli 2.5.1951

1949

CHILDREN OF SPACE	Molly Lake	Brahms	Costumes: Stanley Newby
THE FOUR ELEMENTS (Televised: 28.7.1949)	Lester	Pugni	Costumes: Sylvia Green
THE LAST CURTAIN	Molly Lake	Weber	Costumes: Eva Melova, Decor: Alice Lidderdale
SALUTE TO PETIPA	Molly Lake	Tchaikovsky	Mary Turner

SUITE DE DANSES CLASSIQUES
Pas de Trois from Swan Lake Act I
Carnation Fairy from The Sleeping Princess Act III
Pas de Deux from Giselle Act I
The Fairy of the Humming Birds from The Sleeping Princess Act I
Pas de Deux from Swan Lake Act III

1950			
FALL FROM GRACE Travis — Grandfather (Televised: 18.10.1950)	Molly Lake	John Andrews	Costumes: Joan Nunn, Decor: Stanley Newby
1951			
FADETTE (Was LA PETITE FADETTE)	Molly Lake	Fauré	Costumes: Sylvia Green
1953			
CINDERELLA (3 Act Ballet Pantomime) (CINDERELLA'S DREAM) Molly — Fairy Godmother Travis — Buttons	Molly Lake Lester	Tchaikovsky	Sylvia Green
JEU DE LA DANSE	Molly Lake	Schubert	Costumes: Harry Cordwell 2.5.1951
MUSIC HALL	Molly Lake	Offenbach	
1954			
SICILIENNE Molly and Travis	Lester	Schubert	
Ankara Conservatoire Ballet			
1954 – 1974			
1957			
MUSIC HALL	Molly Lake		
LES SYLPHIDES	Fokine	Chopin	
1958			
SOIREE DE VIENNE	Molly Lake	J. Strauss	
Gala with Nerina and Rassine 1957			
MACAR DANSE	Pyne	Brahms	
SALUTE TO PETIPA	Molly Lake	Tchaikovsky	
SOIREE DE VIENNE	Molly Lake	J. Strauss	
SWAN LAKE Act II	Ivanov	Tchaikovsky	
Gala with Fonteyn and Somes 1958	Ivanov	Tchaikovsky	
CASSE NOISETTE Act II Pas de Deux (Fonteyn and Somes)			

IMPROMPTU FOR TWELVE	Jak Carter	Rossini	
SALUTE TO PETIPA	Molly Lake	Tchaikovsky	
SWAN LAKE (Act II)	Ivanov	Tchaikovsky	
WALPURGIS NACHT	Molly Lake	Gounod	

1959

COMUS A MASKE (Masque)	Molly Lake	Purcell	
FAUST	Lester	Gounod	
THE MUSICIANS OF BREMEN	Molly Lake		
PAGANINI (Opera)	Molly Lake		

Gala with Anya Linden, Maryon Lane, Peter Clegg, David Blair 1959

CASSE NOISETTE (Act II)	Ivanov arr. Molly Lake	Tchaikovsky	
THE DESERTED GARDEN	Molly Lake	Tchaikovsky	Decor: Ulrich Damrau, Costumes: Sylvia Green
DIVERTISSEMENT (Performed by the Guest Artists and Molly)			
CINDERELLA	Ashton	Prokofiev	
COPPELIA Pas de Deux	Ivanov	Delibes	
DON QUIXOTE Pas de Deux	Petipa	Minkus	
SLEEPING BEAUTY Pas de Deux Act III	Petipa	Tchaikovsky	
SOLITAIRE	MacMillan	Arnold	Heeley
TRISCH TRASCH	Cranko	J. Strauss	Briggs
VENEZIANA	Andree Howard	Donizetti	

Johannesburg City Ballet 2.3.1962

WALPURGIS NIGHT	Molly Lake	Gounod	
IMPROMPTU FOR TWELVE	Jak Carter Reproduced: Molly Lake	Rossini	
GISELLE (Peasant Pas de Deux)	Corrali Reproduced: Molly Lake	Adam	

Ballet Transvaal 1963

GISELLE	Coralli Reproduced: Molly Lake	Adam	Costumes: Eileen Sulski, Decor: Raimond Schoop

* Both names are listed as composer, each on a different programme.

** Programme lists Petipa, but attributed to Ivanov in "ANNA PAVLOVA", The London Museum, 1956.

( ) Information not in programmes, but in ANNA PAVLOVA, The London Museum, 1956.

Index